13.95

338.4791
SHS
572

Tourism & Leisure in the Countryside

Tutor's Manual

Exercises, case studies, OHPs and materials to support and extend the textbook. The Tutor's Manual and the book together offer plenty of tested class material for a full year's course.

A4 looseleaf format allows updating and ease of copying.

ISBN I 85450 440 1

Tourism & Leisure in the Countryside

Second Edition

Richard Sharpley

ELM Publications

This second edition of **Tourism and Leisure in the Countryside** is published July 1996 by ELM Publications, Seaton House, Kings Ripton, Huntingdon, Cambs PE17 2NJ.

Tel: 01487 773254   Fax: 01487 773359

Printed by St Edmundsbury Press, Bury St Edmunds, Suffolk, England.

Bound by Woolnough Bookbinding, Express Works, Church Street, Irthlingborough, Northants, England.

ISBN 1 85450 245 X

British Library Cataloguing-in-Publication Data. A catalogue record for this publication is available from The British Library.

Contents

List of Figures

List of Tables

About the Author

Richard Sharpley is a Senior Lecturer in Travel and Tourism at the University of Luton.

As a keen fell-walker, his research interest in tourism and leisure in the countryside developed during many hours walking in the uplands of the UK. His research into the subject developed into a complete Rural Tourism module on the Travel and Tourism degree course at the University of Luton, and it is upon that module that this book is based. He has also researched widely into the social and cultural aspects of tourism and in 1994 wrote a second tourism text book, *Tourism, Tourists and Society*.

In between lecturing and writing, Richard Sharpley is also presently engaged in research for his PhD in Sustainable Tourism Development.

Introduction

The countryside has been an increasingly poplular visitor destination since the late eighteenth century. Recent years, however, have witnessed a dramatic growth in the level and diversity of countryside recreation and a correspondingly greater awareness of the impacts of tourism and leisure on the rural environment. Coupled with the increasing reliance of rural communities on the economic benefits of tourism and leisure, this has served to heighten the need for, and the importance of, effective and sustainable management of the countryside as a resource for recreation.

This revised and updated second edition of *Tourism and Leisure in the Countryside* examines the development, planning and management of tourism and leisure in the countryside. Easy to read and to understand, it is based on a working degree module at the University of Luton and is built on a solid foundation of experience. It is aimed at HND and first degree students majoring in tourism and/or leisure but is equally useful to students in related disciplines with a tourism/leisure component. It can be used on its own as general or background reading or, as at Luton, as an integral part of the course. Many examples are given to illustrate points, with case studies where appropriate, and full references.

This book will also appeal to the general interest reader, and will form a firm basis for project work, where examples and case studies can be followed up and expanded upon.

Dedication

To Julia

Chapter One

Tourism and Leisure: an Introduction

INTRODUCTION

The British countryside has been a popular destination for visitors for over
two hundred years. Beginning with the Romantic Movement in the late
eighteenth century, tourism and leisure has increased to the extent that
today an estimated 900 million day visits (CRN 1995) and over 80 million
visitor nights are annually spent in the countryside. Furthermore, up to 18
million people visit the countryside on a typical summer Sunday, a figure
that falls relatively slightly to 13 million during the winter months.

The dramatic growth in the use of the countryside for tourism and leisure
has brought significant and welcome economic and employment benefits to
many rural communities, in particular those which have been suffering
from a decline in traditional industries. For example, it is estimated that
about £9 billion is spent each year by day visitors and holiday makers in
the countryside (Countryside Commission 1995a). At the same time,
however, the countryside has come under increasing pressure from the
various demands placed upon it, threatening the very qualities that attract
visitors in the first place. There has therefore been a growing recognition
of the need to balance all the demands placed on the countryside, including
tourism and leisure, with the preservation of both the intrinsic character and
quality of the countryside and the well-being of those who live and work
there. The need for balanced and sustainable countryside planning and
management is a major theme throughout this book.

Two points, however, require clarification. Firstly, *tourism* and *leisure*
are traditionally seen as two separate, identifiable areas of activity and
study; within the context of the countryside they overlap to a great extent.

Secondly, although the countryside is a distinct and important resource for tourism and leisure, it should not be viewed in isolation. In other words, the countryside is just one of a number of attractions and destinations that comprise the national tourism industry all of which, in effect, compete for a share of the tourism and leisure market. This chapter defines tourism and leisure and briefly considers the overall tourism and leisure market of which the countryside is a part.

TOURISM
i What is Tourism?
Tourism has existed, in one form or another, throughout history. There have been tourists ever since people were first able to travel, seeking out new lands, building trade links with other countries, making religious pilgrimages or even waging wars. The purpose of these early travellers was, of course, very different from that of most of today's tourists; indeed, mass travel and tourism purely for pleasure is a phenomenon of the second half of the twentieth century.

The rapid increase in participation in tourism over the last forty years has led to the term tourism being generally associated with taking holidays. However, whilst it is relatively simple to categorise particular types of tourism, such as beach holidays or cruises, it is more difficult to define the overall concept of tourism. The first attempt was made in 1937 by the Council of the League of Nations which defined a tourist as someone who travels for twenty-four hours or more outside their normal country of residence. This definition included travel for pleasure, business, health, religion or family reasons, whilst those visiting countries for less than twenty-four hours, for example, people on cruises, were termed excursionists. A major failing of this definition was that it excluded domestic tourism, or tourism in the home country, and therefore a more widely accepted definition of tourism is that proposed by the Tourism Society:

Tourism is the temporary short-term movement of people to destinations outside the places where they normally live and work, and their activities during the stay at these destinations; it includes movement for all purposes as well as day visits or excursions.

2

Thus tourism covers a multitude of activities that can take place at home or abroad and for periods of anything between a day and a year. Going on holiday is, of course, tourism, but it is only part of the overall picture. The list of activities that are included in tourism is virtually endless, but they can be categorised under four main headings:

(a) Holidays

(b) Visiting Friends and Relatives (VFR)

(c) Business (including conference and incentive travel)

(d) Other (including health, education, religion, sport etc)

Overall, then, tourism is a much broader concept than is at first apparent. It includes many categories, such as business travel, that do not conform with the commonly held view of tourism, yet together they comprise one of the world's largest and fastest growing industries.

ii The Tourism Industry
The tourism industry is the term used to describe the collection of businesses which provide the tourism product, or the suppliers of tourism. To use the word industry is, however, somewhat misleading because, rather than being distinct and identifiable, such as the car industry, the tourism industry is made up of a large number of diverse independent businesses of different sizes. In the UK alone it is estimated that there are over 50,000 separate businesses directly involved in tourism and a further 150,000 with an indirect involvement. The great majority are small, privately owned firms, such as restaurants, souvenir shops, guest-houses or independent travel agents, whilst at the other end of the scale there are a number of large national and international organisations. Thus, for example, the owner of a bed and breakfast establishment is as much a part of the tourism industry as is an international hotel chain or an international airline.

Despite this diversity, the tourism industry is divided into five main sectors into which the activities of all tourism businesses can be categorised:

(a) **The Transport Sector** This includes airlines, shipping and cruise companies, bus and coach operators, railways, car hire companies and taxis.

(b) **The Accommodation and Catering Sector** This includes hotels, guest-houses, camping and caravan sites, self-catering and time share appartments, farmhouses, bed and breakfast, holiday villages, restaurants and cafes.

(c) **The Attractions Sector** All the facilities and attractions used by tourists, such as museums, theatres, theme parks, historical sites, nature reserves and national parks.

(d) **The Tourism Organisers Sector** Including tour operators, travel agencies, ticket agencies and conference and incentive travel organisers.

(e) **Tourism Organisations Sector** Usually public sector organisations concerned with the marketing and promotion of tourist destinations. They include national and regional tourist offices and tourist information centres.

The task of planning and managing tourism is complicated by the number and diversity of businesses that are directly and indirectly involved in the industry. There has, therefore, been a growing tendency for larger tourism organisations to integrate their operations to ensure a greater market share and greater control over different sectors of the industry. Thomson Holidays, for example, is part of a larger organisation that owns the Lunn Poly travel agency chain, Britannia Airways and a number of hotels in their major destinations or, in short, all the main elements of a package holiday. The purchase of the Pickfords (now Going Places) travel agency chain by Airtours in 1992 was a further indication of the domination of the holiday industry by a few large companies. Nevertheless, the tourism industry in the UK is still largely made up of small, independent businesses which, together with the major organisations, employ an estimated 1.5 million people.

iii The Development of Tourism

Mass tourism (the general and widespread participation in tourism rather than package holidays in particular) has its roots in the eighteenth century (see Sharpley 1994). Prior to this time people had travelled extensively for the purpose of trade and religion. During the Middle Ages holy days were the earliest form of holiday, although again based on the grounds of religion rather than pleasure. During the 1600s, however, interest in the potential medicinal powers of spa waters was revived by medical writers of the day and by the end of the century spa towns, such as Bath and Scarborough, had become popular places for "taking the waters".

The following century witnessed a gradual change in the character of the spa resorts as, often with Royal patronage, they became social centres for the rich and well-to-do rather than simply health resorts. Bath in particular, with Beau Nash organising the social calendar for the town's visitors, was at the height of its popularity in the early 1700s and by the middle of the eighteenth century places such as Tunbridge Wells, Leamington, Buxton, Harrogate and Epsom had all become popular amongst the leisured classes. Their popularity, however, attracted increasing numbers of an expanding middle class and by the the late 1700s the towns were moving down market and becoming commercial and residential centres.

At the same time, the recuperative effects of seawater were being publicised. In 1753 Dr Richard Russell published a famous paper extolling the virtues of bathing in, and indeed drinking, seawater and he moved to Brighthelmstone (now Brighton) to practice what he preached. Soon Brighton became fashionable and, because of both its proximity to London and a visit by the Prince of Wales in 1783, the town expanded rapidly. In 1760 just 2000 people lived in Brighton; by 1820 its population had risen to over 24,000. A number of northern seaside resorts also began to become popular, in particular those close to the expanding industrial centres. In 1795 the *Blackburn Mail* described Blackpool as:

> *...the first watering place in the Kingdom, whether we consider the salubrity of the air, the beauty of the scenery, the excellence of the accommodation or the agreeable company of which it is the general resort.*

Up until the 1830s the seaside resorts were still the preserve of the wealthy members of society. Travel was restricted to coaches or horseback and the working populations of the expanding urban centres of the Industrial Revolution had neither the time nor the money to travel to the resorts. Paradoxically, however, it was also the Industrial Revolution which finally opened up the possibility of tourism for the masses with the introduction of new forms of transport. By 1830, for example, paddle steamers were carrying Londoners in their thousands down the Thames to the Kent resorts, where the famous piers were originally built for landing passengers rather than for entertainment.

It was the dawn of the railway age that was of most significance. For the first time, cheap, safe and relatively fast transport was available to the majority of the population and, as the rail network spread around the country, the seaside resorts expanded rapidly. The main line from London to Brighton was opened in 1841 and by 1881 the town's population had increased to 99,000, a pattern that was reflected in many other resorts. Nor was this expansion limited to the seaside resorts; the first railway into the Lake District was opened in 1847 and on Whit Monday in 1883 over ten thousand day trippers visited Windermere (Berry and Beard 1980). Furthermore, the development of the railways led to the first package tour when Thomas Cook organised a rail trip from Loughborough to Leicester, carrying passengers to a temperance rally. However, it was the seaside resorts that benefited most, and even in the 1960s they accounted for about 75 per cent of all holidays taken in Britain. The figure today has dropped to about 30 per cent of holidays in the UK, largely as a result of the dramatic increase in overseas holidays, but even so, Blackpool, for example, still plays host to over twelve million visitors each year.

Towards the end of the nineteenth century both domestic and international tourism continued to flourish, although overseas travel was still restricted to the more wealthy members of society. Indeed, many of today's better known tour companies were founded at this time. There was also a growing interest in a more healthy lifestyle and, whilst the seaside was still by far the most popular destination amongst Victorian holiday makers, the invention of the bicycle heralded the beginning of outdoor activity holidays. The Cyclists' Touring Club was founded in in 1878 and soon cycling became a widely enoyed activity. Interest in the outdoors also led to the development of holiday camps which were set up for both health and social reasons. The Cunningham Camp on the Isle of Man, dating back to 1894, was the first ever holiday camp; by the end of the 1930s over 30,000 people annually visited holiday camps. (See Ward and Hardy, 1986, for a detailed history of the British holiday camp). Billy Butlin was the most famous of the holiday camp developers; his first camp at Skegness was opened in 1936 and eventually it was able to cater for up to 10,000 visitors.

During the inter-war years the Britsh seaside resorts were at the height of their popularity. The original resorts of Blackpool, Brighton and Scarborough dominated the holiday scene and many newer resorts flourished, but by the 1960s their popularity started to dwindle with the beginning of the era of international mass tourism. Since then, faced with competition from overseas resorts and newer forms of domestic tourism, such as holiday villages, most have continued to decline and many are now turning to conference tourism to replace their lost holiday business.

The development of the railways from the 1830s onwards was indicative of the first of three major requirements for the emergence of mass tourism, namely technology. The invention of the motor car further increased people's mobility, although until the 1950s the majority of journeys were still by public transport, but it was the technological advances in air transport that led directly to mass tourism as we know it today. From the 1970s onwards improvements in aircraft and engine design, in particular the introduction of wide-bodied jets, combined with the availability of charter flights and all-inclusive package holidays, brought international air travel within the reach of most people. In 1970 less than six million Britons took their holidays abroad; in 1991 the British made over thirty million overseas visits, more than 21 million of which were holidays, and by 1994 the British made almost 40 million overseas trips.

The second factor leading to the growth in tourism is time. Throughout most of the last century people worked a six day week, although in the later 1800s it became more common to have Saturday afternoon off. Thus tourism was limited for the most part to day trips, a situation that was partially improved following the Bank Holiday Act 1871. By 1925 an estimated 1.5 million workers enjoyed paid holidays but it was not until the Holidays with Pay Act 1938 that statutory paid holidays became widely available. Since then both the number of people receiving holidays with pay and the length of holiday has increased dramatically; by 1988, 99 per cent of all full-time manual workers in Britain received at least four weeks paid holiday.

Thirdly, in addition to cheap and efficient transport and sufficient time, people must be able to afford tourism. During the last century most people had relatively little spare money for their leisure time, but from the start of this century, and in particular since the 1960s, both real incomes and the level of disposable income has gradually increased. Between 1981 and 1988 real disposable income increased by 25 per cent, resulting in greater levels of expenditure not only on tourism but on leisure in general. In 1989 an average of almost 16 per cent of all household expenditure was on leisure items, 22 per cent of which was spent on holidays.

In short, then, mass tourism has developed as a result of improvements in technology, time and money although, in recent years, the rate of increase in holiday tourism has slowed down. By 1971 some 60 per cent of the British poplation enjoyed an annual holiday away from home (a holiday being defined as four days or more away) but, over the last 25 years, that proportion has remained the same. Furthermore, the number of domestic, as opposed to overseas, holidays has been in decline for a number of years, although domestic short breaks have been on the increase Thus it is the *pattern*, rather than the overall *volume,* of tourism that is changing. This is largely attributable to a number of factors.

Firstly, the rapid increase in private car ownership has brought greater independence and freedom of movement, removing the dependence on public transport and opening up the whole country, and Europe, to car-based tourism. In 1950, for example, car ownership in the UK stood at two million; the figure today is about 22 million. Current forecasts estimate an increase in vehicle miles of between 80 and 140 per cent by the year 2025, indicating an ever-increasing reliance on the motor car. The drive in the country is a uniquely British form of tourism and 80 per cent of all visits to the countryside are by car. There is already serious concern about the impact of cars on the countryside and these are considered, along with potential solutions, in Chapter Eight.

Secondly, work patterns are changing. In addition to longer paid holidays, the working week is becoming shorter. The working life is also becoming shorter as more people continue on into higher education before starting work and, at the other end of the scale, increasing numbers are taking early retirement. Furthermore, the proportion of women in the workforce has increased over the last forty years; between 1951 and 1991 it rose from 35 to 51 per cent. Other demographic changes, such as people getting married later and having fewer children, have meant that new categories of tourists have emerged in recent years. Both the "dinkies" (double income - no children) and the "empty-nesters" (people whose children have left home and who, perhaps, have taken early retirement) present an important and valuable new market for the tourism industry. As the population as a whole becomes older (it is estimated that by the year 2000, one in four Europeans will be over 55) there are also implications for both the type and seasonality of holiday taking.

Thirdly, leisure in general is becoming more important as the work ethic of the 1980s is being replaced by the quality of life 1990s. At the same time, people are becoming more discerning and quality concious and are starting to reject the off-the-shelf package holiday in favour of more specialised, individual types of tourism. For example, in 1995 the number of overseas package holidays sold in Britain was some 25 per cent down on the 1994 total and by early 1996 British tour operators were bracing themselves for a similar fall in summer holiday bookings. Taken with the other factors, this has meant that, although traditional package holidays are still the mainstream holiday business, there is a growing trend towards independent tourism, including self-catering, car touring, tailor made tours, and out of season tourism. Of most importance, and of great relevance to tourism in the countryside, is the growth in the short break and second, third or even fourth holiday sector of the market. In 1971, for example,12 per cent of British adults took a second holiday each year and three per cent took three or more; by 1989 the proportion had risen to 15 and seven per cent respectively. Surprisingly, perhaps, over 50 per cent of all short break holidays are taken at the seaside.

Overall, then, the development of tourism over the last two hundred years has resulted from the time-money-technology factors, with destinations that were once the preserve of the wealthy and leisured classes becoming popular for mass tourism. The spa towns, the seaside resorts, European resorts and, more lately, long-haul destinations have in turn come into the mass tourism market. The future trends are likely to be a greater seasonal spread away from the normal summer break, more specialised, independent holidays instead of traditional package holidays and continuing growth in short-break, additional holidays. As people become more environmentally aware, there is also likely to be an increase in the supply of, and demand for, more sustainable, environmentally friendly forms of tourism.

iv Tourism in the UK

This section briefly considers tourism as a whole in the UK in order to place the specific sector of countryside tourism in its overall context. (A detailed examination of UK tourism is found in Yale, 1992). The development of, and demand for, countryside tourism is described in Chapter Three.

Tourism in the UK comprises both domestic tourism, the tourism activities of the British within the UK, and international, or incoming, tourism. Incoming tourism includes visits by both foreign nationals who stay in the country for up to one year and by British citizens who live abroad. Since the 1960s the number of overseas visitors to the UK has been gradually increasing; in 1990 a total of 18,013,000 visitors arrived in the UK, spending £7,168 million (see Table 1.1.) In 1991, as a result of the Gulf War and the economic recession, the number of visitors and their level of spending fell by eight per cent. Despite the continuing worldwide recession visitor numbers for 1992 returned to the record levels of 1990 and since then the number of arrivals has continued to rise. In 1994 Britain received over 21 million international arrivals and it has been estimated that by 1996 over 22 million people will visit this country, a figure that is forecast to rise to about 28 million by the end of the century.

TABLE 1.1. OVERSEAS VISITORS TO THE UK

Year	Visits (thousands)	Spending (£m)
1980	12,421	2,961
1982	11,636	3,188
1984	13,644	4,614
1986	13,897	5,553
1988	15,799	6,184
1989	17,338	6,945
1990	18,013	7,748
1991	17,125	7,386
1992	18,535	7,891
1993	19,488	9,354
1994	21,034	9,919

Source: *International Passenger Survey*
Dept. of National Heritage 1995

The major source of visitors to the UK has traditionally been North America, accounting for up to twenty per cent of all visitors. The 1991 drop in visitor numbers was almost entirely caused by nearly one million less arrivals from North America than in 1990. The other principal generating countries for tourism into the UK are Germany, France and other north European countries, with the EU as a whole accounting for 54 per cent of all overseas arrivals in 1994. The dominance of the EU is likely to increase although the Far East, in particular Japan, is seen as a major growth market for overseas visitors during the 1990s. The great majority of visitors to the UK are on holiday, but both business (25 per cent of visitors) and VFR (20 per cent) tourists are important markets.

Thus the UK is an important destination for international tourism. In 1990 its share of worldwide tourism was four per cent of arrivals and 5.3 per cent of spending, although between 1981 and 1991 the rate of growth of both visitors and spending was less than the worldwide average, indicating that the UK is becoming relatively less popular. Indeed, by 1994 the UK's share of worldwide spending on tourism had fallen to 4.7 per cent. Nevertheless, overseas tourism is a significant source of foreign exchange, accounting for around 4.8 per cent of all export earnings in 1994. On the other hand, it must be remembered that the UK is also the world's fourth largest generator of international tourism, in terms of expenditure abroad, after the United States, West Germany and Japan (see Table 1.2.).

Since 1980 the number of Britons travelling abroad has almost doubled but, more importantly, from 1986 onwards the amount spent by the British overseas has been greater than receipts from incoming tourism. In 1994 the deficit on the tourism balance was some £4.2 billion, a situation that can only be reversed in the future by encouraging more international tourists to visit the UK at the same time as persuading a greater number of UK residents to holiday at home.

TABLE 1.2. UK VISITS AND EXPENDITURE ABROAD

Year	Visits (thousands)	Expenditure (£m)
1980	17,507	2,738
1984	22,072	4,663
1986	24,949	6,083
1988	28,828	8,216
1989	31,030	9,357
1990	31,150	9,951
1991	30,808	9,951
1992	33,836	11,243
1993	35,842	12,707
1994	39,897	14,500

Source: *International Passenger Survey*
Dept. of National Heritage 1995

The domestic market is also an important source of income and employment for the UK tourism industry. In 1994, a total of 109.8 million domestic tourism trips generated £14,495 million which, if added to the receipts from incoming tourism and the earnings from international fares on UK carriers (£2,550 in 1994), meant that tourism as a whole contributed just under £27 billion to the UK economy, or 4.0 per cent of GDP. The domestic market, unlike both incoming and outgoing international tourism, has been static, rather than growing, for a number of years. Indeed, it is only the growth in day trips, short breaks and additional holidays that has maintained the overall level of domestic tourism, replacing the loss of main holidays to the overseas market. It is important to note that these figures for domestic tourism do not include day visitor spending, and it is within the day trip sector that the overlap between tourism and leisure arises. Table 1.3. shows the volume and value of domestic tourism by region, with reference to Figure 1.1.

TABLE 1.3. DOMESTIC TOURISM BY REGION 1994

(a)	Trips (million)	Spend (£ million)
England	90.2	11,650
Scotland	8.5	1,310
Wales	9.8	1,075
N. Ireland	1.2	180

(b)		
England	Trips per cent	Spend per cent
Cumbria	3	4
Northumbria	3	3
North West	10	9
Yorks & Humberside	10	10
Heart of England	11	9
East Midlands	8	7
East Anglia	11	10
London	10	9
West Country	17	21
Southern	12	10
South East	9	8

Source: *UK Tourism Statistics*, English Tourist Board

With the exception of the West Country, Northumbria and Cumbria, domestic tourism is spread relatively evenly around the country. This is in marked contrast to incoming tourists, almost sixty per cent of whom spend at least part of their stay in London and who also tend to restrict their visit to the popular 'milk run' cities, such as Oxford, Bath, Stratford-upon-Avon, Cambridge and York. In a sense, therefore, domestic and incoming tourism complement each other as domestic tourists go where incoming tourists do not. The majority of visitors to the popular towns and cities are also domestic tourists but, for example, less than eight per cent of visits to the countryside are made by overseas tourists. The table also highlights the problem of trying to differentiate between tourism and leisure, for although Cumbria is seen as only receiving three per cent, or just over three million, of all domestic visits in England, the Lake District alone plays host to twenty million visitors annually, the majority of whom are on day trips.

Statistics concerning tourism in the UK are available from a variety of sources, including the *Tourism Intelligence Quarterly,* the *United Kingdom Tourism Survey* and the annual *Visits to Tourist Attractions*. It is the changes in the nature of the UK tourism product, however, that are of most relevance to this brief introduction to tourism.

Reference has already been made to the importance of the seaside resorts in the development of tourism. Since the 1960s many of them have seen their popularity wane in the face of competition from overseas resorts which offer better quality, better value, more facilities and attractions and, more often than not, better weather. The seaside resorts have also suffered from the development of new tourism products in the UK. With their outdated, down-market image and lack of investment, the resorts have been unable to maintain their share of the static domestic market.

There are five distinct new products, or types of tourism:

i Heritage Tourism
Heritage is literally defined as what we have inherited from our past. Over the last decade, however, it has become more broadly applied and now the

term is used to describe virtually everything associated with the nation's history, culture, wildlife and landscape. It is therefore not unusual to hear the countryside being described as part of our heritage. Heritage has also become widely used as a marketing tool, forming the basis for what has been described as the heritage industry (Hewison 1987). The UK tourism industry has long been dependent on the country's rich historical past and it has been increasingly packaging heritage as a new type of tourism attraction.

There are two main categories of heritage tourism; tourism in heritage towns and purpose built heritage centres. Heritage towns, such as York, Chester and Stratford-upon-Avon, have a stock of historical attractions and an overall historical atmosphere. They have been popular visitor destinations for many years but more recently they have been taking advantage of the increasing interest in the country's past and also the growth in short break holidays. Heritage centres, on the other hand, are purpose built attractions that utilise modern technology and interpretation techniques to package and present history. The most successful example is the Jorvik Centre in York whilst the Wigan Pier Heritage Centre, which recreates life in a Victorian industrial town, has become increasingly popular since it opened in 1986.

ii Inner City Tourism

In the early 1980s many of Britain's industrial centres were experiencing a decline in their traditional manufacturing base. They were suffering from high levels of unemployment, were becoming run down and were unable to attract investment in new industries. Nevertheless their industrial past was seen as a platform for launching themselves as tourist destinations, thereby using tourism as a catalyst for economic regeneration. One of the first towns to embark on a successful tourism development programme was Bradford. In addition to its rich industrial heritage it also has the attraction of its literary associations of nearby Howarth, home of the Brontës, and its proximity to the Yorkshire countryside. Since then a number of other towns and cities have undertaken similar programmes, collectively marketing themselves as City Breaks.

FIGURE 1.1. UK TOURIST REGIONS

Garden Festivals have been a further means of regenerating inner city areas through tourism. The first was held in Liverpool in 1984, followed by Stoke-on-Trent, Glasgow, Gateshead and finally Ebbw Vale in 1992. Each festival attracted thousands of visitors and created many short-term jobs, although the longer-term benefits have, in most cases, been less evident. The redevelopment of docklands, however, has been one of the most significant innovations in tourism. The docks at Bristol, Portsmouth and Newcastle-upon-Tyne have all become popular tourism and leisure destinations whilst the Albert Dock development in Liverpool is the second most popular tourist attraction after the Blackpool Pleasure Beach in the UK.

iii Industrial Tourism
Industrial tourism can be seen as part of the wider heritage tourism industry for it is based, in part, on the history and development of industrial Britain from the eighteenth century onwards. Interest in industrial heritage is not a new phenomenon. The Great Exhibition of 1851 and the founding of the Science Museum towards the end of the last century were both indicative of a growing awareness of the importance of the country's role in industrial innovation. The last decade, however, has witnessed a remarkable growth in the number of industrial heritage tourist attractions.

Industrial tourism differs from heritage and inner city tourism in that it is site specific. There is a wide variety of attractions ranging from old tin and coal mines, watermills and textile mills to model industrial villages, such as Saltaire near Bradford and New Lanark in the Clyde Valley in Scotland. The Quarry Bank Mill in Cheshire attracts over 150,000 visitors a year whilst the Ironbridge Gorge Museum, based around the world's first metal bridge and the site of the first commercial production of iron, has been a world heritage site since 1986.

Modern industry is also gaining popularity as a tourist attraction. It has been estimated that over five million visits are made annually to breweries, distilleries, pottery companies, glass factories, carpet manufacturers and so on. Nor is tourism limited to production companies; the Thames

Barrier has become a popular attraction for visitors to London whilst the Sellafield nuclear power sation on the Cumbria coast is one of the most popular tourist sites in and around the Lake District.

iv Theme Parks

The United States is generally considered to be the home of the theme park. Disneyland in California and Disney World in Florida, both of which were developed in the late 1950s, are the most famous and attract millions of American and overseas visitors. The market in the US has now reached saturation point with the total number of visits to about thirty American theme parks having remained relatively unchanged in recent years. Some European theme parks, however, pre-date the American parks. De Efteling in the Netherlands, for example, opened in 1951 and today attracts over 2.5 million visitors a year.

Theme parks in the UK are a more recent innovation, dating from the late 1970s. Thorpe Park was one of the first to be established, but Alton Towers, Chessington World of Adventures and Flamingo Land in Yorkshire also all attract large numbers of visitors. In 1994, 3.25 million people visited Alton Towers, making it the most popular paid-entry attraction in the UK; the Blackpool Pleasure Beach, although not strictly a theme park, is the most popular tourist attraction in the UK with over 6.5 million visitors annually. Common to all is the need to invest in new rides and attractions to maintain visitor numbers, particularly since the opening of Euro Disney (more recently re-named Disneyland Paris) in 1992. It is estimated, for example, that the the major British theme parks spent £35 million on new rides and attractions in 1995, although, contrary to initial fears, Disneyland Paris has not proved to be a major threat to UK theme parks. Despite attracting over ten million visitors each year, the development of Disneyland Paris has, paradoxically, resulted in renewed interest in British theme parks, whilst UK theme parks, in comparison to Disneyland, are primarily day visit attractions.

v Inland Resorts

Perhaps the greatest threat to the traditional seaside resorts has been the development of new inland resorts. These are purpose built, self-contained holiday villages based around an all-weather leisure and swimming centre. The first to be established was Center Parcs in Sherwood Forest near Nottingham. It was opened in 1987 at a cost of over £55 million and, despite being able to accommodate up to 3,500 visitors at any one time, it has enjoyed a year round occupancy rate of 98 per cent. (The average occupancy rate for hotels in England is around sixty per cent). In 1989 a second Center Parcs was opened at Elveden Forest in Suffolk and a third, after much local opposition, was opened in Longleat Forest, Wiltshire, in July 1994. Other companies are also planning to enter the holiday village market. For example, the Rank Organisation expect to open their first Oasis Village at Whinfell Forest, Cumbria, in 1997, with two more planned, and it has been suggested that there is sufficient demand for up to ten inland holiday villages in the UK (Biss 1994).

The development and marketing of Center Parcs is described in the case study at the end of this chapter but, in short, the inland resorts are able to satisfy the demand for high quality, self catering short-breaks and holidays at the same time as offering a range of sporting and leisure activities. In recognition of the trends in holiday demand, the traditional holiday camps, such as Butlins, have followed suit by upgrading their accommodation, building new all-weather facilities and changing their name and image.

Overall, then, the tourism industry in the UK is offering a new range of products that are very different from the traditional holiday. The trend is towards short-break, additional holidays that are based on a range of high quality facilties with the emphasis placed firmly on a variety of interests and activities. Many of these new products are also of relevance to tourism in the countryside. The three Center Parcs holiday villages, for example, are located in the countryside and are therefore, in effect, countryside attractions. Likewise many theme parks are to be found in the countryside whilst a number of new types of rural tourism, including rural museums, farm holidays and even conservation holidays, can be categorised under the heading of heritage tourism. Thus, not only is the countryside an integral part of a wider, national tourism product but also tourism in the countryside is responding and changing in accordance with the current trends in UK tourism.

LEISURE

Leisure, like tourism, is a much broader concept than is at first apparent. It is also equally, if not more difficult, to define. Whereas tourism is largely categorised and defined by place and activity, leisure is more a philosophy, or state of being. Thus, whilst tourism is usually a short term obligatory (e.g. business travel) or non-obligatory (e.g. a holiday) activity, leisure is often perceived as a way of life to be strived for, a life free from constraints where people have the choice and ability to work towards self-fulfilment. Inevitably, then, people's perception of leisure is dependent on their individual philosophy of life. To some, leisure might be an ultimate goal in life; others, driven by a desire to succeed in their chosen profession or to complete their life's work, might consider leisure to be a waste of valuable time.

Leisure, therefore, can mean different things to different people. Within the context of the countryside it can refer to anything from a specific activity to developing an understanding of, and harmony with, our natural surroundings. This section, therefore, briefly considers the different approaches to the concept of leisure and the range of activities that it encompasses. (An in-depth study of leisure is found in Torkildsen 1992).

i What is Leisure?

The dictionary defines leisure as *time free from employment*. In other words, leisure may be described as the antithesis to work. Such a definition is, however, rather simplistic. Firstly, it implies that once a person has fulfilled his or her work obligations, whether paid employment, voluntary work or necessary household activities, then any time left over is leisure. This could be described as *disposable* time. Most people, however, have other obligations, such as family commitments, and so not all time free from work is strictly free. Thus, a better description of leisure might be *discretionary* time, or time when people are free to choose how they occupy themselves.

Secondly, by generalising leisure as the opposite to work, the definition of leisure as free time from employment makes certain assumptions about the relationship between work and leisure and the nature of work itself. If leisure is seen as the desirable aim in life then work becomes a means to an end and something to be endured. Certainly work, at a basic level, is concerned with earning money on which to live, but for many people work has a deeper meaning. It is a means of achieving self-fulfilment, of achieving recognition or status or, more generally, doing something useful in life. Research has shown that even if people became financially independent by, for example, inheriting a large sum of money or winning a national lottery they would still continue in employment. Thus, work can be an equally important part of life as leisure and, during the 1980s, it was the work, as opposed to leisure, ethic that was dominant.

The relationship between work and leisure is also becoming less distinct. For many people work, such as DIY or part-time education, is a form of leisure whilst voluntary work is an increasingly popular way of utilising free time. In the extreme, work and leisure may be one and the same thing but, generally, an individual's perception of leisure is dependent on his or her perception of, and motivation for, work.

Another popular way of trying to define leisure is in terms of participation in specific activities that can be regarded as leisure activities, or those which are not motivated by life's basic needs. In other words, leisure encompasses a vast range of activities which may be active, passive, educational or entertaining but which are unified by the fact that they are voluntary, or determined by choice rather than necessity. Defining leisure by activity, however, again raises the problem of the work/leisure dichotomy because what is leisure to one person may be work to another. Furthermore, if leisure is seen as a means of achieving a complete, fulfilled life then many passive activities, such as watching television or playing video games, may be regarded as undesirable, time-filling activities rather than leisure pursuits.

A common theme to the time, non-working and activity based definitions of leisure is the notion of choice and freedom from the needs of daily life. Leisure is normally seen as a source of relaxation and enjoyment that either complements or provides relief from work. Therefore it may be concluded that leisure is best defined as an individual's state of being characterised by freedom of choice, relaxation and entertainment.

ii The Development of Leisure

Leisure has probably existed since earliest times although, as with tourism, it is only during the twentieth century that it has come to be enjoyed by the population as a whole rather than by a privileged minority. However, whilst tourism gradually developed and expanded from the early 1800s onwards, leisure has played varying roles in society throughout history. During the ancient Greek civilisation, for example, leisure was regarded as a means of self-development through education, sport and music whilst work, on the other hand, was associated with manual labour. The Greek philosophers considered leisure to be the basis of civilised society. Leisure became central to the Roman way of life with the emphasis on health and fitness rather than learning, whereas during the Middle Ages the puritanical work ethic took precedence with leisure, at least for the masses, restricted to religious feasts. Indeed, leisure was regarded as an evil. The Industrial Revolution again restricted leisure to the upper levels of society and it was only towards the end of the last century that leisure for the workers was considered to be socially desirable. From the 1930s onwards the factors that led to the development of mass tourism, in particular greater amounts of free time and personal income, likewise heralded the arrival of mass leisure as we know it today.

iii Leisure in the UK

It is virtually impossible to describe the full range of activities that are classed as leisure. There are, for example, over 200 activities alone that can be described as sports. In general, though, leisure can be divided into five distinct categories. By far the most popular is home-based leisure, with a particular emphasis on watching television and videos and listening to music. Gardening and DIY are also important growth sectors in the home market. Social leisure outside the home includes activities such as shopping, drinking, bingo and going for a drive. A major trend in this area has been the development of indoor leisure complexes, such as Meadowhall in Sheffield, which include shopping, eating and entertainment facilities. The third category is entertainment and the arts, covering visits to the theatre, cinemas and museums.

Sport is an expanding sector of the leisure market. It has been estimated that over 21 million people participate in sport and exercise at least once a month and in 1989 almost £9 billion was spent on sports-related goods and services. The most popular sport is walking (2 miles (3.2 km) or more). Passive participation in sport, such as watching football matches, is included in this category. The fifth category is travel and tourism although certain types of tourism, such as business or religious travel, should not be included under the general heading of leisure.

Overall leisure in the UK accounts for almost 16 per cent of household expenditure, or over £100 billion annually. The *Leisure Day Visits Survey 1988-89* was the first survey to estimate the volume and value of day trips away from home, filling the gap in tourism statistics in which figures for day trips do not appear. It found that, during the survey period, 630 million day trips generated £5.2 billion in spending. If this figure is added to those for tourism (i.e. trips including at least one night away), domestic tourism spending is increased by fifty per cent to almost £16 billion. Total tourism spending in the UK (i.e. both domestic and incoming tourism and the receipts of UK carriers) thus, in 1990, amounted to some £25 billion annually, twenty per cent of which was accounted for by leisure day trips.

With specific relevance to tourism and leisure in the countryside, the survey found that the most popular reason for a day trip (28 per cent of all day trips) was outdoor activities, including outdoor sport, walking, fishing, sailing and so on. As many of these activities, by their nature, take place in the countryside, the survey indicated the importance of the countryside as a resource for leisure. Yet this is not the full picture. The *Leisure Day Visits Survey* defined a day trip as one which lasts for three hours or more involving a round trip of 20 miles (32 km) or more. Around a quarter of all trips were between 20 and 29 miles (32 and 47 km) with the average length of trip being 68.4 miles (110 km). However, an earlier survey of countryside recreation (Countryside Commission 1985) found that half of all trips to the countryside involved a round trip of *less than* 20 miles (32 km) and one third were under 10 miles (16 km). In other words, the *Leisure Day Visits Survey* included figures for only half of all day trips to the countryside.

More recently, the *1993 UK Day Visits Survey* (CRN 1995) rectified this by no longer applying the three hour time or the distance travelled limits. A total of 2,200 million day visits were recorded, generating total spending of £15 billion. The average length of trip was just 15 miles (24 km) and one third of all trips were made on foot. Almost 41 per cent of all day visits were to the countryside (including forests/woods, canals/rivers and coastal areas), and the second most popular activity overall was walking or rambling. Average spending on a trip to the countryside was £8.50 but, because this figure excludes non-spenders (potentially a relatively high proportion of visits), it is not possible to calculate an accurate figure for spending on day trips specifically to the countryside. Thus, although the *1993 Day Visits Survey* is not directly comparable with earlier day visit surveys, it is, nevertheless, further confirmation of the popularity of the countryside as a leisure destination. The demand for tourism and leisure in the countryside is considered in greater detail in Chapter Four.

TOURISM AND LEISURE IN THE COUNTRYSIDE

It is clear from these brief, separate descriptions of tourism and leisure that they overlap to a great extent. Indeed, with some exceptions, tourism is just one of a number of activity categories that comprise leisure in its broadest sense, yet tourism and leisure are often considered as distinct areas of study and research. Statistical surveys treat them separately, with tourism figures excluding leisure day visits and *vice versa*. Within the context of the countryside it is possible to maintain this distinction. Some activities, such as outdoor sports or visiting a country pub, would normally be categorised as leisure activities whereas weekend breaks or camping holidays, for example, come under the heading of tourism.

The study of tourism and leisure in the countryside, however, should be based around the resource, the countryside itself, rather than on the activities that take place within it. It is concerned with the effective planning and management of tourism and leisure as one of the many demands and pressures on the countryside, optimising the benefits to visitors, rural communities and the countryside itself whilst, at the same time, maintaining a balance between the exploitation and conservation of the countryside's natural and cultural qualities. Furthermore, many of the problems associated with developing countryside tourism and leisure, such as improving access, conservation issues and visitor management, are of equal relevance to both areas of activity. Throughout this book, therefore, tourism and leisure are considered together as the combined *recreational* use of the countryside.

It is also evident that the countryside is an integral part of the overall tourism and leisure product in the UK. There are three factors which are likely increase the importance of the countryside in comparison to other destinations and attractions. Firstly, as the trends continue towards more free time, greater participation in an increasing variety of outdoor activities, a healthier lifestyle and an expansion of the types of tourism, the countryside is likely to play an increasingly important role as a resource for tourism and leisure. Secondly, the decline in traditional rural industries and the more recent need to limit agricultural production has raised the profile of tourism and leisure as a source of income and employment for rural communities. Increasing emphasis is therefore likely to be placed on developing and promoting countryside recreation. Thirdly, and in contrast, greater awareness of environmental issues in general and the need to conserve the countryside in particular has highlighted the potentially damaging effects of unrestrained tourism development. Therefore the growing demand for countryside recreation and the promotion of its economic benefits is likely to come increasingly into conflict with the needs of conservation, with sustainable development becoming more widespread.

Central to all these issues is the role of the countryside as the basic resource which supports a variety of demands including tourism and leisure. Chapter Two examines the nature of the resource and highlights the difficulties in managing and balancing those demands placed upon it.

Case Study: Center Parcs - Tourism in the Countryside?

The Center Parcs concept originated in 1967 when a Dutch company, then known as Sporthuis Centrum Recreatie, opened its first, small holiday village of thirty villas in the South of Holland. Since then the organisation has expanded to the extent that there are now fourteen Center Parcs holiday villages in North West Europe. Most are in Holland but there are also two villages in France, one in Germany, two in Belgium and three in England. By 1987 the organisation was playing host to an annual two million guests, 70 per cent of whom were repeat visitors, although one of the Dutch holiday villages was sold in January 1995, perhaps as a result of over capacity in the region.

The original purpose of Center Parcs was to offer short break holidays on a year-round basis, as well as longer holidays during the traditional holiday seasons, in a purpose-built, self-contained environment. The emphasis was on the provision of activity based holidays in a natural or rural location, in effect creating a country club atmosphere. To achieve this the Company has developed holiday villages which provide high quality accommodation and leisure facilities with the central attraction being an all-weather, sub-tropical dome. Originally the all-weather centre was based around a water activity environment. Since the mid 1980s, however, the all-weather concept has been expanded to include the Park Plaza, a totally covered area containing shops, restaurants and bars. Thus Center Parcs revolutionised the holiday market, setting the trend for the development of inland resorts. Their success is demonstrated by an average occupancy rate of 95 per cent for all their villages.

The first Center Parcs village in the UK, situated in 440 acres (178 hectares) of land in Sherwood Forest near Nottingham, opened in July 1987. Costing over £55 million it has 709 stone-built villas, six restaurants, four retail outlets and an extensive range of indoor and outdoor sport and leisure facilities based around a 20 metre high sub-tropical swimming dome. Following its immediate success a second

Centre Parcs was opened in Elveden Forest in Suffolk in August 1989. With 650 villas this village cost about £75 million to develop, the extra cost mainly arising from the incorporation of the Park Plaza concept. The roof covering the plaza area can be opened during good weather in the spring and summer. Finally, a third village was opened at Longleat Forest in Wiltshire in July 1994. It is of a similar size to the Elvedon Forest complex but, unlike the two earlier villages, its facilities are distributed amongst three main centres. All of the UK villages have achieved close about 95 per cent occupancy rates with over 40 per cent of their business being repeat visitors, although agressive discounting in 1996 indicates that high occupancy rates will be increasingly difficult to maintain.

The marketing of Center Parcs in the UK has two main themes. Firstly, the villages are marketed as short-break (3-day weekend or 4-day midweek breaks) activity holiday centres, directed mainly towards the ABC1 market segment. This is in response to the growing trend towards additional holidays with the main, long holiday being taken overseas. In particular, the marketing is directed towards younger families, whilst the emphasis on professional/managerial level visitors is reflected to a degree in the relatively higher prices charged compared with those for holidays in the new style seaside holiday villages, such as the up-graded Butlin's camps.

Secondly, the marketing of Center Parcs emphasises the natural countryside setting of their villages. As their brochures state, Center Parcs *combine the finest sports and leisure provision with the tranquility of a beautiful, natural setting. Two worlds in perfect harmony.* Furthermore, the development of the villages is promoted as not only conserving but enhancing the natural enviroment. Great care is taken to preserve existing natural features during construction, whilst extensive tree planting and the creation of lakes and waterways is also undertaken to provide a natural environment and a variety of wildlife habitats. In 1988 Center Parcs were awarded not only the English Tourist Board's England for Excellence Award and the British Tourist Authority's Come to Britain Trophy, but also the Business and Industry Environment Award.

Center Parcs are therfore marketed as sustainable and appropriate rural tourism attractions. There is no doubt that they have done much to improve the environment and that, according to the principles for sustainable development (see Chapter Nine), they have contributed significantly to local employment and income. The three UK villages employ over 2000 staff, most of whom were recruited locally, and it is estimated that each village generates about £10 million a year in the local economy through increased local trade, increased employment and so on. However, in context of sustainable countryside tourism, a number of points must be raised.

Firstly, despite the emphasis on environmental factors, the creation of a large village and a sub-tropical dome is not necessarily appropiate in a rural setting, whatever the original quality of the location. The proposed development at Longleat Forest, in particular, caused widespread controversy, largely as a result of the site falling within an Area of Outstanding Natural Beauty (AONB). The Government's support for the project appeared to contradict its own policy guidance for rural development whilst also raising serious questions about the effectiveness of AONB designations (see Chapter Six). Secondly, although the villages undoubtedly contribute to local income and employment, much of the profits are returned to the parent company. Thirdly, the villages are not small scale developments. They attract large numbers of visitors who must travel there (usually by car) and who generate large amounts of rubbish that must be disposed of. Finally it could be argued, depending on perceptions of what is real countryside, that there is nothing natural about the artificially created environment of a Center Parcs village. Nevertheless, Center Parcs have been hugely successful and, despite possible criticisms, the benefits they have brought to visitors, local communities and the environment represent an important addition to the countryside tourism product.

Chapter Two

The Countryside as a Resource

INTRODUCTION

The countryside is the basic resource that supports rural tourism and leisure. Its intrinsic character and quality are the primary attractions for most visitors who, in turn, are a valuable source of income and employment for rural communities and businesses. Thus, to maintain a healthy, thriving tourism and leisure industry the resource itself must be maintained; a less attractive environment will result in fewer visitors. In other words, tourism and leisure should exist, and be developed, in harmony with the countryside environment.

Yet tourism and leisure are not the only demands made on the countryside. Agriculture, forestry, housing, industry, power generation, roads and the armed forces all compete for a share of, and have an impact on, the resource. The effective management of the countryside is, therefore, dependent on a balanced relationship between the users of the countryside, including visitors, those who live and work in rural communities and the countryside itself. Furthermore, the countryside is a living, working environment which is in a constant state of evolution and change. Centuries of human influence have left their imprint on the landscape that now attracts millions of visitors each year. Thus an understanding of the character of the countryside as a resource is of fundamental importance to the study of countryside tourism and leisure. In particular it is necessary to define what is meant by countryside as a reference point for the rest of this book.

WHAT IS THE COUNTRYSIDE?

The word countryside is commonly used and understood, yet there is no general consensus as to what is or is not countryside. It collectively describes such a variety of land forms and associated land uses that no single definition will suffice. Indeed, any definition of the countryside is as dependent on individual perceptions and experience as it is on the physical or geographical characteristics of the land. To one person, for example, the countryside might signify a particular type or area of landscape, but to another a whole way of life.

The countryside, then, is a vague concept which can mean different things to different people. Furthermore, it may be considered simply as a way of describing the physical, tangible characteristics of a particular area or region, or it may be seen as representative of certain social and cultural structures. However, in a general sense the countryside is usually taken to refer collectively to rural, as opposed to urban, areas, although this again is problematic as it raises the question of where is the line drawn between urban and rural areas. Different parts of the countryside may be more or less rural in both the physical and social sense of the word, whilst the countryside itself is dynamic and in a constant state of change and development. For this reason, it has been suggested that the distinction between urban areas and the countryside is best considered within the parameters of an urban-rural continuum along which different types of countryside may be placed (see Lane 1994). For the purposes of this book, however, countryside is described in terms of its recreational use.

Traditionally the countryside, as a resource for recreation, was restricted to the wilder, more remote parts of the country, including those which have now been designated as national parks. Since the late 1960s there has been an expansion of recreational countryside in terms of both the legal definition of countryside and the remit of those organisations, such as the Countryside Commission, concerned with the management of the countryside. This has resulted from the increasing demand for tourism and leisure in the countryside, the perceived need to provide recreational facilities and opportunities closer to major centres of population, and the diminishing role of farming and agriculture in the rural economy.

The urban-rural fringe, including green belt land, has also been recognised as a valuable resource for recreation (see Chapter Eight). The countryside is literally on the doorstep of larger towns and cities and many countryside, or urban-fringe, projects are working to both conserve and improve the landscape and to promote its enjoyment by the public. The case study at the end of this chapter describes one such project.

Thus the countryside, in recreational terms, refers to all land touching and beyond larger towns and cities. It includes all agricultural, forested and open land and lakes, rivers and coastal areas. Any town or village with less than 10,000 inhabitants is generally accepted to be a rural, rather than urban, settlement and is, therefore, also included in the definition of countryside.

CATEGORIES OF COUNTRYSIDE
As we have seen, there is no single way of defining the countryside. It is made up of such a variety of land forms, from high mountain areas to coastal regions, that it would be impossible to describe it. It is, however, possible to categorise the countryside by a number of broad characteristics. These indicate its varying potential as a resource for tourism and leisure in different rural areas.

i   Rural Population Density
The countryside can be divided into three broad categories on the basis of population density.

(a)   Low Density. No part of Britain can be described as true wilderness yet many remote, upland and moorland areas are very sparsely populated. These have traditionally been the most popular destinations for countryside visitors and many, such as national parks or Areas of Outstanding Natural Beauty, are now formally protected. This has led to stricter planning controls which determine the level and type of tourism and leisure development. Owing to the special qualities of these areas, their intense recreational use is likely to lead to conflict between the demands of visitors and the need for conservation, whilst the arrival of large numbers of visitors can also have serious implications for the social and cultural well-being of remote rural communities. It is also important to note that low population density and the small scale of rural settlements are two important attractions of the countryside to visitors, the majority of whom live in built-up, urban areas.

(b) Medium Density. The areas of the countryside that lie between the remote uplands and the major centres of population have a low to medium population density. Within this category the countryside is made up of small villages and towns surrounded by large areas of intensively farmed land, perhaps most closely conforming to the traditional image of the British countryside. Recreation has not been a major land use in these areas in the past but the growing demand for new and different leisure activities in the countryside, such as four-wheel off-road driving, will increase their recreational value. As most farmland is privately owned, conflict is most likely between visitors and landowners.

(c) High Density. The more highly populated areas of the countryside are found on the urban-rural fringe, in green belts and in commuter belts, areas which may be described as suburbanised countryside. Recreation has traditionally been a low priority in these areas although in recent years there has been a growing emphasis on the provision of tourism and leisure facilities closer to major towns and cities.

ii Economic Prosperity

The countryside can also be categorised by different levels of economic prosperity and diversity. As was discussed in Chapter One, the prime motivating factor behind tourism and leisure development is the perceived economic and employment benefits it can bring to an area or region. Within the context of the countryside, therefore, the role of tourism and leisure as alternative sources of income varies in importance.

The less prosperous areas of the countryside are those which, as a rule, depend on traditional rural industries, such as hill farming. They have been unable to benefit from modern intensive agricultural techniques and the shift of manufacturing and service industries away from the cities into rural locations. In these areas, therefore, tourism and leisure play an important role in improving economic prosperity and diversification. It has been estimated, for example, that tourism accounts for over 20 per cent of all economic activity in the Scottish Highlands and Islands and over one third of all employment in the Lake District National Park is tourism related. Traditional agrarian activities may also be considered an attraction to visitors and it is no coincidence that the more marginal, less prosperous rural areas in the UK where modern intensive farming techniques have not been introduced are amongst the more popular countryside destinations.

At the other end of the scale are those parts of the countryside that enjoy a diverse and prosperous economy and relatively higher levels of employment. By implication, there is no need to develop and promote tourism and leisure in these areas and there may, in fact, be a policy for discouraging tourism development.

iii Accessibility

As we saw in Chapter One, the growth in tourism and leisure has resulted from the three enabling factors of time, money and technology. In particular the dramatic increase in car ownership and use and the corresponding development of the road network has opened up most of the countryside for recreation. Over eighty per cent of all visitors to the countryside travel by car and those parts of the countryside which are more accessible to the main centres of population attract the greatest numbers of visitors. Over 20 million people, for example, live within a three hour drive of the Lake District and most visitors to the Lake District are on day trips. The greater the accessibility of a rural area, the greater are the impacts of tourism and leisure. Indeed, some see the motor car as the most serious threat to the survival of the countryside, an issue that is explored in detail in Chapter Eight.

Access *within* the countryside also determines recreational use and value and is, therefore, a further means of categorising rural areas. Areas with restricted public access, such as privately owned moorland estates, attract less visitors but there is likely to be greater conflict between landowners and those demanding access. The improvement of access within the countryside is central to current countryside recreation policy (see Chapter Seven).

iv Social/Cultural Characteristics

A final means of categorising the countryside as a resource for tourism and leisure is by the social and cultural structure of an area. Rural society is considered by many to have retained a variety of characteristics or attributes that have been lost in modern, urban societies, such as a sense of community or living and working closer to nature, and it these characteristics which are a further attraction of thge countryside to visitors. In other words, the people and communities that live in the countryside are as much a part of the resource as is the physical landscape and any tourism and leisure development should take into account the needs and requirements of local communities. At the same time, different communities may have varying attitudes towards visitors. The inhabitants of a commuter village, for example, having moved from the city to their rural idyll, may have a negative attitude towards sharing the countryside with tourists. In contrast, remote rural communities might welcome tourism and leisure for its economic benefits but may, on the other hand, suffer more from its impacts.

Common to these four categories is that tourism and leisure have an impact on the countryside environment. The degree of impact is dependent on the different characteristics of particular countryside areas and, indeed, it can be both positive and negative. The management and control of these impacts is central to the efficient and sustainable use of the countryside as a resource for recreation and is a theme throughout this book. Most importantly, however, the countryside is not a static, inanimate object, nor is it a museum. It is a living, working and constantly changing environment that has evolved over thousands of years. Its attraction as a resource for recreation is largely dependent on both its special quality and character and on what some see as the uniquely British perception of the countryside.

As a basis for understanding the traditional motivation behind tourism and leisure in the countryside it is necessary, therefore, to consider briefly how the countryside has evolved and developed and how attitudes towards it have adapted in response to changes in rural industry and society. (For a detailed history of the English landscape see Hoskins, 1955).

THE DEVELOPMENT OF THE COUNTRYSIDE

No part of the British countryside is entirely natural. From earliest times, the landscape has been shaped and altered by the influence of people living and working on the land. The complex pattern of fields, villages, woods, hedgerows, walls, roads and footpaths that together create the unique character and atmosphere of the countryside has evolved over the centuries as a result of people's use and exploitation of the land.

Just as the landscape has changed, so too have the needs and requirements of society. Indeed, landscape change is directly related to societal change. At the beginning of civilisation land was used for survival; it was a source of shelter, fuel and food. For centuries the land supported, and was adapted by, an agricultural based society. However, the last two hundred years or so have witnessed the rapid evolution of an increasingly affluent and mobile industrial society. This has inevitably further influenced both the character and use of the countryside; recreation is one of the latest in a long list of demands made on the countryside resource. Moreover, it is a continuing process of change and evolution that must be recognised. It has been argued, for example, that much countryside planning in general, and recreation planning and development in particular, is based on an historical, pre-industrial vision of the countryside. Rather than trying to preserve the past, it is argued, the countryside and its recreational use should be allowed to develop according to the requirements of modern society. (See Fairbrother, 1972 and Harrison, 1991). The sociological arguments are beyond the scope of this book but, in short, the development of the countryside is inextricably linked with both its use and the needs of society as a whole.

The influence of people on the countryside can be traced back to Neolithic times (around 2,500 BC), and up until the mid-eighteenth century the evolution of the countryside was a slow, gradual process of transformation resulting from the increasing use of the land for agriculture. The earliest settlers had only primitive tools and were therefore limited to those parts of the country which were easiest to clear. The Neolithic population of Britain numbered only about 20,000 and thus had a minimal impact on the countryside. They were essentially nomadic people and it was not until the early Iron Age, around 500 BC, that the first villages began to appear. The clearance of land continued through to Roman Britain but again the majority of the countryside remained largely untouched by man. Indeed, the legacy of the Roman occupation is more visible in their towns and roads than any extensive land cultivation. It has been estimated that, during this period, only two or three per cent of potential farmland, excluding the uplands, had been cleared.

The Anglo-Saxon period, between the departure of the Romans and the Norman invasion in 1066, is notable for the appearance of large numbers of villages over the English countryside. The majority of rural villages that now exist, with the exception of those that developed as a result of the Industrial Revolution, had been established by the late eleventh century. The agricultural life of these early villages was based on the open-field system, large open fields divided into strips which were owned and worked by individual villagers. The method of ploughing created ridges along the centre of the strips whilst each strip was separated from the next by a double furrow. The resulting ridge and furrow texture of the landscape is still visible today in some parts of the country.

The farming of the land was generally limited to the fertile, lowland areas of the countryside and vast tracts of land remained in their natural state. Over the centuries leading up to the Agricultural Revolution, however, the destruction of the country's woodlands continued with increasing rapidity. Greater areas of land were required for farming, especially sheep farming. At the start of the sixteenth century, for example, the population of England was outnumbered three to one by sheep. Furthermore, in pre-industrial Britain, wood was the most important natural material available. It was used not only for fuel but also for the construction of houses and ships. Even by the Middle Ages there was serious concern over the increasing shortage of timber and it is estimated that over one million acres (405,000 hectares) of woodland were destroyed between 1500 and 1700. During the eighteenth and nineteenth centuries extensive re-planting of trees was undertaken and many present-day woodlands date from this period.

Until the early eighteenth century, then, the evolution of the countryside was a gradual process of replacing forests and woodlands with open fields. About half of the country's farmland had been enclosed by hedgerows by 1700, the remaining half consisting of medieval open fields and commons. The system of roads, farms and villages was well established and probably about three quarters of the countryside of England and Wales was used for agriculture. From the mid-eighteenth century, however, the transformation of the countryside, in terms of both the physical appearance of the landscape and rural society, has been more rapid and dramatic.

The Agricultural Revolution, from around 1750 onwards, signified the emergence of modern farming methods with more efficient crop rotation, the introduction of winter fodder for livestock, the expanding use of fertilisers and so on. The open field system was unsuitable for these new methods and, therefore, the following century saw the enclosure of millions of acres of open farmland, creating the patchwork of fields, hedgerows and stone walls that is the unique characteristic of the British countryside. Between 1761 and 1844 more than 2,500 Acts of Parliament led to the enclosure of over 4 million acres (1,619,000 hectares) of open fields. Additionally, the advances in agricultural techniques meant that previously unusable land, such as heaths and moors, could now be cultivated and a further 1.25 million acres (506,000 hectares) of marginal land were enclosed.

More recently a second agricultural revolution has again transformed large areas of the countryside. The system of subsidies and support payments to farmers introduced since the Second World War, initially as a national policy and latterly under the Common Agricultural Policy (CAP), has acted as an incentive for the introduction of more intensive and large scale farming methods. The most visible effect on the landscape has been the creation of large prairie farms, paricularly in eastern England, whilst technological advances have enabled the cultivation of marginal land such as wetlands and moorlands. The destruction of the traditional rural landscape and the resulting impacts on nature and wildlife habitats are well documented (see Shoard 1980), but the figures are alarming. Between 1947 and 1980, for example, the total length of hedgerows fell by

22 per cent, semi-natural vegetation declined by 25 per cent and the area of broad leaved woodland decreased by forty per cent.

The Industrial Revolution also had a profound effect on the countryside. It brought physical changes, such as the building of canals and railways and the development of industrial communities, including mining villages and mill towns. More importantly, it heralded the change from an agricultural to an industrial, urban based society. At the start of the 1800s most of the population lived in rural towns and villages and about thirty per cent of people worked in agriculture. By 1850 half the population lived in the expanding towns and cities and in the early twentiethth century only twenty per cent of the population still lived in the countryside. Since then the number of people dependent on agriculture for a living has continued to decline to the extent that less than five per cent of the rural population is now employed in farming.

In recent years, however, the population in countryside areas has begun to increase again and the loss of jobs in agriculture has been compensated by the diversification of the rural economic base. Many manufacturing companies, attracted by cheaper rents, have relocated from urban to rural areas whilst many new service industries have been established in the countryside. By 1987 almost two thirds of rural employment was in private and public sector service industries and a further quarter was in manufacturing. Technological advances in communications and a growing trend towards a service, as opposed to manufacturing, industry based economy will continue to reduce the distinction between urban and rural societies and economies.

One effect of the urbanisation and industrialisation of society which occured during the nineteenth century was that the countryside became, for a growing proportion of the population, the antithesis of life and work in the city. They were faced with poor housing and long hours of work in appalling conditions and thus people's perceptions of the countryside began to change. It was no longer a place where they lived and worked but a symbol of times past, of a way of life lost. It has been suggested that the English have an idealised, romantic vision of the countryside (see

Lowenthal and Prince, 1965). Variously associated with history, art, poetry and the rustic lifestyle, the countryside, it is argued, is seen as the true nation, the real England, a green and pleasant land (Newby 1985).

As discussed in Chapter Three, the romanticising of the countryside was a major influence on the early growth of tourism and leisure in the countryside, as was the industrialisation of society itself. It is also probably true to say that people's perception of the countryside is, in many cases, as important as its physical attributes in determining its attraction as a resource for recreation. Many countryside visitors are motivated by their perceived image of a rural utopia, a place to escape from the stress of modern life into a nostalgic past; for the urban dweller, the countryside represents a *refuge from modernity* (Short 1991:34). Furthermore, current policies for both conservation and the provision of facilities and opportunities for tourism and leisure in the countryside appear to be based on this traditional *countryside aesthetic* (Harrison, 1991). In other words, conservation policies are symptomatic of the present interest in heritage. They are designed to protect the scenic quality of the landscape and the rural way of life which, perhaps, belong to another, pre-industrial, age. As a result, emphasis is placed on the promotion of more traditional and appropriate quiet, contemplative pursuits whilst the demands of newer activities have not been catered for. The degree to which the countryside and its use is being allowed to continue to evolve is a matter of debate but the policies of those organisations entrusted with the planning and management of the countryside would certainly seem to conform to the aesthetic ideology.

DEMANDS ON THE COUNTRYSIDE

The countryside is a finite resource. Throughout the centuries it primarily supported the agricultural needs of a gradually increasing population and, in simple terms, there was plenty of land to go round. The last two hundred years, however, have witnessed a population explosion and a great increase in the variety of demands made on the countryside, all of which, in effect, compete for a share of the resource. Thus, the tourism and leisure industry does not enjoy exclusive rights to the use of the countryside. Rather, it is one of many competing claims between which a balance must be maintained.

i Farming and Agriculture

The dominant land use of the countryside has always been farming. As we have seen, farming has been largely responsible for the evolution of the countryside and the creation of the traditional rural landscape and even now about eighty per cent of the countryside is farmland. Modern, intensive farming methods introduced since the Second World War have, however, had a dramatic and, in places, destructive effect on both the natural and visual qualites of the landscape. The extensive loss of hedgerows and woodland, the drainage of wetlands and the ploughing over of moors and downland have done much to destroy the traditional countryside. Nor have protective measures, such as national park designation, been able to control the activities of farmers. It has been estimated, for example, that more than twenty-five per cent of the North York Moors have been converted to either forest or farmland *since* the area was designated as a national park.

Until recently, intensive farming has been officially encouraged through the system of subsidies, support payments and capital grants. Government policy itself was conflicting, with incentive payments available to either convert land to agriculture or to conserve it. During the 1980s, however, a number of schemes were introduced to limit, if not reverse, the intensive use of farmland. The first Environmentally Sensitive Areas were designated in 1987 (see Chapter Six) and with continuing excess in production over demand, resulting in the EU's butter and grain mountains, farmers have been encouraged to take land out of production under the set-aside scheme. Both this and the more recent Countryside Stewardship Scheme place the emphasis on conservation and quiet enjoyment.

Therefore, in the 1990s there is likely to be a reversal of the excesses and policies in farm production of the previous four decades. It has been estimated, for example, that up to fifteen per cent of land currently used for cereal production is surplus to requirements. Indeed, the Countryside Commission sees the reduction in farm output as an opportunity for farmers to diversify into other businesses, particularly tourism and leisure. In the uplands, however, there is a need to preserve farming on environmental grounds because the grazing of animals helps preserve the semi-natural vegetation.

ii Forestry

By the beginning of the twentieth century less than five per cent of the countryside was forested and the destruction of Britain's forests and woodlands was almost complete. Therefore the Forestry Commission was established in 1919 with the purpose of replenishing the nation's timber supply. The Forestry Commission is now the country's largest landowner and the proportion of land under forest has risen to ten per cent.

For many years the Commission was primarily concerned with the commercial production of timber with little attention being paid to either the visual or recreational amenity of the forests. This resulted in large areas of the countryside being planted with dense forests of fast growing conifers. These had a dramatic impact on both the scenic quality of the landscape and also the wildlife habitats within the forests. From the 1960s the planting of forests has been more sensitive to the landscape and there has also been more emphasis on planting a mixture of trees. Since 1967 the Forestry Commission has had a positive policy towards recreation provision and many forests and woods are now popular visitor destinations. The future trend is towards specially developed, multi-purpose forested areas, known as Community Forests, providing for timber, recreation, nature conservation, land reclamation and housing. In early 1992, proposals for a new National Forest and twelve regional Community Forests were announced, thirty year projects which together form part of the Countryside Commission's overall strategy for the development of a multi-purpose, sustainable countryside into the twenty-first century (Countryside Commission 1995b).

iii Water

The lakes, rivers, canals, reservoirs and coastal waters which together comprise the country's water resources are an integral element of the countryside. They visually complement the character and atmosphere of the countryside whilst, like the rural landscape, they support a wide range of uses. Not only do they satisfy domestic and industrial water demand but also they are part of the land drainage and flood control system, they are used for transport and for waste and sewage disposal and they also play a vital role in nature and wildlife conservation. Furthermore, water is an increasingly important resource for recreation (see McCormack 1994). Navigable rivers and canals are widely used for a variety of activities such as cruising, sailing and canoeing whilst lakes and reservoirs also support a number of water-based sports. It is estimated that 3.9 million people now participate in angling, spending a total of £1,746 million directly and indirectly in 1990, whilst flooded gravel pits are increasingly being used for recreation. Nor is it just the use of the water itself that attracts visitors; riverbanks, canal towpaths, lakesides and coastal areas are all popular sites for informal activities, such as walking, cycling, photography and bird watching.

As the various demands for the use of water continue to increase, the management of water resources in terms of both space and water quality will be central to many countryside issues. In some parts of the country, in particular the south-east, the continuing drought situation throughout 1992 brought about by high levels of demand and below average rainfall over a number of years was a matter of serious concern until the wet winter that year. Similarly, many parts of the country, in particular Yorkshire, experienced severe water shortages during the hot summer of 1995. On the other hand, some areas of the country have an over-supply of water; the Kielder Reservoir in Northumberland, for example, was built in anticipation of a rapid increase in water demand in the north-east of England but is now surplus to requirements.

Competition between the various users of existing water resources and concern for water quality are likely to be the main areas of water resource management in coming years. Windermere in the Lake District, for example, has become seriously polluted owing to its intense recreational use and over 500 sacks of litter were removed from its shores in 1991. There are now plans to reduce the speed limit for motor craft on certain parts of the lake whilst some people believe that some water sports, such as water skiing and jet skiing, are inappropriate in a national park setting and should be banned altogether. (A public enquiry into the Windermere proposal was held between May 1994 and January 1995 but, by early 1996, no decsion had been made). Likewise, the scenic and natural qualities of many coastal areas are under threat from recreational developments, such as marinas, and intensive farming. In short, the management of the country's water resources will be centered on balancing the various demands for the use of water with the need to maintain adequate supplies, water quality and conservation of the water environment.

iv Military Use
The Ministry of Defence (MOD), which owns or leases nearly 600,000 acres (243,000 hectares) of land, is the second largest landowner in the country. It uses extensive tracts of the Dartmoor, Northumberland and Pembrokeshire Coast National Parks and, in fact, has a presence in every national park apart from Exmoor. Probably no other use of the countryside attracts as much criticism as its use for military training. The firing of live ammunition scars the landscape, disturbs people and wildlife and restricts access to some of the most beautiful and wild areas of the country. Nor is the training restricted to land; low flying military jets are a common feature in many parts of the country, particularly in the Lake District and over North Yorkshire. On the other hand, it has also been argued that, by restricting access, military use of the countryside can benefit the conservation of wildlife.

The public are allowed access to most training areas at certain times. In fact in 1992 the MOD published a booklet entitled *Walks on Ministry of Defence Lands*, including walks on Dartmoor and Salisbury Plain. Nevertheless, the ending of the Cold War and cut-backs in the armed forces generally are likely to lead to further questions being raised over the necessity for such a large land area to be used for military training.

v Housing
The increase in the amount of housing required nationally is determined not by the actual size of the population but by demographic changes within the population. Therefore, although the overall population of the country

is expected to grow relatively slowly, the number of households is likely to increase more rapidly. The major growth is in the single person household category, although longer life expectancy, increasing numbers of single-parent families, the high divorce rate and the trend towards younger people buying homes also contribute to higher demands for housing.

Much of this demand will be catered for in urban areas but there will be, nevertheless, increasing demand for new housing in the countryside as the urban-rural population shift continues. In fact, a survey in 1992 found that one in five city residents planned to move to the countryside within five years and that two thirds of those questioned would prefer to live in the country. This will give rise to a number of pressures and impacts in rural communities. Firstly, much of the recent increase in rural households has been absorbed within existing town and village limits, but further demand will necessitate new housing developments in the wider countryside. Secondly, the popularity of living in the countryside has resulted in dramatic increases in the price of rural housing, causing severe problems in some rural areas. Thirdly, traditional rural villages, particularly in more remote areas, tend to be close-knit communities that date back many generations. As more and more people move away from the cities, though, these traditional communities may be swamped, or even lost. Many small communities in the south-east of England, for example, have become no more than commuter dormitory towns and villages.

Traditional village life is an integral part of the countryside and an important element in the attraction of the countryside for tourism and leisure. Rural crafts, the farming industry, country pubs and so on are all attractions in their own right and the income from visitors is vital to their continuation. Therefore it is essential that policies for housing in the countryside take both the use of the land and the social and economic well-being of rural communities into account, factors which were to some extent recognised in the government's White Paper, *Rural England: a nation committed to a living countryside*, published in October 1995.

vi Conservation
As public concern for environmental matters in general, and for the

countryside in particular, continues to grow there will be increasing demands for areas of the countryside to be protected from inappropriate development and change. Surveys have shown that people are generally becoming more concerned about the need to protect the countryside (see British Social Attitudes 1986 and 1987). It has been found, for example, that not only do increasing numbers of both rural and city dwellers feel that the countryside has changed a lot in the last twenty years but also that a majority feel it has changed for the worse. Urbanisation, industrialisation and the agricultural use of chemical pesticides and fertilisers are seen to be the greatest threats but, most interestingly, increased recreational use is not perceived as a threat. The surveys also found that a majority of people believed that best use for land taken out of agricultural production was the creation of national parks and wildlife reserves.

In a strict sense conservation is not a demand on the countryside but setting aside areas for protection restricts other uses and is, therefore, a claim on the countryside resource. The purpose of most land designation in Britain is conservation (see Chapter Six). Nature Reserves and Sites of Special Scientific Interest are specific conservation designations but development and change is also restricted in national parks and Areas of Outstanding Natural Beauty. Furthermore, the policies of most organisations concerned with the management of the countryside and its use for recreation are dominated by the perceived need to conserve and protect rural landscape and communities. Thus, conservation is both a physical claim on the land and also an ideological demand on the resource.

There are, of course, many other demands and claims on the countryside. Quarrying and mining can have localised impacts, both visually and in terms of noise, pollution and transport, whilst the generation and supply of power makes use of the countryside's resources. Elecricity transmission lines are considered by many to be a visual intrusion whilst new developments, such as the windfarms on Kikby Moor in the Lake District, are an indication of the constantly changing and evolving use of the countryside. It has been forecast that car ownership could increase by up to 48 per cent by 2005; unless there is a dramatic reversal in the government's continuing policy of extending and improving the road network to satisfy this demand, yet more of the countryside will be lost, to say nothing of the pollution and congestion caused by an increasingly car dominated society.

In short, the countryside is a resource supporting a multitude of demands, all of which have an impact on both the environment and, to a greater or lesser extent, the other users of the countryside. These demands also depend on a healthy, attractive and thriving countryside; there is an underlying need for the countryside resource to be protected and for the uses of it to be sustainable. That is, the overall use of the countryside should be planned and managed in a way which not only minimises the depletion of the resource but optimises the benefits to the environment, rural comunities and those who make use of the countryside. In other words, countryside management in general is concerned with maintaining a balanced relationship between the physical and social characteristics of the countryside and the demands made upon it. More specifically, countryside recreation must also be planned so that the intrinsic quality and attractiveness of the countryside is preserved whilst the benefits to visitors and local communities are optimised. The advent of mass tourism and leisure has, however, brought serious impacts which threaten the future of the countryside as a resource for recreation.

THE IMPACTS OF TOURISM AND LEISURE
The prime motivating factor behind the development of tourism and leisure, both nationally and internationally, is the perceived economic and employment benefits that can arise. Thus, for example, many developing countries have turned to tourism as a means of expanding and diversifying their economies as the basis for wider economic growth. Similarly, tourism is being promoted in many countryside regions in Britain to replace the loss of jobs in traditional industries and, as we have seen, tourism and leisure can be a significant source of income and employment for rural communities. More specifically, tourism and leisure contribute to economic and social regeneration through their potential for job retention and creation, pluriactivity (the opportunity to supplement incomes by individuals or families having more than one job) and service retention (for

example, local shops, facilities and public transport), as well as the contribution they can make towards conservation and to the regeneration of local arts and crafts (OECD 1994).

There has, however, been increasing alarm amongst both conservationists and the tourism industry about the potentially destructive effects of uncontrolled tourism development. All tourism is dependent on the environment in which it exists, whether natural or man made, and unless that environment is protected then, in the extreme, the longer-term negative impacts of tourism can outweigh any shorter-term economic benefits. In other words, excessive or inappropriate development can destroy those things that attract visitors in the first place, with serious economic and social consequences in the destination region. (See Mathieson and Wall, 1982, for a complete consideration of tourism impacts.)

The impacts of tourism are normally associated with the development of mass tourism to overseas destinations. There has been much publicity, for example, surrounding the rise and fall in the popularity of the Spanish seaside resorts and the effects of the rapid growth of tourism on the culture and society of developing nations. The fragile ecology of places such as the Galapogos Islands and the Himalayas is threatened by tourism; the Everest Base Camp, a popular destination on trekking holidays in Nepal, is said to be the highest rubbish tip in the world. Furthermore, the economic dependence of some countries on the income from tourism has been described as a form of neo-colonialism.

Of equal concern, however, are the impacts of tourism and leisure on the British countryside. Some areas, of course, are more resilient than others and different activities have varying impacts on the environment but there are generally two categories, or types, of impact; physical impacts and social/cultural impacts.

i Physical Impacts
The physical impacts of tourism and leisure are those which have an effect on the physical environment of the countryside. These can occur in a number of ways.

(a) Erosion

One of the most visible and publicised effects of recreation in the countryside is the erosion of footpaths. The fells of the Lake District, the mountains in the Snowdonia and Brecon Beacons National Parks and many other popular trails, such as the Pennine Way and the Lyke Wake Walk, are in a serious state of disrepair. The paths on what are known as the Three Peaks in the Yorkshire Dales, Ingleborough, Penyghent and Whernside, have been so heavily used that on average they are over 37 feet (11.2 metres) wide. An estimated 120,000 walkers climb Ingleborough each year and all-terrain mountain bikes are now a common sight on many upland paths. The problem of footpath erosion has also been compounded by the increasing popularity of walking as a year-round activity. Vegetation damaged by walkers' boots no longer has a chance to recover during winter months. The implications for the maintenance and repair of footpaths are enormous in terms of both finance and time. In the Lake District, for example, the National Trust employs four footpath-repair teams at an annual total cost of £160,000 and it has been estimated that could take 45 years for all the Lakeland footpaths to be repaired.

Erosion is not limited to footpaths. Illegal parking causes damage to grass verges; the provision of extra car parks goes some way to alleviating the problem, although more parking facilities attracts more visitors thereby putting more pressure on the countryside. The erosion of river banks by the wash from motor cruisers is also a major problem, paricularly in the Norfolk Broads.

(b) Pollution

Tourism, by implication, involves travel. Whether by bus, train, aeroplane, boat or car, the movement of people has some impact on the environment. Over eighty per cent of all visits to the countryside are made by car and it is the car which is the greatest source of air pollution. About 19 per cent of the UK's carbon monoxide emissions and 45 per cent of nitrogen oxide emissions are caused by traffic. Studies in Germany have found that much of the damage to the forests has been caused by car emissions. Rivers and lakes can also be polluted by oil and fuel leaks from motor craft and most forms of motorised transport also give rise to noise pollution.

Litter and rubbish also pollute the countryside and can be dangerous to livestock whilst graffiti and other intentional damage to ancient monuments and buildings are also a form of pollution. Overcrowding in honeypot destinations and traffic jams can be described as people pollution and can have a serious impact on both local residents and on the enjoyment of other visitors.

The development of tourism and leisure facilities can also give rise to what can be termed visual or architectural pollution. The prime attraction of the countryside is its scenic quality but as more and more facilities are built to cater for increasing numbers of visitors that quality can become polluted by inappropriate developments. The national chains of roadside restaurants, often with brightly coloured signs, can look out of place beside a country road and much roadside furniture, such as road signs, advertisements and the increasingly popular white-on-brown tourist signs, tend to mar the visual character of the countryside. Indeed, road developments and improvements could also be categorised as visual pollution. On a larger scale, holiday villages, time-share developments, leisure complexes, caravan and camping sites, ski lifts and and so on could all be seen as polluting the visual amenity of the countryside, although much is dependent on individual perceptions of what the countryside should be used for. That is, if the *countryside aesthetic* is applied, then all new, modern developments could be argued as polluting the countryside.

(c) Physical and Ecological Damage

The physical impact of tourism and leisure is also evident in the damage that is caused, often by the sheer volume of vistors, to countryside attractions. Stonehenge, for example, had to be cordoned off to prevent further damage to the ancient stones and many National Trust houses and gardens, such as Sissinghurst in Kent, are in danger of becoming victims of their own popularity. The ecology of the countryside can also be threatened by tourism and leisure developments and the activities of visitors in the countryside. Vegetation and wildlife habitats can be damaged, for example, by people picking wild flowers or wandering off footpaths onto open country.

ii Social and Cultural Impacts

The social and cultural impacts of tourism and leisure are normally associated with the effects of mass tourism in lesser developed countries. The clashes between different cultures and value systems, the ostentatious display of relative wealth and the commercialisation and trivialisation of culture, art and religous festivals are just some of the problems that arise from the influx of large numbers of visitors in some countries. Though less marked, countryside tourism and leisure can also have a number of sociocultural impacts on rural communities.

Recreation can bring economic and employment benefits to rural communities and small numbers of visitors will have little, if any, adverse impact on the lives of local people. Larger scale tourism, however, can impact on rural life in a variety of ways. Traditional village shops serving the day to day needs of the local community may be converted into souvenir shops or tea shops to benefit from the income from visitors, thereby reducing the level of local services. Crowds and congestion on the streets and in shops and pubs may inconvenience local residents, who then begin to resent the presence of visitors. Clovelly in Devon, for example, has a population of 400 yet plays host to 370,000 visitors a year, many of whom peer through windows and even try to enter into local residents' homes (ETB 1991).

The purchase of houses and cottages as second or holiday homes in rural areas tends to inflate the price of housing and land as well as reducing the number of homes available for local residents. In the Lake District some 16 per cent of all properties are second/holiday homes and in the Langdale valley the proportion is 37 per cent. The value of properties in the national parks in particular can be as much as 25 per cent above the national average while local income is, generally, lower than average. Thus, younger people are unable to find affordable places to live and may therefore move to the cities. Widespread ownership of rural properties by outsiders can also cause resentment and a loss of local culture and identity. The fire-bombing of holiday homes in North Wales during the 1980s, for example, was as a reaction to the growth in the number of properties owned by English people.

As rural communities become more dependent on tourism and leisure as a source of income and employment it is possible that, in the extreme, they will lose their local identity and become objects of curiosity to visitors. Furthemore, that economic dependence itself can have a serious social impact; the greater the dependence on the income from visitors, the greater will be the hardship if the number of visitors declines. Thus, a wet summer season can have serious implications for the economic prosperity of popular rural destinations.

iii Positive Impacts

In addition to income and employment generation, tourism and leisure can also bring positive benefits to the environment. Many historical buildings, for example, depend on the income from visitors for their upkeep. Tourism can also bring a new lease of life to old or redundant buildings in the countryside. Disused farm buildings can be converted into bunk-barns or other forms of accommodation and old mills are often converted into restaurants or craft centres. Darley Mill near Pately Bridge in North Yorkshire, for example, was a ruined water mill but it now houses a furniture and craft shop and a tea room and restaurant.

SUSTAINABLE DEVELOPMENT

Throughout this chapter it has been emphasised that the countryside is a resource that supports a variety of demands and that these demands have an impact on the physical and social character of the countryside. Concern for the environment and the conservation of the world's natural resources as a whole is becoming more widespread and as a result sustainable development is being proposed as the way forward. Sustainability is a difficult concept to define but in essence it is concerned with minimising the destruction and wastage of natural resources, preserving them for the benefit and use of future generations. Thus, reducing air pollution, searching for alternatives to fossil fuels, preventing the destruction of the rain forests and recycling paper are all forms of sustainable development.

The same principles may be applied to the use of the countryside. Sustainable farming methods, for example, are those which minimise the

51

use of chemical fertilisers and pesticides, avoid the destruction of the natural and wildlife features of the countryside and preseve its productivity for the future. Likewise, countryside recreation should be sustainable, ensuring that the negative impacts described above are minimised and that the countryside and its communities benefit from the development of tourism and leisure. Conversely, any activity that incurs a cost on the countryside, whether erosion, pollution or a disruption to local communities, is non-sustainable. It would be logical to conclude, therefore, that countryside recreation can never be sustainable because every activity has some degree of impact.

Nevertheless, the tourism and leisure industry has become increasingly concerned about the impacts of tourism on the environment. It has proposed that the solution lies in the adoption of sustainable tourism development policies, although there is some debate as to what those policies should be and, indeed, whether or not the industry is simply jumping on the environmental bandwagon as a marketing ploy (Wheeller 1991 and 1992). Many organisations concerned with tourism and leisure in the countryside are also adopting a sustainable approach to the planning and management of the countryside. For example, the Countryside Commission recently published *Sustainable Rural Tourism*, a booklet designed to encourage and suggest ways of developing rural tourism which *can be maintained in the long term without degrading the environment in which it takes place* (Countryside Commission 1995c). The principles of sustainable tourism and specific management schemes are examined in Chapter Eight.

The basis of sustainable planning and management of countryside recreation lies in the inter-relationship between four factors, at the heart of which lies the resource, the countryside itself (see Figure 2.1.). The activities of visitors and the tourism and leisure industry impact on the people who live, work and own the countryside and the physical landscape. Conversely, the countryside and its communities must be maintained in order to continue to support the industry and to attract visitors. This relationship is cental to the provision and management of tourism and leisure in the countryside.

FIGURE 2.1. THE RURAL INTER-RELATIONSHIP

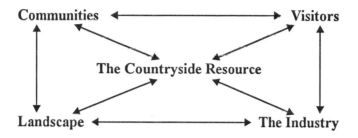

CARRYING CAPACITY

Every resource, including the countryside, is finite. In other words, there is a limit to its use. One of the means of measuring the level of recreational use that the countryside can absorb, hence providing a basis for countryside planning and managing, is the concept of carrying capacity. This may be defined as the level of use that the countryside can sustain before the landscape, the experience or enjoyment of the visitors and the prosperity and well-being of its communities is impaired. There are four categories of carrying capacity.

(a) Physical Carrying Capacity

Different destinations or attractions have different physical capacities to absorb people. There is a limit to the number of visitors who can be accommodated in a country house, in a pub, in car parks and so on. Therefore, physical carrying capacity is of more relevance to individual destinations within the countryside rather than the countryside as a whole.

(b) Ecological Carrying Capacity

The ecological capacity of the countryside is the degree to which it can sustain recreation before its ecology, or natural and wildlife characteristics, are damaged. The erosion of footpaths or river banks, the pollution of lakes and rivers and the destruction of wildlife habitats are all indications that the ecological capacity of an area has been exceeded.

(c) Social Carrying Capacity

All communities will be able to absorb the influx of visitors to some extent. Much will depend on the type of visitor and the location and size of the community. However, the level of tourism and leisure development beyond which the social and cultural well-being of the local comunity is adversely affected is defined as the social carrying capacity.

(d) Psychological Carrying Capacity

Psychological carrying capacity is less easy to measure as it depends to a great extent on the needs of individual visitors and the characteristics of the area or site. Essentially it refers to the level of congestion that will be tolerated by visitors before their experience or enjoyment is impaired. A theme park, for example, has a high psychological capacity; vistors would expect to be amongst a crowd and it may, in fact, contribute to the enjoyment of the visit. On the other hand, the psychological capacity of some countryside areas may be very low. For a hiker in an upland area the sight of other hikers might spoil his or her sense of peace and solitude and, for that individual, the psychological capacity of the area has been exceeded. Indeed, different visitors to the same site may have different perceptions of its psychological capacity.

Some types of carrying capacity are more easy to define and measure than others and the basis of measurement can largely be dependent on value judgements. All recreational activity involves a degree of impact and therefore the question arises, for example, of what amount or level of impact is acceptable? Nevertheless, the concept of carrying capacity is a useful tool for both countryside and visitor management and, as such, underlines the fragile and finite nature of the countryside as a resource for tourism and leisure.

SUMMARY

This chapter has introduced the concept of the countryide as the basic resource that attracts and supports tourism and leisure and the necessity of maintaining it for the benefit of visitors, rural communities and the landscape itself. It has defined the countryside, for the purpose of this book, as including all open, agricultural and forested land outside and fringing urban areas, towns and villages of less than 10,000 inhabitants, rivers, lakes, canals and reservoirs and coastal areas. A number of important points have emerged.

i   The countryside is a living, working environment that has evolved and changed throughout history, and continues to change, as a result of human influence and exploitation and economic and social trends.

ii The countryside as a resource for tourism and leisure may be categorised by a variety of physical, economic and social characteristics which determine the type and level of recreational use. Its attraction lies in both its physical, cutural and visual amenity and in individual perceptions of the countryside.

iii The countryside is a multi-purpose resource that supports a broad range of demands and uses. These demands are inter-related inasmuch as the policy and management of one use inevitably has effects on others. The effective and sustainable management of the countryside is dependent on maintaining a balance between these demands and uses.

iv Tourism and leisure have both positive and negative impacts on the rural environment. The key to sustainable recreational use of the countryside is to minimise the physical and social impacts whilst optimising the benefits to local communities and visitors and ensuring that tourism and leisure contribute to the protection and conservation of the countryside.

Recreation is just one of many demands made on the countryside, yet it is becoming one of the major sources of income and employment for many rural areas. It also has many impacts on the countryside and there is an increasing need for effective planning and management so that the resource is protected for future generations. Chapter Three describes the past and present trends in demand as an introduction to the following chapters on the legal and organisational structure of countryside management.

Case Study: The Luton and Dunstable Countryside Project

Bedfordshire is the third smallest of the 39 English Shire Counties and, with a population of some 540,000, the sixth most densely populated. The major urban centres are Bedford, lying in the centre of the county, and the Luton and Dunstable conurbation at its southern tip. Some 77 per cent of Bedfordshire's land area is farmland whilst urban and industrial use accounts for a further seventeen per cent. The landscape of Bedfordshire includes chalk downland, river valleys and clay vales and the southern end of the county forms part of the Chilterns Area of Outstanding Natural Beauty. The county is, perhaps, better known for its brick-making and car industries rather than its countryside but, nevertheless, the County Council has adopted a countryside strategy based on conserving wildlife and historical sites, increasing the area of woodland and improving access for recreation. Four areas in particular have been identified for priority action; Marston Vale (one of twelve Community Forests in England), the Ivel Valley, major road and rail corridors and the Luton and Dunstable Urban Fringe.

Luton, Dunstable and Houghton Regis together form one of the largest urban areas in south east England outside Greater London. The urban/rural fringe surrounding the towns is beset with problems common to many such areas; new housing developments intrude on the countryside, farming is hampered by vandalism and trespass, rubbish is illegally dumped and access to the countryside is poorly provided for. To counter these problems the County Council, in partnership with the Countryside Commission, has established the Luton and Dunstable Countryside Project.

The Project employs two full-time Project Officers. Its main purpose is to work towards the improvement of the countryside within the project area and to promote its enjoyment by both local people and visitors. To achieve this aim the Project's work is based on negotiation, assistance and direct action where necessary. Fundamental to the success of the Project, however, is the involvement of local people and therefore the Project works closely with the Luton and Dunstable Wildlife Project, local schools, other local voluntary groups and the British Trust for Conservation Volunteers (BTCV). There are four main areas of activity in which the Project is involved.

i Environmental Improvement
The Project Officers undertake small-scale work themselves or arrange for volunteer groups or, if necessary, contractors to improve the local rural environment. They are also able to organise the payment of grant aid where appropriate. Their environmental improvement work includes activities such as planting trees, assisting in landscape management, removing rubbish and abandoned cars, resolving conflicts resulting from vandalism and trespass and improving the appearance of buildings in the countryside.

ii Improving Access
Much of the Project's work is concerned with repairing, clearing and waymarking footpaths, replacing stiles and bridges and ensuring proper use. Particular attention is paid to improving access and attending to the special needs of certain user groups, such as the disabled. For example, paths need to be suitably surfaced with gentle gradients for wheelchair users.

iii Nature Conservation
The Project works closely with the local Wildlife Project and other voluntary groups to protect existing wildlife habitats and to create new ones. Luton Borough Council has also developed a Nature Conervation Strategy, identifying different categories of sites for conservation in and around the town.

iv Improving Awareness
Perhaps one of the most important parts of the Project's work is improving local people's awareness of the surrounding countryside, in terms of both attracting new users and promoting the need for conservation and appropriate use. The Project Officers work closely with schools, colleges,

57

community groups and volutary organisations, giving talks, arranging activities and leading guided walks.

The work of the Luton and Dunstable Countryside Project is, therefore, essentially the same as that undertaken by national organisations, such as the Countryside Commission, but on a local scale. It is, perhaps, at the local level that the most effective work can be done in the urban/rural fringe, as reflected in the emphasis placed by the Countryside Commission on community involvement (see Chapter Five). Nevertheless, the continuing success of the Project is equally, if not more, dependent on adequate funding and the enthusiasm and commitment of the Project Officers as it is on the support of local people.

Chapter Three

Countryside Recreation:
Demand and Supply

INTRODUCTION

Countryside recreation encompasses a wide range of activities and pursuits, many of which are unplanned, spontaneous and informal. Everything from a summer holiday in a country cottage to a short visit to a village pub can be categorised as tourism and leisure in the countryside whilst a multitude of traditional and more modern sporting activities, such as hang-gliding and jet-skiing, can also be included. If the context of the countryside itself, as defined in Chapter Two, is also taken into consideration it becomes clear that calculating the number of people who participate in countryside recreation in all its forms would be an enormous, if not impossible, task.

It is, of course, possible to determine the volume of visits to some destinations or attractions within the countryside. Where an entry fee is charged, such as at some historical properties, it is a relatively simple matter to keep an accurate record of visitor numbers, whilst surveys at car parks can indicate the level of use of particular, defined areas, such as country parks. The same cannot be said, however, for the wider countryside and therefore an assessment of the overall demand for countryside recreation is necessarily dependent on surveys of selected samples of the population. Such an approach is fraught with difficulties. Not only are many countryside activities undertaken by a relatively small proportion of the population, but demand levels are also determined by economic and social factors, seasonality and frequency of participation. There may also be conflicting views amongst survey respondents as to what actually constitutes tourism and leisure in the countryside.

Without surveys of large samples of the population over an extended period of time, therefore, figures for the demand for tourism and leisure in the countryside are likely to be, at best, reasonable estimates. Furthermore, whilst the overall volume and value of countryside recreation serves as a useful comparison with other types of tourism and leisure, it is of little interest in the context of planning and managing the recreational use of specific areas of the countryside. Thus, for example, expressing demand as the total annual number of visits to the countryside tells us nothing about who goes where, how often and why. Of greater importance are demand factors such as social and economic status, trends, motivations, perceptions, frequency of participation and so on. These greatly assist in planning and catering for the needs of countryside visitors at the same time as minimising the more detrimental effects of tourism and leisure in particular areas. This chapter, therefore, considers those factors which determine the level of participation in countryside recreation and to what extent the tourism and leisure industry responds to them.

WHAT IS DEMAND?

The measurement of demand is complicated by the fact that demand itself can be defined in a number of ways. That is, it refers not only to what people actually do but also to what they intend to do, or even to what they would do if they could. In its simplest form, the demand for countryside recreation is a measurement of current levels of participation, known as *expressed* demand. Thus, for example, the expressed demand for recreation in country parks is the total number of visits made to country parks, normally over a period of one year.

Taking this approach implies that everyone has the same opportunity or ability to visit a country park and that the number who do is a fair indication of the demand for them. The ability to paticipate, however, is constrained by various factors. There may, therefore, be a number of people who want to visit a country park but are unable to do so because of, for example, financial or time constraints, a lack of mobility, or family commitments. In other words, the potential demand for visits to country parks exists, but it is *suppressed* demand, or a demand that has not been satisfied. There might also be a proportion of the population who are unaware of the existence of country parks but would, nevertheless, visit one if they were better informed. This third category of demand is known as *latent* demand.

If it were possible to accurately determine the total expressed, latent and supressed demand for countryside recreation it is likely that the overall level of demand would be many times greater than current levels of participation. Indeed, the activities of many organisations involved in the promotion and provision of countryside recreation, such as project groups working on the urban/rural fringe, are concerned with satisfying both supressed and latent demand. On the other hand, the increasing concern for the protection and conservation of the countryside is likely to result in greater emphasis being placed on the management and control of current, expressed demand rather than accommodating supressed or latent demand. The policy of most national park authorities, for example, is to discourage inappropriate, noisy pursuits in favour of the more traditional quiet, contemplative countryside activities.

Within the context of this chapter we shall be concerned with the current, expressed demand for tourism and leisure in the countryside whilst measures for satisfying supressed and latent demand are discussed in Chapter Eight. As with tourism and leisure as a whole, however, although mass participation in countryside recreation is a phenomenon of the second half of the twentieth century, it has its roots in the late 1700s and early 1800s. Before examining the characteristics of current demand and participation it is important, therefore, to trace the development of countryside recreation and to determine the historical influence on present demand and motivation.

THE DEVELOPMENT OF COUNTRYSIDE RECREATION

The history of tourism and leisure in the countryside dates back to the end of the eighteenth century. Prior to this time the countryside had been the setting for recreational activities, but participation in these was restricted to a privileged minority of the population. During the eleventh and twelfth centuries, for example, large areas of the countryside were set aside as forests for hunting, one such area being the New Forest in Hampshire which was created by William I in 1079. Other landowners used their estates for hunting and riding but for the majority of the population the countryside was the place where they lived and worked. They had no access to the large, private estates and their right of access to common land was primarily for the purposes of grazing, cutting peat and gathering fuel (see Chapter Seven).

Even by the early 1800s some eighty per cent of the population still lived in the countryside and were dependent on agriculture for a living. Recreation as such was limited to holy days and time free from the necessities of work on the land and thus, as a distinct form of leisure activity, countryside recreation for the masses did not exist. It was only with the Industrial Revolution and the rapid urbanisation of society that the distinction between urban and rural life evolved. Technological improvements in transport, in particular the development of the railways, provided the means by which different parts of the country became more widely accessible but the opportunities for tourism and leisure were restricted by low incomes and a lack of free time. Furthermore, as we saw in Chapter One, it was to the seaside resorts rather than to the countryside that the railways and the cheap excursion trips took the trippers, although the Lake District became increasingly popular as the nineteenth century progressed.

It was also in the Lake District that true countryside tourism and leisure probably evolved. The author Daniel Defoe had passed through the region on his tour of Great Britain between 1724 and 1726 and found it *a country eminent only for being the wildest, most barren and frightful of any that I have passed over in England, or even Wales itself.* The scenic qualities of the countryside meant little to the travellers of pre-industrial England although just forty years later the poet Thomas Gray undertook a short ten-day excursion in the Lake District and is commonly regarded as the first tourist (Rollinson 1967). His narrative provided the inspiration for many writers and artists to follow in his footsteps and signified the start of the Romantic Movement which was to so influence people's perceptions of the countryside and rural life.

Not a single red tile, no gentleman's house, or garden walls, break in upon the repose of this little unsuspected paradise; all is but peace, rusticity and happy poverty, in its neatest, most becoming attire.

(Grey 1884: 226)

Thomas West, a local Jesuit priest, published the first guide book to the Lake District in 1778 in which he described 21 viewing stations from which to appreciate the landscape. The artists Turner, Constable and Gainsborough all spent time in the Lakes but it is William Wordsworth who is most closely associated with the the region. His own *Guide to the Lakes* was published in 1810 and it was he who first proposed the concept of national parks. Common to all the Romantics, however, was the idea that the countryside was a place for quiet contemplation and solitude and Wordsworth in particular was opposed to, and fearful of, the arrival of the masses in his beloved Lakeland. It was a view that was widely held amongst the educated classes and which, along with the threat posed by industrial expansion and exploitation of the countryside, led to the beginning of the conservation movement. The Lake District Defence Society was formed in 1883 after the then Manchester City Corporation won the right to use Thirlmere as a reservoir. One of its founders, Canon Rawnsley, went on to head the Kendal and District Footpath Preservation Society, with the aim of maintaining access over footpaths, before becoming one of the founder members of the National Trust in 1895. It was from these early beginnings that the national conservation organisations, such as the Council for the Protection of Rural England (CPRE), were to emerge.

During the nineteenth century an increasingly prosperous middle class turned to the countryside for sporting and leisure activities. Sports such as fox-hunting and shooting, once the preserve of the aristocracy, became more popular and land owners were quick to recognise the potential financial rewards from leasing shooting rights to those who could afford it. Cycling also became a popular activity following the founding of the Cyclists' Touring Club in 1878. Meanwhile, in response to the appalling working and housing conditions in nineteenth century towns and cities, open-air recreation for the urban masses was provided for by the creation of urban parks and recreational areas on the urban fringe. Indeed, many of London's famous parks date from the mid-1800s. People, however, were still restricted by low pay, long working hours and restricted mobility and thus, even by the start of the twentieth century, little recreational use was made of the wider countryside.

It was the period between the two World Wars that witnessed the first major increase in the use of the countryside for recreation and leisure. People enjoyed more free time and the Holidays with Pay Act 1938 ensured that the majority of workers enjoyed paid time off work. Transport and mobility were improving; by the start of Second World War private car ownership had risen to about two million. The range of activities that took place in the countryside also increased rapidly during this period. Camping, cycling and fishing became popular and many organisations, such as the Ramblers Association and the Youth Hostel Association, were established during the 1930s. Attitudes towards the countryside were also changing. Not only was there increasing emphasis on healthy, outdoor activities but also there were growing demands for greater access to the wider countryside.

Walking and rambling became increasingly popular during the 1920s and 1930s, particularly amongst the working populations of the northern industrial towns and cities. Inspired by both the desire to escape from the cities and to regain access to land over which many believed they had a right to wander at will, the ramblers rapidly came into conflict with landowners in what was to become the freedom to roam campaign. Centred around the Peak District, where about seventy-five per cent of the moors were privately owned and closed to public access, various groups came together to participate in mass trespasses over private land. The most famous of these was the 1932 trespass on Kinder Scout which resulted in a number of the leaders being imprisoned. The mass trespasses were undoubtedly motivated to an extent by the political desire to see privately owned land returned to the people but, nevertheless, they were an important factor in the move towards an official policy for access and recreation in the countryside. With the conservation organisations, such as the CPRE, the access groups presented a strong and united front in the fight for greater provision of recreational opportunities and for conservation, twin policies that have not always remained in harmony.

The years following the Second World War were notable for the introduction of legislation for the provison of access to the countryside and for conservation, in particular the designation of national parks (see Chapter Four). The second major period of growth in the demand for countryside tourism and leisure, however, was between 1960 and 1980, reflecting the increase in participation in all forms of tourism and leisure. Rising prosperity and more free time during the 1950s meant that, by the early 1960s, a new leisured society was emerging. In particular the rapid growth in private car ownership led to a dramatic increase in outdoor recreation. It has been estimated, for example, that the number of day trips to the countryside on a typical summer weekend doubled between 1968 and 1977 (Harrison 1991). One result of this increase in participation was that countryside recreation became viewed as something to be contained and managed rather than widely promoted and policies were designed to channel visitors away from threatened, more fragile rural areas.

Since the late 1970s participation in countryside recreation has levelled off. Indeed, it has been found that between 1977 and 1980 the total number of people visiting the countryside actually declined by 22 per cent (Harrison 1991), although the figure rose again between 1980 and 1984. More regular surveys have been conducted since 1980 and these have found that, despite continuing increases in personal wealth and more widespread car ownership, demand for countryside recreation has remained largely static over the last decade. This is probably attributable to a number of factors.

i   The demand for domestic tourism and leisure as a whole has also been static over the same period whilst the number of overseas visits made by UK residents increased by over seventy per cent. As more people take overseas holidays the shortfall in the domestic market has been made up for by the increase in second and third holidays and short breaks. Only eight per cent of overseas visitors to the UK visit the countryside so little benefit has accrued from the increase in incoming tourism.

ii The countryside as a destination has faced competition from new attractions and destinations, such as heritage towns and dockland attractions, all of which take a share of the static domestic market.

iii The number of activities that comprise tourism and leisure in the countryside has broadened. This has had the effect of diluting and spreading demand although the need for access to the countryside to accommodate new and different activities has increased.

iv As the urban/rural population shift continues, less people may feel the need to visit the wider countryside.

v It could be argued that there is a limit to the number of people who actually wish to visit the countryside. Just as the proportion of the population who do not take a holiday away from home has not changed between 1971 and 1991 (see Chapter One), so too must there be a finite number of people who will participate in outdoor, rural activities.

Recreation in the countryside, then, has evolved over the last 200 years for the same reasons that tourism and leisure in general have developed. More free time, increases in personal income and technological advances have all contibuted to the growth in the number of people visiting the countryside. In fact during the major growth period of the 1960s and 1970s there was a close correlation between the rate of increase in countryside recreation and increases in car ownership and the level of disposable income (Fitton 1979). Importantly, though, the perception of the countryside has also played a role in the development of tourism and leisure. The influence of the Romantics, the vision of the countryside as the antithesis to the harsh working and living conditions of the nineteenth century cities and the rejection of the Victorian work ethic all contributed to a perception of the countryside that remains to this day. In more recent times it is the variety of countryside activities, rather than the total demand, that has increased. Therefore it is more useful to consider the trends, motivations and enabling factors of demand, rather than overall demand figures, as a basis for the management and planning of countryside recreation.

THE DEMAND FOR COUNTRYSIDE RECREATION

It has been frequently emphasised that a multitude of activities and pursuits comprise tourism and leisure in the countryside. Just as the countryside resource itself is varied, so too are the recreational opportunities that it offers. The Sports Council, for example, lists 28 categories of countryside sports that it officially recognises (Sports Council 1990). If all other formal and informal activities are taken into account it soon becomes apparent that the list is virtually endless. There is little purpose in compiling a complete list of all recreational activities that take place in the countryside. Nevertheless, the breadth and scope of countryside tourism and leisure can be indicated by a number of categories into which the various activities fall, thereby serving as an introduction to an assessment of current participation and demand.

i Categories of Countryside Activities

There are seven broad headings under which countryside tourism and leisure activities may be categorised. These can be the sole purpose of a visit to the countryside (i.e. during a day visit) or one of a number of activities undertaken during the course of a longer stay.

(a) Touring

This category covers all methods of moving or travelling around the countryside. Thus, cycling, pony trekking, rambling and hiking, cross-country skiing and caravanning are touring activities, as are all types of motorised travel. The latter includes trail-bike riding, off-road four-wheel driving and, of course, the traditional drive in the country.

(b) Water-based activities

Many tourism and leisure activities take place on inland and coastal waters. Fishing, sailing and swimming are the more traditional type of pursuit whilst water-skiing, jet-skiing, power boat racing and windsurfing have become increasingly popular. Water-based tourism includes cruising on canals and rivers and the new all-weather inland resorts, such as Center Parcs, have water activities as their central attraction.

(c) Land-based activities

Included in this category are both formal sporting activities, such as pot-holing, climbing, orienteering, shooting, hunting, golf and a multitude of other sports, and also informal land-based activities. The latter may include picnics, socialising in a rural location, camping, visiting a theme park, wildlife park and so on.

(d) Aerial activities

These may not be traditionally thought of as countryside pursuits but, nevertheless, many take place in, or are dependent on, a rural setting. Hang-gliding, for example, takes place in hilly areas or from cliffs and safe hot-air ballooning is dependent on the wider open spaces in the countryside.   Other aerial pursuits include traditional gliding and microlight flying.

(e) Cultural activities

Many historical houses and gardens are to be found in the countryside and visits to rural museums, archaeological sites, country fairs and shows, musical or theatrical events and even to country restaurants may be categorised as cultural activities.

(f) Educational activities

There is some overlap between educational and cultural activities. A visit to a craft workshop, for example, can be both cultural and educational. This category, however, includes educational holidays, such as painting or photography weekends and courses in local crafts, and visits to outward-bound schools. Farm tourism, visits to rural industries and country viilage weekends can also be classified as educational, or discovery, activities. Country camps, such as those organised by the Boy Scouts, are a further example of educational uses of the countryside.

(g) Conservation activities

With the emphasis on local community involvement in countryside management and the growing awareness of environmental issues, conservation work has become a distinct category of countryside activity. Thus, conservation holidays, as offered by the British Trust for Conservation Volunteers (BTCV) and voluntary work with national and local organisations, such as the Woodland Trust or local Groundwork Trusts, are an increasingly popular and important category of countryside recreation.

This list is neither complete nor exhaustive and many activities can be included under different category headings. Nevertheless it outlines the range of tourism and leisure activities that take place in the countryside and highlights the potential difficulty in trying to determine the demand for countryside recreation as a whole. The Countryside Commission lists eighteen different activities as a basis for its surveys on countryside recreation (see Figure 3.1.).

ii Participation in Countryside Recreation

Relatively little research has been undertaken into the general demand for countryside recreation, undoubtedly owing to the difficulties mentioned above. The annual *General Household Survey* (GHS) periodically includes statistics concerning overall participation in leisure activities, although countryside recreation is not treated as a separate field of leisure. Leisure activities are grouped under the three separate headings of active sports, games and physical activities, open-air outings and sightseeing but no distinction is made by location. Thus, for example, the 1986 GHS found that walking for 2 miles (3.2 km) or more was the most popular outdoor activity, enjoyed by nineteen per cent of the population in the four weeks prior to the survey, although this covers both urban and rural walking. The category *visits to the countryside* accounted for only three per cent of the population but many activities that would be included as countryside recreation are assessed separately. Therefore, although the GHS is a useful guide to overall leisure trends and participation by age, gender and social class, it tells us little about participation in countryside recreation in particular.

FIGURE 3.1. COUNTRYSIDE ACTIVITIES

Visited the sea coast or cliff tops (but not seaside resort)

Visited historic buildings, stately homes, museums, gardens or parks in the countryside (excluding country parks)

Visited country parks

Visited zoos, safari or wildlife parks in the countryside

Visited nature reserves in the countryside

Been on drives, outings, picnics etc in the countryside (including visits to attractive villages)

Been on long walks, hikes or ramblesof at least 2 miles (round trip) in the countryside, either from car or home

Been birdwatching/nature study in the countryside

Been fishing in the countryside

Been horseriding or ponytrekking in the countryside

Been shooting in the countryside

Been hunting in the countryside

Taken active part in other organised sport (e.g. football, cricket, cycling, golf, sailing, running, climbing, motor sport etc.) in the countryside

Taken active part in other informal sport (e.g. jogging, kicking a ball about, beach games, throwing frisbees etc.) in the countryside

Watched any organised sport in the countryside (in person, not on TV)

Visited friends or relatives in the countryside

Carried out any organised conservation or recreation work in the countryside (e.g. tree planting, clearing of footpaths etc.)

'Picked your own' (fruit, vegetables etc.) in the countryside

Source: Countryside Commission 1985

The Countryside Commission has undertaken its own surveys of tourism and leisure in the countryside. The last major survey was carried out in 1984 (The *National Countryside Recreation Survey 1984*), consisting of household interviews over six separate periods during the year, with different people being interviewed in each period. A total of 6,302 people between the ages of 12 and 75 were questioned about their participation in various countryside activities (Figure 3.1.). Although follow-up surveys have been conducted on a reasonably regular basis since then, the 1984 survey is still the most complete examination of the demand for rural recreation. Therefore, much of the following analysis is based upon the findings of the 1984 survey, although reference is made to more recent work where relevant.

The most notable trend since 1984 has been a gradual decline in both the number of trips made per person and the proportion of people visiting the countryside in each of the four-week periods throughout the year (see Tables 3.1. and 3.2.).

TABLE 3.1. VOLUME OF TRIPS TO THE COUNTRYSIDE
(Number of trips per person in each four week period)

Month	1984	1985	1986	1987	1988	1989
February	2.5	2.0	2.0	2.2	2.13	2.31
May	4.3	3.7	3.4	3.5	n/a	3.65
June	4.4	4.0	4.2	3.4	3.95	3.44
July	6.0	4.1	4.6	3.8	4.38	3.86
August	5.9	4.9	5.0	4.1	5.00	3.67
October	3.6	2.4	2.7	2.4	2.94	2.12
Monthly Av.	4.5	3.5	3.7	3.2	3.68	3.17

Source: Countryside Commission 1985

The fall in numbers in 1985 and 1986 was attributed to the poor summer weather in those years after the long, hot summer of 1984. However, the longer term trend is still a decline in the number of visits to the countryside, in particular during the high season months of July and August. The tables also show the seasonal variation in countryside recreation. In 1984, for example, there were 18 million trips on a typical summer Sunday but only two million on a typical winter weekday. The most recent figures (1990) indicate that, in a typical four-week period, people made, on average, three visits to the countryside (Countryside Commission 1995a).

71

TABLE 3.2. PROPORTION OF TRIPS TO THE COUNTRYSIDE BY PER CENT (In each four week period surveyed)

Month	1984	1985	1986	1987	1988	1989
February	44	37	34	37	36	43
May	59	56	52	51	n/a	52
June	61	56	58	54	57	52
July	70	55	60	53	59	53
August	69	62	59	56	60	51
October	54	44	41	40	44	37
Monthly Av.	60	52	51	49	51	48

Source: Countryside Commission 1985

The total number of trips is a rather misleading indication of the demand for countryside recreation because it does not show how these trips are distributed amongst visitors. In other words, some people visit the countryside frequently whereas others only occasionally participate in countryside recreation. Furthermore, a proportion of the population never visit the countryside. It is therefore necessary to look at the percentage of trips made by frequent and infrequent visitors (see Table 3.3.).

TABLE 3.3. PERCENTAGE SHARE OF TRIP MAKING TO THE COUNTRYSIDE

Trips made per average four week period	1984	1985	1986
No trips	40	48	49
1 Trip	11	10	10
2-4 Trips	20	19	19
5-8 Trips	12	10	10
9-15 Trips	9	7	6
16 or more Trips	8	6	6

Source: Countryside Commission 1985

In 1984, the 17 per cent of people who were frequent visitors to the countryside (nine or more trips) accounted for 68 per cent of all trips. By 1990, just 11 per cent of people who visit the countryside frequently made 61 per cent of all trips (Countryside Commission 1995a). Conversely, forty per cent of people made no visits to the countryside over an average four week period, a figure that rose to 49 per cent in 1986 and to fifty per cent in 1990. Thus, the great majority of trips are made by a relatively small section of the population whilst a significant minority never visit the countryside. In fact, over an average year it is estimated that about twenty per cent of the population do not participate in countryside recreation. Therefore, the trend indicates that an increasingly small proportion of the population account for the great majority of countryside trips, whilst just thirty per cent of people are occasional visitors.

iii Factors of Demand
There are a number of factors which determine the extent to which people visit the countryside. At a practical level, demand will be dependent on the amount of leisure time available, levels of income, location and mobility, whilst the ability to participate in countryside recreation may also be constrained by such things as family responsibilities or age. On the other hand, individual motivation and preference are equally important demand factors. That is, people's perception of the countryside as a tourism and leisure destination and the relative importance placed on countryside recreation as compared to other forms of leisure activity also play a role in determining overall levels of demand. In short, therefore, the demand for tourism and leisure in the countryside is a function of a variety of factors, many of which are inter-related and which, to a great extent, are dependent on occupation and social class.

The *National Countryside Recreation Survey 1984* highlighted five main influences on the demand for countryside recreation, confirming the findings of earlier surveys.

(a) Car Ownership
Much of the countryside is only accessible by road. As public transport services in rural areas continue to decline it is, therefore, inevitable that personal mobility is the single most important enabling factor for countryside recreation. The 1984 survey found that a person with the use of a car is almost three times as likely to visit the countryside as someone

with no car available to them in the household. Table 3.4 shows the percentage of trips in relation to car ownership.

TABLE 3.4. COUNTRYSIDE TRIP-MAKING BY CAR OWNERSHIP

	Percentage of Population	Percentage of Trips
Use of Own Car	46	63
Car in Household	20	19
No Car in Household	34	18

Source: Countryside Commission 1985

Thus, 82 per cent of all trips to the countryside are made by the 66 per cent of the population who have use of a car. The results of the 1990 survey mirrored these figures; over half of those interviewed had use of a car and they accounted for almost 70 per cent of all visits. The 1984 survey also found that travelling by car, either with friends or relatives or by hiring a car, is the most popular form of transport for those people without a car in their household. Conversely, only five per cent of trips are made by public transport, half as many as in 1977. Therefore, not only is the car the dominant means of reaching and travelling around the countryside but also public transport is becoming increasingly less popular. This has important implications both from an environmental point of view and also in terms of increasing the accessibility of the countryside for certain sections of the population.

(b) Social Class
Social and occupational status are important determinants of the demand for countryside recreation. It has been found that people in professional and managerial positions are three times as likely to visit the countryside as those who are either unemployed or on minimum incomes (see Table 3.5.). In 1990, 42 per cent of the population were ABC1s but they made fifty-two per cent of visits.

TABLE 3.5. COUNTRYSIDE TRIP-MAKING BY SOCIAL CLASS

Social Class	Percentage of Population	Percentage of Trips
A	2	2
B	13	20
C1	23	28
C2	27	27
D	16	12
E	12	7
E (unemployed)	7	4

Source: Countryside Commission 1985

Although it is the professional and managerial groups that are the most frequent users of the countryside, the overall volume of trips is largely accounted for by those in clerical and skilled manual occupations (C1 and C2). However, it is important to point out that, although the higher social groups are more likely to visit the countryside, there is little difference in the frequency of trip-making between the different social groups that actually visit the countryside. Social status and car ownership are, of course, inter-related because those on higher incomes are more likely to own at least one car.

(c) Housing Location

The 1984 survey showed that the type and area of housing are important influences on the level of participation in countryside recreation. Perhaps not surprisingly, people who live in rural areas, affluent suburbs and modern family housing are much more likely to visit the countryside than those who, for example, live on poorer council estates.

The survey also found that membership of countryside related organisations and ownership of recreational equipment, such as tents, boats or caravans is reflected in a higher frequency of countryside visits. It is likely, however, that both of these characteristics result from, rather than lead to, a greater interest in, and use of, the countryside.

Overall, then, the most frequent countryside visitor is a car owner in a professional occupation who probably lives in or near the countryside in good quality housing, who probably owns recreational equipment and who is likely to be a member of a countryside related organisation (see Curry 1994 for an in-depth examination of participation in countryside recreation).

iv Motivations for Visiting the Countryside

The figures relating to the levels, frequency and trends in the demand for countryside recreation are of both use and interest in the planning and management of the countryside. They are, however, just part of the picture. It is equally important to know *why* people visit the countryside. Some people might visit the countryside to participate in a particular activity, such as fishing or walking, whereas for others the attraction might simply be the rural environment. Thus, the reasons for visiting the countryside can be assessed under two headings; how the countryside is used and the motivation for visiting the countryside.

(a) How the countryside is used

The 1984 survey looked in detail at the various activities that people pursue in the countryside. It found that the great majority of visitors participate in informal activities, with drives, outings, picnics, long walks or hikes over 2 miles (3.2 km) in length and visiting friends and relatives being the most popular pursuits (see Table 3.6.).

TABLE 3.6. PARTICIPATION IN COUNTRYSIDE RECREATION ACTIVITIES

Activity	Percentage of Trips
Drives, Outings, Picnics	19
Long Walks	18
Visiting Friends and Relatives	14
Sea Coast	8
Informal Sport	12
Organised Sport	7
Pick Your Own	4
Historic Buildings	4
Country Parks	4
Watched Sport	3
Others	7

Source: Countryside Commission 1985

In particular, the survey highlighted the popularity of the wider, unmanaged countryside as opposed to managed sites, such as country parks or historic houses. It found that three times as many visits are made to the open countryside as to specific, managed destinations or attractions. By 1990, it was found that twice as many activities took place in a general countryside setting than at purpose-built facilities, but this figure is not directly comparable as outdoor urban leisure activities (e.g. visiting a park or urban open space) were included in the 1990 survey. In other words, the countryside is predominantly used for casual, informal activities. This was confirmed by the fact that, of those people who actually stopped in the countryside rather than just driving through it, over half stopped in the wider countryside. Furthermore, the number of visits to attractions with entry charges fell during 1991, largely as a result of the recession. For example, wildlife attractions, historic properties and steam railways all experienced a reduction in demand, though this trend has since reversed. Thus, managed countryside sites are of relative unimportance within the context of overall countryside recreation whilst the overwhelming demand for recreation in the wider countryside has important implications for the future provision of recreational opportunities and facilities.

On the other hand, it must be stressed that, although the level of participation in formal activities or visits to managed sites is low when expressed as a percentage of all countryside visits, there is a significant demand for specific activities in terms of volume. The traditional country sports of hunting, shooting and fishing, for example, are far more popular than the relative demand figures imply. Between 1983 and 1991 the number of people participating in angling increased by 175,000 to a total of 3.9 million and, despite the efforts of various pressure groups, hunting with hounds now attracts 243,000 direct participants, an increase of some 13 per cent since the early 1980s. Furthermore, over £1.4 billion was spent directly on these country sports in 1991, double the amount spent on live arts and cinema admissions. Almost 11 million people visit National Trust properties, many of which are in countryside locations, nine country parks attracted over one million visitors in 1991 and the larger rural-based theme parks also played host to well over one million visitors each. In other words, a greater proportion of the population use the countryside for informal tourism and leisure activities but, nevertheless, significant numbers of people participate in specific, organised and planned activities.

(b) Motivation

Any attempt to assess the motivation for visiting the countryside is fraught with difficulties. Not only do most visitors participate in informal activities but also most trips are spontaneous. Over half of all visits involve a round trip of less than twenty miles (32 km), for example, and 78 per cent of trips are undertaken in fine weather (Countryside Commission 1985). Furthermore, a visit to the countryside may be motivated by a desire to escape *from* a particular environment rather than a positive need to go *to* the countryside. Nevertheless, qualitative research has been undertaken into the motivation for countryside recreation.

The *National Countryside Recreation Survey 1984* found that almost two thirds of trips are made to the countryside specifically because of the environment rather than to participate in a particular activity (see Table 3.7.).

TABLE 3.7. MOTIVATION FOR LAST TRIP FROM HOME TO THE COUNTRYSIDE

	Percentage of Trips
Wanted to go to that particular place	29
Just wanted to go somewhere in the countryside	28
Wanted to take part in that particular activity	19
To be with the family	10
Because something there at the time	2
Other reasons	12

Source: Countryside Commission 1985

Further research carried out in 1986 on behalf Countryside Commission (Qualitative Consultancy, 1986) found that it is the intrinsic qualities of the countryside that often attract people. That is, many visitors are looking for a sense of space and freedom and for relaxation from the pressures of modern living. Over eighty per cent those interviewed said they visit the countryside because it is peaceful, quiet and rarely busy, whilst a similar proportion said that it was a nice place to be with friends.

Another study in 1986 (Harrison *et al.* 1986) looked at the motivations for visiting the countryside amongst a wide cross-section of residents of the London Borough of Greenwich, the majority of who were infrequent countryside visitors. (See Harrison 1991, for a detailed discussion of the study.) A number of points emerged from this research. Firstly, the appeal of the countryside to many people was found to be the variety of sounds, smells, sights and other experiences of nature offered by the countryside which were in marked contrast to urban life. Secondly, perceptions of the countryside varied between different groups of people. Some held the traditional view that the real countryside is limited to wilderness upland or moorland areas whereas for others it is synonymous with agricultural areas. Thirdly, some people felt that the countryside can only be enjoyed in solitude or with close friends but the experience of the countryside for others was enhanced by the presence of other people. Finally, the study found that, to many people, the countryside symbolises a different, and better, way of life to that found in towns and cities. That is, rural society is perceived to have retained many qualities of life that have been lost in modern, urban life.

In short, the Greenwich study found that the motivation to visit the countryside varies greatly between different people and that the use and perception of the countryside is dependent on social and cultural factors as well as previous experience. The view of the countryside as the symbol of a better, although mostly past, way of life is widely held and, despite the fact that only a minority of the population are frequent countryside visitors, most people, including infrequent visitors, feel a strong attachment to the countryside. This, of course, is in direct contrast to the evidence presented by the quantitative research into the demand for countryside recreation.

These findings have been reinforced by a more recent survey undertaken by the Countryside Commission (Countryside Commission 1996). Over ninety per cent of those questioned believed that the countryside is an important part of the country's heritage and that society has a moral duty to protect the countryside for future generations. At the same time, the main benefits of visiting the countryside were found to be the sense of relaxation and well-being, fresh air and the peace and quiet of the countryside. Interestingly, the study also demonstrated that *people benefit from the countryside, even if they have little or no physical contact with it* (Ashcroft 1996). It was found that 93 per cent of people value the countryside, whether or not they visit it.

In general, then, the demand for tourism and leisure in the countryside is a function of a variety of factors and constraints. The dominance of a relatively small proportion of frequent visitors tends to belie a widely held attachment to the countryside whilst the research into the motivation for visiting the countryside challenges the traditionally held views of countryside recreation. Furthermore, the attraction of the countryside goes beyond the aesthetic appeal of the landscape and, therefore, the intrinsic natural and social character of the wider countryside needs to be considered in the planning and provision of countryside recreation opportunities.

THE SUPPLY OF COUNTRYSIDE RECREATION

So far in this chapter we have looked at the historical and current demand for tourism and leisure in the countryside, the various factors that determine that level of demand and the motivation for visiting the countryside. The purpose of this section is to briefly assess how far this demand is catered for by the suppliers of countryside recreation. The supply of tourism and leisure in the countryside is, in effect, the overall subject of this book. That is, the following chapters are concerned with the legislation, organisations, policies, planning and management related to the use of the countryside as a resource for recreation. Nevertheless, it is important to introduce the supply side of the countryside recreation demand/supply equation within the context of the overall management of the countryside. In particular, it is necessary to examine the extent to which the motivations and needs of countryside visitors are satisfied.

The supply of countryside recreation can be divided into two broad categories; public sector supply and private sector supply. Generally the public sector, in the form of national and local government and the various public organisations involved in the environmental, social and economic planning management of the countryside, operates at a macro level. That is, it is responsible for the provision of recreational opportunities and facilities for the benefit of society as a whole. At the same time, it strives to balance the requirement of recreation provision with other, often conflicting, demands and pressures on the countryside.

On the other hand the private sector operates at the micro level. In other words, the thousands of small businesses that comprise the tourism and leisure industry are concerned with making a profit from satisfying the demand for the various activities that together make up the rural tourism and leisure market. Indeed, many businesses, such as some farms, have turned to supplying tourism and leisure facilities as an alternative source of income and employment. These businesses, therefore, are more concerned with their individual areas of activity rather than with the overall supply of countryside recreation. However, many public sector organisations, such as the Countryside Commission, now place much emphasis on ensuring that the private sector as a whole works towards the common goal of sustainable development.

i Public Sector Supply

The policies and activities of the principal public sector organisations concerned with the provision of tourism and leisure in the countryside are discussed in detail in Chapter Five. In general, however, public sector provision of countryside recreation has broadened in scope over the last forty years. At the time of the designation of the national parks during the 1950s countryside recreation was limited to traditional activities, such as walking and rambling, in the more remote, wilderness areas of the countryside. Thus, public sector provision was largely concerned with designating areas of the countryside for recreation. As the demand for recreation expanded rapidly during the 1960s and 1970s the supply of recreation was dominated by the policy of containing and managing demand through the provision of new facilities closer to urban centres. This was motivated by the desire to protect and conserve the more popular, yet fragile, areas of the countryside, in particular the national parks. As the demand data show, however, these managed sites account for a relatively small proportion of countryside visits, calling into question the effectiveness of this policy.

In more recent years the wider appeal of the countryside, as evidenced by the qualitative research into the motivation for visiting the countryside, has been recognised. This has resulted in a number of organisations adapting their policies to include the wider countryside in their supply of recreational opportunities. The Countryside Commission, for example, is committed to both increasing access to the countryside, with particular emphasis being placed on the improvement of the public rights of way network, and promoting countryside recreation to a broader section of the population. Other public sector organisations positively promote the use of rural resources for recreation whilst the Tourist Boards and most local authorities also support and encourage the wider provision of facilities and opportunities for countryside recreation.

A number of points need to be raised, however, with particular reference to the extent to which the public sector is satisfying, or supplying, the demand for countryside recreation.

(a) Much of the current promotion and provision of tourism and leisure in the countryside is motivated by the perceived economic and employment benefits that result from an influx of visitors. Tourism and leisure are also seen as a positive force in the conservation of the countryside and, therefore, the emphasis is on creating a demand to the benefit of an area or region rather than satisfying a broader social need.

(b) The widely supported principal of sustainable development favours the more traditional type of countryside activity whilst discouraging those which have an adverse impact on the environment. Many national parks, for example, promote quiet, contemplative activities that are seen to be appropriate to the setting. The dominance of the informal use of the countryside (see Table 3.6.) undoubtedly reinforces the view that the appeal of the countryside lies in its aesthetic scenic qualities and, therefore, the future planning and supply of recreation is likely to be guided by the traditional perception of the countryside.

(c) The public sector relies to a great extent on existing planning laws and agreement and co-operation for the implementation of its policies. Thus, the supply of recreation, in terms of improved opportunities and access, is largely dependent on the interests and co-operation of landowners.

(d) The degree to which the demand for countryside recreation is seen to be met by the public sector depends on how countryside recreation itself is viewed. It may be argued, for example, that the opportunity to enjoy the countryside should be afforded and promoted to the entire population as of right. On the other hand, should the supply of countryside recreation, like many other forms of tourism and leisure, be dominated by the private sector and, thus, be subject to market forces? The respective arguments are beyond the scope of this book, yet the supply of recreation in the countryside is increasingly being guided by conservation and economic, as opposed to social, objectives.

ii Private Sector Supply

The private sector is made up of thousands of small businesses that together supply the various needs of visitors to the countryside. Many satisfy the basic requirements of visitors, such as providing accommodation, food and drink, transport, souvenirs, maps and so on. As such, they play a supporting role in the supply of countryside recreation although they account for a large share of the estimated £9 billion earnings from tourism and leisure in the countryside. Others, however, are more directly involved in the provision of recreation, offering a huge variety of activities and attractions. A number are tourism and leisure attractions in their own right, such as holiday villages, historic houses and gardens, steam railways, theme parks and museums. In some cases their rural location adds to the visitors' experience, although it is not necessarily the initial attraction, whereas in other cases it might be purely incidental.

Of greater interest in the context of this chapter, however, are those private sector attractions and destinations which, in effect, are part of rural life. In other words, their appeal lies in the opportunity they offer to experience a different, or better, way of life which, as the qualitative research identified, is one of the primary motivations for visiting the countryside. One such attraction is the Whitbread Hop Farm in Kent which is described in the case study at the end of this chapter.

Many rural industries have diversified into tourism and leisure, either out of necessity or as a means of supplementing their income. For example, the *Countryside Directory*, a publication which lists over 2000 different countryside recreation attractions, includes 55 vineyards in the UK which welcome visitors. Rural craft centres, potteries, pick-your-own centres and farm shops are also popular destinations but there are three types of development in particular that both satisfy the motivational demands identified in the research and lead to a greater understanding and knowledge of rural life.

(a) Farm Tourism

Farms have been supplying tourism and leisure facilities for many years. Camping and caravan sites are often to be found on farmland and many farms have always offered bed-and-breakfast accommodation. Over the last ten years or so, however, the farming industry has suffered from falling incomes and recent changes in EU policy have further increased the pressure on farms to diversify and to seek alternative sources of income. Furthermore, some environmental improvement schemes, such as the Countryside Commission's *Countryside Stewardship Scheme*, includes the incentive for farms to open up land to public access. Thus, increasing numbers of farms now offer a variety of farm holidays, ranging from simply serviced or self-catering accommodation to actually working on the farm. It has been found that between ten and fifteen per cent of farms in England have diversified into tourism, most commonly offering various forms of accommodation. In the West Country, however, over 23 per cent of farms are involved, earning some 36 per cent of their total income from tourism (Denman 1994).

The Farm Holiday Bureau (FHB), established in 1983 by a number of tourism and agricultural organisations to promote farm tourism amongst both farms and the public, now has a membership of over 1000 farms. Most of these offer accommodation and, in addition, the opportunity to participate in sports and farming related activities. In fact the most successful tourist attraction in Wales in 1992 was a dairy farm near Tenby in Pembrokeshire. It attracted 90,000 visitors who came to watch cows and goats being milked, walk along a nature trail or to visit the restaurant and souvenir shop. The FHB promotes farm tourism through *Stay on a Farm*, a guide book which produces about a quarter of all bookings for FHB members.

On a smaller scale, since 1993 the Cumbria Farm Tourism Initiative (CFTI), a strategy prepared jointly by the Agricultural Development and Advisory Service (ADAS), the Cumbria Tourist Board and the Rural Development Commission, has been working towards the development and marketing of farm tourism in Cumbria. Its overall aim is to increase income and employment on farms by advising individual farms or existing marketing groups on how best to develop farm tourism. The first CFTI guide to farm accommodation in Cumbria was published in 1994.

For most visitors, the attraction of staying on a farm is the traditional image of a warm welcome, plentiful and wholesome food and the rustic farm environment. However, the most important feature of staying on a farm has been found to be the opportunity to enjoy the peace and quiet in an attractive rural setting (Denman 1994), largely confirming the fact that the majority of people who visit the countryside are looking for space, feedom and relaxation. Importantly, farm accommodation is also seen as offering value for money.

(b) Country Village Weekend Breaks

Another innovation in countryside tourism and leisure has been the introduction of Country Village Weekend Breaks (CVBW). CVWB was a co-operative marketing consortium that, since 1984, helped small rural communities to market themselves as weekend tourism destinations. The purpose of CVWB was to give visitors an experience of present-day village life, breaking down the usual barriers between visitors and local people. Visitors stayed in the homes of villagers or farmers, ate local food and were given craft demonstrations and guided tours around farms and the surrounding countryside. The weekends were organised by the villagers themselves and were designed to supplement, rather than replace, their normal work and income. By 1990, eight villages in the Hereford, Shropshire and Staffordshire area were offering over fifty different weekend breaks. Owing to a number of problems, including local administrative difficulties and the perceived high cost of the breaks during a period of recession, CVWB no longer operates in England although a similar scheme, supported by the Wales Tourist Board, still exists in Wales. Neverthless, the CVWB scheme remains one of the best examples of sustainable tourism in practice, as well as highlighting some of the potential pitfalls.

(c) Conservation Holidays

As concern for the environment has grown, increasing numbers of people are choosing to spend their leisure time working on conservation projects in the countryside. The major organisation which provides the opportunity to participate in conservation holidays is the British Trust for Conservation Volunteers (BTCV). Being a charity BTCV is not strictly a private sector organisation yet for over thirty years it has been involved in conservation work. Each year it trains over 50,000 volunteers who work at more than 15,000 sites, undertaking practical work such as repairing footpaths and walls and protecting natural habitats. During the 1980s the number of people participating in BTCV's Natural Break conservation holidays increased five-fold, indicating not only increasing environmental concern but also a greater willingness and desire amongst the public to learn about, and be involved in, practical conservation work.

Overall the private sector supply of tourism and leisure in the countryside is restricted to a minority of visitors. As the surveys have shown, the greatest demand for countryside recreation is for informal, spontaneous activities such as driving, walking and visiting friends and relatives and, therefore, the supply of countryside recreation, for the majority of visitors, is dependent on the maintenance of the physical, natural and social characteristics of the countryside.

SUMMARY

Countryside recreation as a distinct category of tourism and leisure has its roots in the late eighteenth century but the major period of growth in demand was between 1960 and 1980. This was as a result of increases in free time, income and, in particular, car ownership. Since 1980 demand has remained static with the countryside facing increasing competition from overseas tourism and newer categories of domestic tourism and leisure attractions. A number of points have emerged from the assessment of the demand for recreation in the countryside.

i The demand for countryside recreation is determined by a variety of inter-related factors including car-ownership, social and occupational status and place of residence. A person in a professional or managerial occupation is three times more likely to visit the countryside than someone who is unemployed or on a minimum income.

ii Although up to eighty per cent of the population visit the countryside at least once a year, the great majority of visits are made by a small minority of frequent visitors. This indicates that there is a significant level of latent demand amongst people who never or infrequently visit the countryside.

iii Most visitors to the countryside participate in informal activities such as walking, driving or visiting friends and relatives. Visits to managed sites, though significant in terms of visitor numbers, account for a minority of countryside activities.

iv Qualitative research into the motivation for visiting the countryside has revealed a variety of perceptions of the countryside dependent on experience and social and cultural factors. For many people the countryside is synonymous with a better way of life that can no longer be found in towns and cities.

v Public sector supply of countryside recreation has tended to manage and contain expressed demand rather than creating new opportunities. Current policies recognise the need to promote the wider countryside but, within the context of sustainable development, are dominated by economic and conservation issues.

Case Study: The Whitbread Hop Farm

The Whitbread Hop Farm is situated in the Kent countryside between Paddock Wood and Tonbridge. Since it opened its doors to tourists in 1982 it has become one of the county's most popular rural visitor attractions.

The Hop Farm dates back to 1836 when it was known as Beltring farm. Its then owner had purchased it for £550 and when he died he left the land to the Drapers Company, a London based charitable organisation. From 1887 the land was farmed by E. A. White, a hop grower, who became internationally recognised for his research into hop production. It was he who built the four large Victorian oast houses which form the centrepiece of the farm and are reputed to be the best example of oast houses in the country. Since 1920 the farm has been owned by Whitbreads. The company developed the site into one of the largest working hop farms in Kent and until 1968 large numbers of hop pickers stayed on the farm each summer to work on the annual hop harvest.

The Whitbread Hop Farm is now a good example of a countryside tourism and leisure destination that is based on a traditional rural industry. The four original oast houses, known as Bells 1, 2, 3, and 4, house a number of attractions including a rural museum, a pottery workshop, a conference and banqueting centre and a family restaurant. There is a small aviary housing owls and birds of prey which are used in regular demonstrations for visitors, and the farm is also home to the famous Whitbread Shire horses. The central, and most recent, attraction is an exhibition called *The Kent Hop Picking Story*. Opened in 1992, it uses photographs, videos and modern interpretative techniques, such a recreating the smell of hops, to describe the history of the farm, the development of hop growing, the brewing process, and life on the farm as a hop-picker.

The range of activities offered by the farm is not limited to exhibitions and displays. In 1991 the farm joined forces with the Kent Trust for Nature Conservation, the county's wildlife conservation charity, and developed a nature trail. In addition to affording visitors the opportunity to walk in the Kent countryside it also plays an important role in educating school children and other young people about the countryside, wildlife, and the importance of nature conservation. There is also an animal village, which houses a variety of animals, and a camping and caravan site which allows visitors to use the farm as a base for short breaks and longer holidays in the countryside.

The Whitbread Hop Farm derives a substantial amount of business from offering country pursuit days to corporate clients. Visitors spend a day on the farm, during which they are able to participate in a range of activities which include clay pigeon shooting, falconry, parascending, four-wheel driving courses, archery, and, weather permitting, hot-air ballooning. Furthermore, the number of special events are organised, such as jazz and classical music evenings, hot-air balloon festivals, vintage air displays, classic car shows and even tug-of-war championships.

Thus, the Whitbread Hop Farm has been transformed from a working hop farm into a multi-purpose visitor destination. Tourism and leisure have contributed to the conservation of an important example of traditional rural architecture whilst the farm provides the opportunity for visitors to participate in a range of activities. It plays an important role in education, satisfying visitors' desire to learn about and experience a traditional rural industry, and it provides a dramatic rural setting for a variety of special events. Overall its success undoubtedly lies in its heritage, the range of attractions and activities it offers, and a successful marketing strategy.

Chapter Four

Countryside Recreation and the Law

INTRODUCTION

Virtually all activities undertaken by visitors to the countryside are constrained to some extent by law. Even a simple drive in the country, for example, with a visit to a pub followed by a walk along a footpath is subject to a multitude of driving, licensing and access regulations. At the same time the planning, development and provision of tourism and leisure in the countryside is guided by a complex legal framework; the development of land, building design, access, the designation of special areas and the protection of wildlife are all controlled and regulated by law. To cover all aspects of what may be described as Countryside Law is beyond the scope of this book (see, for example, Garner and Jones 1993). However, much of the present system for the planning and management of countryside recreation has its foundations in law. The purpose of this chapter is, therefore, to highlight the major legislation that has facilitated the positive development of the countryside as a resource for tourism and leisure rather than those laws that control or restrict activities. It thereby serves as an introduction to the more detailed discussions of countryside organisations and policies in subsequent chapters.

THE DEVELOPMENT OF COUNTRYSIDE LAW

There has been a rapid and unprecedented rise in the level of participation in countryside tourism and leisure over the last forty years; this same period has witnessed the introduction of the main legislation concerning the countryside. Indeed, many of the planning and management procedures enshrined in the legislation can be seen as reactive responses to the increased demands and pressures on the countryside, rather than proactive attempts to anticipate and manage demand. As will be discussed shortly, this has resulted in some parts of the legislation being less effective than they might otherwise have been.

However, whilst legislative, or statute, law (law that is embodied in Acts of Parliament) which relates to the management of the countryside is a feature of the second half of the twentieth century, countryside law in a more general sense is as old as the common law of England. In contrast to statute law, common law is the term used to describe those principles of law based on the decisions made by judges in particular cases, a process that continues to this day. From early times a judgement or decision made in any particular case was recorded, setting a precedent by which other similar cases could be judged, and in this way a body of law was developed over the centuries. In 1386, for example, a traveller staying at an inn had his possessions stolen from his room. The traveller claimed that the innkeeper was liable for the safekeeping of his belongings while he was a guest at the inn. The judge upheld the claim that the innkeeper was responsible and also found that the innkeeper had not committed a criminal offence. This decision created a precedent that still holds today. Certain aspects of countryside recreation are still subject to common law, in particular issues relating to trespass and rights of access to common land, and these are examined in Chapter Seven.

Prior to the Industrial Revolution of the eighteenth and nineteenth centuries England's society and economy was largely based on the countryside and thus much of the law was concerned with the land and agriculture. Following the Industrial Revolution, however, the urbanisation of society, improvements in working conditions and the mechanisation of transport led to dramatic changes in demands and pressures on the countryside. In particular there was a growing awareness of the need to reconcile the traditional agricultural use of the countryside with the increasing demands for recreation as described in Chapter Two. Certain groups were, at the same time, increasing pressure both to maintain public access to the countryside and to conserve the landscape from creeping industrialisation and urbanisation. The Commons, Open Spaces and Footpaths Preservation Society, Britain's first and longest surviving conservation organisation, was formed in 1865 and, as the Open Spaces Society, it continues today to campaign to free all areas of common ground for legal public access. Likewise the original aim of the National Trust, founded in 1895, was to secure continued public access to places of natural beauty or historic interest.

It was not until 1949 that the first major piece of legislation, the National Parks and Access to the Countryside Act, was passed, forming the platform for other legislation in following years and laying the foundations for the present-day structure of administration and management of the countryside for conservation and recreational purposes.

In short, then, the law relating to the countryside has broadened from its early beginnings as a regulatory process developed to serve the needs of a rural, agriculture based society into the machinery for resolving the potential conflicts between farming, the demands of an increasingly leisure orientated society and the need to conserve and protect the countryside as a fragile and finite resource satisfying a variety of needs.

CONFLICTS WITHIN THE LAW

Essentially the main objective of countryside law with regard to tourism and leisure is to promote public access to and enjoyment of the countryside whilst at the same time seeking to protect the intrinsic qualities of the countryside. More recently, protecting and enhancing the economic, social and cultural well-being of those who live and work in the countryside has also been included as a necessary policy objective, and as seen in Chapter Five these aims are translated into the roles and activities of the main organisations concerned with countryside recreation.

Yet it is perhaps inevitable that these objectives conflict. A protected, beautiful landscape will continue to attract visitors who contribute to the local economy, but ever-increasing numbers of visitors may have negative impacts on the environment that, in the long run, could destroy those very qualities sought by visitors in the first place. The need to maintain the balance, to minimise the potential conflicts at the same time as maximising the benefits, is a major theme throughout the rest of this book and is the prime objective of the efficient and effective development and management of tourism and leisure in the countryside.

Farmers – Guardians of the Countryside?
Before looking at each relevant piece of legislation separately, one further point needs to be emphasised. In 1942 the Report of the Committee on Land Utilisation in Rural Areas, otherwise known as the Scott Report (HMSO 1942), was published. Its purpose was to suggest ways in which the social and economic conditions in rural communities could be revived following the decline of the Depression years. Importantly, its findings were largely based on the belief that both the physical landscape of the countryside and its communities could be preserved by a prosperous and traditional farming industry. In other words, it failed to anticipate the rapid post-war adoption of intensive, efficient farming methods and their potential effects on the landscape, such as the destruction of hedgerows and woodland (see Shoard 1980). In short, the recommendations of the Scott Report placed the future of the countryside firmly in the hands of the farming industry.

Interestingly, the Scott Committee also favoured access for all in the countryside as long as it did not interfere with proper use of the land and, furthermore, its report also suggested that all public footpaths should be recorded by local authorities, a proposal that found its way into the National Parks and Access to the Countryside Act 1949 and which now is a major element of public rights of way policy (see Chapter Seven). However, the main thrust of the Report was concerned with the central role to be played by farming and forestry in the countryside.

This central theme was carried through into the major planning and countryside legislation of the following years. In 1947 the Town and Country Planning Act was passed. It effectively "nationalised" the right to develop land for the first time by introducing the requirement for landowners to obtain planning permission from their local council before undertaking any development. This requirement was not extended to the farming industry; any change or development of either land or buildings for agricultural or forestry purposes, and indeed any change in the agricultural use of land, was exempted from planning control. Thus, arguably, the 1947 Act effectively placed the farming industry above the law. Any change of use for non-agricultural purposes, such as the conversion of barns into holiday homes or the development of farmland into a golf course, was, of course, still to be subject to planning consent.

The result of this exemption was twofold. Firstly, it allowed for the controversial planting of vast areas of conifer forests, the creation of prairie farms, the uncontrolled removal of hedgerows and the drainage of wetlands, threatening the future of both the countryside's wildlife and its traditional character. In recent years over-production, grain mountains and environmental concern have led to a reversal of policy. Through a range of schemes and financial incentives farmers are now encouraged to play a more active and positive role in landscape and wildlife conservation (see Chapter Eight).

Secondly, the exemption of farmers from planning control meant that the legislation from 1949 onwards concerning the protection, promotion and enjoyment of the countryside was, in effect, attempting to manage a resource that was outside legislative control. In 1980, for example, it was estimated that some 96 per cent of the total land area of the national parks, the prime resource for countryside tourism and leisure, was being used for agricultural or forestry purposes (MacEwan and MacEwen 1981). As will be seen, this assumption of the farming industry's guardianship of the countryside has given rise to a management system for both recreation and conservation that relies heavily on voluntary co-operation and agreements rather than statutory power. This, in turn, has had a limiting effect on the degree of control and authority of those organisations entrusted with the management of both recreation and conservation in the countryside.

COUNTRYSIDE LEGISLATION
Since 1949 there have been a number of important pieces of legislation designed to both conserve and protect the countryside and to promote and manage it as a resource for tourism and leisure. The following two Acts are of most concern:

National Parks and Access to the Countryside Act 1949
Countryside Act 1968

Four further Acts are of direct relevance to both recreation and conservation in the countryside:

Highways Act 1980
Wildlife and Countryside Act 1981
Environmental Protection Act 1990
Environment Act 1995

All of the above legislation has to a greater or lesser extent had an influence on tourism and leisure in the countryside. At the same time the countryside is a part of the national tourism and leisure product, the promotion of which is the responsibility of the national and regional tourist boards. The Development of Tourism Act 1969 will therefore also be considered briefly. It is important to note that the countryside legislation applies only to England and Wales; Scotland has its own separate legal system and, as a result, for example, has no national parks (a subject of debate that continues to this day). Reference will therefore be made to the Scottish system where relevant.

i National Parks and Access to the Countryside Act 1949

The 1949 Act was first major piece of legislation concerned directly with both conservation and enjoyment of the countryside and, almost fifty years later, it still forms the basis for the management of tourism and leisure in the countryside. The provisions contained within the Act are wide ranging and indeed are somewhat broader than its title would suggest, and can be seen as the result of a process that started almost one hundred and fifty years earlier.

As we have already seen, the first seeds of the conservationist movement were sown in the Lake District. The National Trust originated in Lakeland and the Friends of the Lake District was one of a number of preservationist groups that merged to form the Council for the Preservation (now Protection) of Rural England (CPRE) in 1926.

95

Likewise the concept of national parks was first proposed in the Lake District by William Wordsworth, who concluded his 1810 *Guide to the Lakes* with his now famous wish that:

> *...the author will be joined by persons of pure taste throughout the whole island, who, by their visits (often repeated) to the Lakes in the North of England, testify that they deem the district a sort of national property in which every man has a right and interest who has an eye to perceive and a heart to enjoy.*

Interestingly it was also Wordsworth who first expressed concern about the possible effects of mass tourism and leisure in the countryside. Worried about the influx of visitors that would result from the opening of the railway to Windermere, he wrote in 1844:

> *Is then no nook of English ground secure from rash assault?*

His misgivings demonstrated a rather elitist, class-orientated opinion as to which members of society should be able to visit the Lake District or would be able to appreciate its undoubted scenic qualities. The preservationist groups of the late nineteenth and early twentieth centuries similarly tended to be dominated by a generally middle-class, educated and urban-based membership. Nevertheless they were instrumental in leading a number of campaigns to protect the country's highly valued landscapes from the development of quarries, housing, road improvements, reservoirs and so on.

In contrast to these groups, during the 1920s and 1930s walking and rambling was rapidly growing in popularity amongst the working populations of the industrial cities, particularly in the north of England. Their campaigns for the freedom to roam (see Hill 1980) over the privately-owned grouse moors of Derbyshire culminated in the famous mass trespass on Kinder Scout in the Peak District in 1932, whilst the fight to secure greater access to the countryside is continued to this day by the Ramblers Association. Thus pressure was being exerted on two fronts;

the preservationist groups working for the protection and conservation of the countryside and the ramblers demanding greater freedom of access.

The first official move towards establishing national parks came with the Addison Committee's 1929 enquiry into the feasibility of national parks and the improvement in general of recreational facilities in the countryside. The Committee's report included proposals for the establishment of nature reserves and sanctuaries and, although its recommendations were not acted upon in the prevailing economic climate, it nevertheless provided the impetus for further pressure. In 1936 the CPRE, the Ramblers Association and a number of other amenity groups joined forces to form the Standing Committee for National Parks, presenting a united front to campaign for both the protection of and access to the countryside. It produced a report assessing the existing planning legislation which concluded that the responsibility for ensuring both the preservation of the country's most outstanding yet threatened landscapes and the promotion of access to them lay with central government. The report recommended that an authority should be set up to designate and manage national parks.

It was probably the Second World War that was the decisive factor leading to the introduction of countryside legislation. There was a political and national desire for a new and better Britain to replace the gloom and depression of the 1930s and the concept of national parks and nature reserves were included in the post-war development plans. Therefore John Dower, an architect and active member of the Ramblers Association, was asked by the then Minister of Town and Country Planning to write a report on the establishment of national parks. It was Dower's 1945 Report on National Parks in England and Wales, followed by the 1947 Hobhouse Committee's Report accepting the majority of Dower's proposals, that led directly to the National Parks and Access to the Countryside Act 1949.

The Act itself covers six main areas:

(a) National Parks
Of primary importance, the Act enabled the designation of specified areas

97

of the countryside as national parks. In his 1945 report Dower defined a national park *as an extensive area of beautiful and relatively wild country in which:*

(a) *the characteristic landscape beauty is strictly preserved,*
(b) *access and facilities for open-air enjoyment are amply provided,*
(c) *wildlife and buildings and places of historic interest are suitably protected while*
(d) *established farming use is effectively maintained.*

Dower thus saw the national parks fulfilling two roles: the conservation of the natural and man-made landscape and the provision of opportunities for recreation. These aims were echoed by the Act which stated that national parks were to be designated to *preserve and enhance the natural beauty of the areas specified, and for the purpose of promoting their enjoyment by the public.* The areas to be designated would be characterised by their natural beauty, their potential for recreation and their location with respect to centres of population, essentially extensive tracts of open country which the Act defined as *mountain, moor, heath, down, cliff or foreshore.*

Dower originally proposed ten areas to be designated as national parks, a list increased to twelve by the Hobhouse Committee. Eventually, ten of those twelve areas were designated as national parks between 1951 and 1957, the first being the Peak District and the process culminating with the Brecon Beacons (see Table 4.1). The total area covered by the parks extended to some 13600 square kilometres, or roughly 9 per cent of the land area of England and Wales. The remaining two areas proposed by Hobhouse were the Norfolk Broads and the South Downs. Although no further national parks have been designated since 1957 the Broads were awarded the equivalent of National Park status as a result of the Norfolk and Suffolk Broads Act 1988 and as a result are considered by some to constitute an eleventh national park. Furthermore, it was announced in early 1992 that the New Forest in Hampshire was also to be accorded similar status. However, in July 1994 that decision was reversed by the

Government and, rather than giving extra recognition to the particular qualities of the area, the Forest was simply to become subject to improved planning control.

TABLE 4.1. NATIONAL PARKS IN ENGLAND AND WALES

Park	Designation Date	Area (sq. km)
Peak District	1951	1404
Lake District	1951	2280
Dartmoor	1951	945
Snowdonia	1951	2170
Pembrokeshire Coast	1952	583
North York Moors	1952	438
Exmoor	1954	686
Yorkshire Dales	1954	1716
Northumberland	1956	1031
Brecon Beacons	1957	1350

Source: *Protected Landscapes. The United Kingdom Experience*
(IUCN 1987)

The influence of the Scott Report is also visible in the 1949 Act. Whilst Dower called for the maintenance of traditional farming practices in the proposed national parks, the Act itself stated that due regard should be given to the needs of the farming and forestry. By so doing, the scene was immediately set for potential conflicts between the public interests of recreation and conservation of the landscape and the private interests of the farming and forestry industries within the Parks. The Hobhouse Committee had recommended that each national park should be administered by an independent Parks Committee, whilst the Act envisaged that Joint Boards made up of representatives of local authorities and centrally appointed members, with a high degree of autonomy from local authority control, would oversee the planning and management of the parks. In practice only the Peak District and, to a lesser extent, the Lake District were given the necessary autonomy and independence whilst the remaining eight parks effectively came under the control of the local authorities within whose boundaries they lay. Only in September 1991 was it announced that these remaining eight parks would be granted freedom from local authority control, a move designed to alleviate many of the conflicts that, as discussed in Chapter Six, since their designation the national parks had failed to reconcile. This decision was finally translated into legislation in 1995. Nevertheless, despite the controversy surrounding the effectiveness of the national parks, their creation remains the single most important piece of legislation in the provision of countryside tourism and leisure.

(b) The National Parks Commission
Part 1 of the Act covered the setting up of the National Parks Commission (NPC), the body responsible primarily for the designation of the national parks and other protected areas of countryside as defined elsewhere in the Act. Responsible to the then Ministry of Town and Country Planning (now the Department of the Environment), the Commission was, however, relatively powerless with no management or administrative functions, effectively confirming that the management and control of the new parks would be decentralised to the relevant local authorities. In 1968 the NPC became the Countryside Commission.

(c) Nature Conservancy
In addition to the designation of national parks for the promotion of recreation and the preservation of what may be described as the *scenic* quality of the landscape, the Act included provisions for nature conservation, effectively the landscape's *natural* qualities. This arguably illogical split dated back to 1947 when, alongside the Hobhouse Committee, a Special Committee for Wildlife Conservation (the Huxley Committee) published its report recommending that important or threatened wildlife habitats should be managed by a central body for the purpose of both conservation and scientific research. Following this report and prior to the 1949 Act the Nature Conservancy (later the Nature Conservancy Council, (NCC)) was established by Royal Charter in 1949 with the prime objective of setting up Nature Reserves in Great Britain. The Act provided the Conservancy with new powers to establish and manage National Nature Reserves (NNRs) by either entering into agreements with landowners or by purchasing land, and also to create

100

bylaws for their protection. Furthermore the Conservancy was also empowered to designate Sites of Special Scientific Interest (SSSIs), although these did not enjoy the protective status of NNRs. It also became the Conservancy's duty to undertake scientific research and to offer advice on nature conservation and it was given the appropriate authority and independence to do so. In 1990 the overlap in the roles of the NCC and the Countryside Commission was officially recognised by the merger of the two organisations into Countryside Councils for Scotland and Wales. In England, however, the Countryside Commission and the NCC have retained their separate identities, the NCC now known as English Nature.

(d) Rights of Way

Although the most dramatic and visible result of the 1949 Act was the designation of the national parks, of equal importance in terms of public access for recreation and leisure were the provisions it contained concerning Public Rights of Way. Indeed a greater number of sections in the Act were devoted to this single issue than to the combined legislation for national parks, nature reserves and SSSIs. The rights of way network is of central importance to the provision and management of tourism and leisure in the countryside; as the Countryside Commission (Countryside Commission 1989a) states:

The national system of...rights of way is the single most important means of access to and enjoyment of the countryside.

Also, in addition to the continuing campaigns for improved public access to the countryside much of the work undertaken by countryside organisations today is concerned with the effective management and maintenance of rights of way. The issues concerning rights of way and access in general are considered more fully in Chapter Seven.

The 1949 Act is of vital importance as it set in motion a process that was designed to unravel the complex and often confusing regulations surrounding the legal status of rights of way (for a comprehensive guide to rights of way and the law see Riddell and Trevelyan 1992). The existence and use of many roads, footpaths and bridleways that together constitute the rights of way system dates back over many centuries. Over the years some routes ceased to be used, others were lost to building development or to the plough, and in many cases there was confusion as to whether the public could use a particular route as of legal right or whether access was "permissive" (i.e. with the express permission of the landowner over whose property the route crossed). Therefore the main objective of this part of the Act, as originally suggested by the Scott Committee in 1942, was to introduce legislation to lead to the clarification and confirmation of the existence and status of rights of way.

Essentially, through the Act all local highway authorities (usually county councils, metropolitan district councils and London borough councils) became duty bound to prepare a definitive map of all roads, footpaths, bridleways and roads used as public footpaths (RUPPs) in their region. This was to be achieved by producing, in consultation with local parish councils, a draft map and written statement for consideration by the public. Closures or new routes would then be made, followed by the publication of a provisional map and statement. After further consultation a final, definitive map and statement of a county's rights of way would then be published.

With over 140,000 miles (224,000 km) of rights of way in England and Wales the enormity of the task is self-evident; almost fifty years since the Act was passed many highway authorities have yet to complete their definitive maps. Both the Countryside Commission and the Ramblers Association have set the year 2000 as the target date for the completion of definitive maps and for the entire network to be open, well-maintained and signposted/waymarked as required. The next few years are therefore likely to witness a flurry of activity and a concentration of resources to achieve this aim.

(e) Footpaths and General Access
Part V of the Act dealt with general access to the countryside as a separate issue from the specific problems surrounding the rights of way network. Despite the efforts of the Ramblers Association and other amenity organisations during the 1920s and 1930s, and indeed the

recommendations of the Hobhouse Committee, the Act provided that the public should **not** enjoy a universal right of access to open countryside. Rather, access should be gained on a permissive basis through agreements with landowners. Where necessary, the Act empowered local authorities to enter into access agreements with landowners to secure public access to open country and to pay compensation to landowners for any expenses incurred in undertaking such an agreement.

In practice relatively few access agreements have been implemented, with over half being in the Peak District. However, this part of the Act is of great significance to the provision of countryside recreation for it firmly gave precedence to the legal, proprietorial, rights of landowners over what many see as the socially desirable right of the public to wander at will in the countryside. (See, for example, Shoard, 1987 and Harrison, 1991). In contrast, the public in some Scandinavian countries, such as Sweden, enjoy what is known as *Allemansratten*, or the legal right of access to all land whether publicly or privately owned. Access to the countryside is still largely dominated and controlled by the interests of landowners although, as will be seen, the attitudes of landowners have been modified in recent years by the emergence of tourism and leisure as the new rural growth industry. Nevertheless the debate over public access to the countryside continues to be centred as much on the social desirability of a universal right of access as it is on the actual legal mechanism.

(f) Other Provisions
A number of other powers were included in the 1949 Act which have a bearing on countryside tourism and leisure. The NPC, in addition to its role in the creation of the national parks, was empowered to designate Areas of Outstanding Natural Beauty (AONBs). These are areas of countryside outside the national parks which, due to their particular scenic qualities, warrant both recognition and protection. In contrast to the recreational objectives of the national parks AONB designation is primarily intended for the purpose of conservation. Additionally, the Act allowed for the creation of long-distance footpaths (National Trails) and the provision of information and warden services for visitors to the national parks.

Overall, then, the National Parks and Access to the Countryside Act 1949 was a far-reaching piece of legislation. At one stroke it sought to set down procedures for the conservation of the scenic qualities of countryside, for the provision and promotion of recreation (albeit in line with the prevailing scope and extent of participation in tourism and leisure in the countryside), and for nature and wildlife conservation. It also set in motion the mechanism for the definition and management of the rights of way system. With hindsight the assumption of the farming industry's guardianship of the countryside and the lack of authority and power conferred onto the NPC and the bodies entrusted with the administration of the national parks was, as is discussed in the next chapter, an arguably fundamental flaw. Nonetheless, the importance of the Act cannot be overstated.

ii Countryside Act 1968

The two decades following the 1949 Act saw an increasingly affluent society's demands for power, water and natural resources place ever greater pressure on the countryside, pressure that the national parks in particular appeared ill-equipped to deal with. It was, however, the unforeseen (in 1949) explosion in tourism and leisure as described in Chapter Three that began to bring the twin aims of conservation and recreation provision in the national parks into conflict. As more and more people ventured into the countryside, resulting in particular from the dramatic increase in private car ownership, concern began to grow about the potential impacts on the countryside of the leisure boom, what John Dower's son Michael described as *The Fourth Wave* (Dower, 1965). Consequently during the 1960s three *Countryside in 1970* conferences highlighted the need to balance the use of the countryside as a resource for tourism and leisure with its conservation and protection. The objective of these conferences was to consider ways and means of harmonising the needs of both the rural and the urban populations, in effect introducing the concept of sustainable development.

In 1966 the White Paper *Leisure in the Countryside* was published which led directly to many of the provisions contained in the second major piece of countryside legislation, the Countryside Act 1968. The White Paper emphasised the concern that leisure in the countryside would continue to increase and that not only would traditional recreational areas, such as the national parks, begin to suffer damage through overuse but also the visitors themselves would spill over into the wider countryside. Furthermore it was feared that increasing numbers of car-borne visitors would bring the problems of litter, vandalism and trespass, thereby threatening the livelihood of the farming community. Thus the planning philosophy of the day became one not of the harmonisation and balancing of needs but one of containing the problem. In other words the proposed solution, as evidenced by the provisions contained in the 1968 Act, was to divert demand to newly created facilities, thereby reducing the pressure on traditional areas. In short, to control or reduce the numbers of urban visitors to the countryside the plan was, effectively, to take the countryside nearer to the towns. This was to be achieved by creating country parks. To an extent this can be seen as making generalised assumptions about the motivations of visitors to the countryside and the resulting success of country parks is still a subject of debate (see Chapter Six).

The two principal features of the Act were:

(a) The Countryside Commission
The 1968 Act transformed the National Parks Commission into the Countryside Commission. This reflected a broadening of the functions of the original body to take in the conservation and enhancement of the countryside as a whole and to encourage the promotion and provision of wider countryside recreation. The Commission was also given the power to undertake or to grant aid research work and to initiate management projects in the countryside, a first step towards its becoming the major and most influential organisation concerned with countryside conservation and recreation that it is today.

(b) Country Parks
The central thrust of the Act was to facilitate the development of new countryside recreation areas to act as a kind of pressure valve for the most popular, and hence threatened, areas of the countryside. This it did by empowering local authorities to either develop or purchase land for the

purpose of creating country parks. The Act also included powers for local authorities to develop recreational facilities such as picnic areas and car parks and to undertake building work for the provision of, for example, visitor centres and restaurant facilities. These provisions were not only limited to the public sector; private landowners were also enabled to develop or establish country parks on their land. Grant aid of up to 75 per cent for private landowners or fifty per cent for local authorities was made available through the new Countryside Commission.

Whilst mainly being concerned with the mechanism for the development and funding of country parks, the 1968 Act also made some refinements to definitive map procedures detailed in the 1949 Act. At the same time certain provisions were introduced regarding the duty of highway authorities to maintain and to signpost rights of way. All rights of way, for example, were to be signposted where they leave a metalled road, a duty that, along with the completion of definitive maps, has yet to be fully complied with. Also of significance within the Act were the sections that broadened the definition of open country to include woodlands, rivers and canals and those which empowered the Forestry Commission and the then public Regional Water Authorities to provide facilities for leisure and sporting activities on their property. Finally, there was a stated requirement for all concerned individuals and organisations to have due regard for the conservation of both the natural beauty and amenity of the countryside.

The Countryside Act 1968 is therefore notable for broadening and extending many of the principles of the 1949 Act, in particular the definition of the countryside and the range of facilities to be provided for recreation. As such it built upon the earlier Act and together they form the basis for much of the present day planning and management of countryside recreation.

iii Highways Act 1980
All public rights of way are technically highways. The Highways Act 1980 is therefore of direct relevance to the provision of countryside recreation as it contains the most important legislation concerning the

creation, dedication and diversion of rights of way. The statutory duties of highway authorities and landowners with respect to the maintenance of public rights of way are also detailed.

iv Wildlife and Countryside Act 1981
As with earlier countryside Acts, the Wildlife and Countryside Act 1981 continued the tradition of relying on cooperation and agreement with landowners in its provisions for the protection of nature and wildlife. It was mostly concerned, as its name suggests, with conservation and indeed Part 1 of the Act covers the protection of specific species of animals, birds, plants and other wildlife.

Under the general heading of nature conservancy, the NCC was given powers to designate Marine Nature Reserves and to grant aid work undertaken by individuals or organisations involved in nature conservation work whilst relevant authorities, such as local councils, were empowered to enter into management agreements with landowners for the purpose of both conservation and promoting its enjoyment by the public. The most contentious sections of the Act were those which required the NCC to effectively give landowners and local authorities three months notice of their intention to designate a Site of Special Scientific Interest. In practice this meant that the NCC had to re-notify all SSSIs while in effect landowners, perhaps worried about either restrictive planning controls or visitors on their land, were allowed three months to destroy the proposed site. By 1985 almost ten per cent of SSSI re-notifications had been damaged prior to re-notification being finalised (Bromley 1990). Furthermore, the NCC was required to compensate landowners for any loss of income or reduction in land value resulting from SSSI designation; in other words, the NCC had to 'buy' land that was of scientific importance.

Other provisions in the 1981 Act included powers for local authorities to appoint wardens for any area of countryside, including national parks, where public access is permitted. The refinement of rights of way legislation was also continued with the definitive map procedure being transformed from a once-off to a continuous up-dating process.

v Environmental Protection Act 1990

This Act was primarily concerned with introducing measures for the protection of the environment as a whole rather than the countryside in particular. It covered a wide range of issues including provisions for the control of pollution, such as the emission and disposal of industrial waste. Perhaps of particular interest to motorists in the countryside were the measures designed to regulate farmers' practice of stubble burning after harvesting. However, the provisions of most relevance were those which, in Wales and Scotland, transferred the responsibilities of the Countryside Commission and the NCC to a single Countryside Council for Wales and, from 1992, Scottish Natural Heritage. For some this was seen as a desirable move towards a more unified approach to countryside management, removing some of the overlap of functions carried out by the two separate agencies. Others, however, felt it would lead to a dilution of the responsibility and authority of each body, particularly the standing of the NCC as a scientific agency, while posing a threat to the balance of attention given to the separate issues of recreation, scenic preservation and nature conservation. At present it is still too early to determine the longer term effects of this amalgamation, although a move to combine the work of the Countryside Commission and English Nature is currently under consideration.

vi Environment Act 1995

In 1991, following the publication of the Report of the National Parks Review Committee (Edwards 1991), it was announced that all national parks would become free-standing planning authorities, independent from local authority control. The Environment Act 1995 includes provisions allowing for the strengthening of the status of all National Park Authorities, at the same time as redefining and widening the purpose of national parks. This signifies an important move towards the establishment of a system of national park administration similar to that envisaged by both Dower and Hobhouse in the 1940s, yet many believe that the 1995 Act still does not go far enough in its attempt to resolve the conflicts in national parks. These issues are discussed in greater detail in Chapter Six.

COUNTRYSIDE LAW IN SCOTLAND

As was pointed out at the beginning of this chapter Scotland has an entirely separate legal system from that in England and Wales. Therefore, although many of the conflicts that surround the countryside as a resource for tourism and leisure are of equal relevance in Scotland as they are south of the border the means of resolving them in many cases are completely different. Two issues in particular need to be considered, namely landscape conservation through land designation and rights of way.

i Scottish Land Designation

Much of planning and management of the countryside in England and Wales for both conservation and its enjoyment by the public is based on the principle of land designation as legislated for in the National Parks and Access to the Countryside Act 1949. However, although similar legislation for Scotland was considered during the same period (in 1947 the Ramsay Committee reported on National Parks and the Conservation of Nature in Scotland alongside the Hobhouse Committee in England) no part of Scotland has ever been designated as a national park. The 'National Parks for Scotland' debate has continued ever since and the main arguments are considered shortly in a case study.

With no national parks there was of course no need for a National Parks Commission and so environmental issues were dealt with directly by the Scottish Secretary until the Countryside Commission for Scotland was formed in 1967 through the Countryside (Scotland) Act. The lack of national parks, and indeed other designated areas such as AONBs, was compensated to some extent in 1978 when the Commission nominated forty National Scenic Areas (see Figure 4.1). Covering areas mostly to the north and west of Scotland and totalling almost 13 per cent of the country's land and inland waters, the NSAs were officially designated through the Town and Country Planning (Scotland) Act 1978. Their purpose is primarily for conservation with a number of planning restrictions applying to designated areas. Thus, although some NSAs cover popular visitor destinations such as Loch Lomond, Ben Nevis and Glencoe, and the Cuillin Hills on the Isle of Skye, overall they approximate more to the concept of AONBs rather than national parks.

FIGURE 4.1. NATIONAL SCENIC AREAS IN SCOTLAND IN 1990

Source: Countryside Commission

ii Scottish Rights of Way

The law concerning access to the Scottish countryside in general, and public rights of way in particular, differs considerably from the system in England and Wales. The premise of *once a right of way, always a right of way* (see Chapter Seven) does not exist and at the same time the complicated and lengthy legislation concerning definitive map procedures has no counterpart in Scottish law. This has led to a degree of confusion surrounding the status of the rights of way network, so much so that Ordnance Survey maps of Scotland do not, in fact, show any rights of way. Furthermore this uncertainty over public rights of access have given rise to two popular misconceptions: firstly, that there are no rights of way in Scotland and secondly, that the public enjoy free access to the Scottish countryside (and hence that there is no law of trespass).

Public rights of way do exist in Scotland, although the law does not recognise the rigid categories such as footpaths, bridleways and so on that exist in England and Wales. Their status is defined by use. There is also a legal procedure for establishing a public right of way, where six requirements must be satisfied:

(a)   there must be a public place at either end of the claimed right of way
(b)   the claimed right of way must have been used by members of the public to get from one public place to another
(c)   there must be a sufficiently definite route
(d)   there must have been continuous use of the route by the public
(e)   the use must have continued for twenty years
(f)   the use must not be by tolerance or permission of the landowner affected.

The lack of certainty about the rights of way network in Scotland results more from the fact that there is no equivalent to the Acts applying to England and Wales requiring the production of definitive maps and no legal duty on planning authorities to establish the status of a right of way. There is a duty to *assert, protect and keep open* any public right of way but in practice the planning authorities have tended to rely on agreements with landowners at the cost of an actual public right of access. It is this widely enjoyed permissive access, either actual or implied, that has given rise to the popularly held belief of a Scottish freedom to roam; the public, in fact, have no automatic right of access to the countryside. Without significant changes to the law concerning the definition of the rights of way network, access to the countryside in Scotland is likely to remain largely based on the permission of landowners and as demand for access grows the number of disputes over a right of access is also likely to increase. (See Scottish Rights of Way Society 1986 for a detailed analysis of the law in Scotland).

COUNTRYSIDE LAW: A EUROPEAN PERSPECTIVE
Since joining the European Community in 1973 British legislation as a whole has increasingly been set in a European context. Indeed where there is any conflict between Community law and the domestic statute law of individual member states then there is a presumption that Community law will prevail.

In general European (EU) law is mainly concerned with facilitating the free movement of goods, services and labour and the elimination of unfair competitive practices. However, following the formation of the Single Market in 1992 and the Maastricht Treaty in 1993, greater emphasis has been placed on the harmonisation of environmental and social considerations in the member states. A large number of directives have been issued by the EU in recent years that have been related to environmental issues, some of which have had a direct effect on countryside management. (All EU member states are obliged to introduce legislation to meet the aims and objectives of directives). For example, a European directive in the mid 1980s led to provisions in the Agriculture Act 1986 for the establishment of Environmentally Sensitive Areas (ESAs).

Under the ESA scheme, Community funding was made available to protect the landscape and wildlife in valuable or important areas which were vulnerable to changes in farming practices. In England five areas were originally designated in 1987 where farmers were invited, in return for incentive payments, to enter into agreements not to undertake

112

environmentally detrimental practices or to revert to more environmentally friendly farming methods. Following the success of the scheme a further six areas, including Exmoor and the Lake District, were proposed in March 1992 and by 1994 a total of 24 ESAs had been designated, covering some 2,839,198 acres (1,149,008 hectares) of English farmland.

Likewise it was a European directive which led to the concept of Environmental Impact Assessment being included in the planning process. Essentially this requires that, in a limited number of major development projects, the environmental and social impact of a project must be assessed before work is commenced.

It remains to be seen what effects increasing political and economic union within the EU will have on countryside conservation and recreation in the UK. Potentially, however, the greatest benefit may accrue from Community-wide policies on tourism in general, and rural tourism in particular. The development of tourism is seen as an effective means of reversing economic decline at the same time as protecting the heritage and environment of less favoured rural areas around the continent. Thus funds are already available through the Common Agricultural Policy and the Community's Regional Development Funds for the development of tourist facilities, for promotion and for vocational training within the rural context. In 1987 an EEC-sponsored report was published suggesting a European strategy for the development of rural tourism (Grolleau 1987), whilst the Organisation for Economic Co-operation and Development (OECD) also views tourism as a powerful vehicle for the social and economic regeneration of rural areas (OECD 1993 and 1994). Therefore, it is likely that tourism and leisure in the countryside will play an increasingly important role within EU regional development policies. (See Hoggart *et al* 1995 for a detailed consideration of rural development issues in Europe).

THE DEVELOPMENT OF TOURISM ACT 1969
So far this chapter has considered the main legislation constituting what may be categorised generally as countryside law, the body of law which is focussed primarily on the overall planning and management of the

countryside resource and within which the provision of recreation is legislated for to a greater or lesser extent.

It has already been emphasised, however, that tourism and leisure in the countryside cannot be viewed in isolation. The countryside is just one of the many attractions or destinations that make up the tourism product and therefore, in effect, competes with other destinations and attractions for a share of the tourism and leisure market. At the same time the continued success (in an economic sense) of the countryside in attracting visitors may well be dependent on external factors; the popularity of the overseas package holiday during the 1980s, for example, had a drastic effect on domestic tourism and leisure. In order to obtain a complete picture of the relevant legislation it is therefore necessary to consider the law relevant not only to the *resource*, the countryside, but also to the *activity*, namely tourism. The major, indeed only, piece of legislation regarding this is the Development of Tourism Act 1969.

The Government's recognition of the economic benefits of tourism, and hence the desirability of promoting tourism, both nationally and internationally, dates back to 1929 when the then Travel Association of Great Britain and Northern Ireland (an organisation made up largely of representatives of the tourism industry) first received an annual grant of £5000 from the Board of Trade to assist with the promotion of tourism to Britain. The following forty years witnessed an explosion in tourism and by the 1960s a growing level of out-going tourism was exacerbating an already serious Balance of Payments problem. The devaluation of the pound in 1967 made Britain increasingly attractive (i.e. cheap) destination for overseas tourists and so the promotion of tourism was seen as a relatively simple way of increasing foreign earnings. Therefore, with the calls for greater investment in tourism and for the establishment of nationally recognised tourist boards, the Development of Tourism Act was passed in 1969.

Although the Act contained many provisions for financial aid for the tourism sector its most important and long-lasting effect was to create the statutory tourist boards, namely the British Tourist Authority (BTA) and

FIGURE 4.2. REGIONAL TOURIST BOARDS IN ENGLAND AND WALES

FIGURE 4.3. AREA TOURIST BOARDS IN SCOTLAND

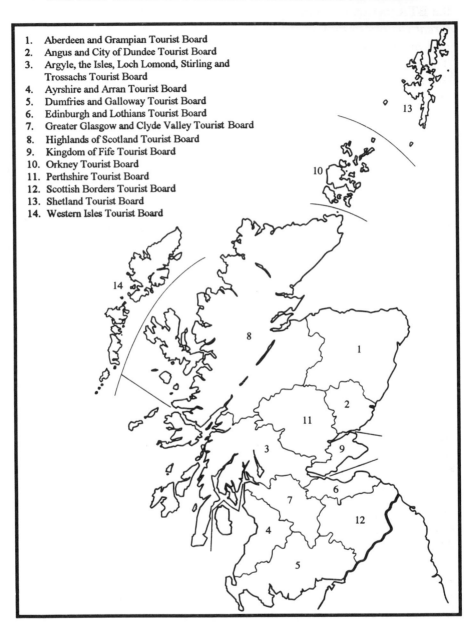

1. Aberdeen and Grampian Tourist Board
2. Angus and City of Dundee Tourist Board
3. Argyle, the Isles, Loch Lomond, Stirling and Trossachs Tourist Board
4. Ayrshire and Arran Tourist Board
5. Dumfries and Galloway Tourist Board
6. Edinburgh and Lothians Tourist Board
7. Greater Glasgow and Clyde Valley Tourist Board
8. Highlands of Scotland Tourist Board
9. Kingdom of Fife Tourist Board
10. Orkney Tourist Board
11. Perthshire Tourist Board
12. Scottish Borders Tourist Board
13. Shetland Tourist Board
14. Western Isles Tourist Board

the national English, Wales and Scottish Tourist Boards. The functions of the BTA were to *encourage people to visit Great Britain and people in Great Britain to take their holiday there* and to *encourage the provision and improvement of tourist amenities in Great Britain* (Development of Tourism Act 1969). The three national Boards were given *the like function*. In essence, the BTA assumed responsibility for promoting Britain abroad whilst the national Boards were responsible for tourism development and promotion at home. From 1984 the Scottish Tourist Board (STB) was empowered to undertake its own international marketing and promotion.

The administrative system was further broadened by each national Board establishing regional authorities. In England twelve Regional Tourist Boards were created, since reduced to eleven, each supported by a combination of English Tourist Board, local council and local tourism trade funding (Figure 4.2.). In Scotland 32 Area Tourist Boards were established, and three Regional Boards in Wales. In April 1996, the structure of public sector tourism administration in Scotland was rationalised, with the number of Area Tourist Boards being reduced to fourteen (Figure 4.3.). A more detailed description of the structure and activities of the tourist boards may be found in Lavery 1990.

With some minor changes the system of public sector tourism administration resulting from the 1969 Act remains the same today. Many of the activities of the BTA and ETB have been amalgamated whilst there has been a general decentralisation of authority to the regional boards. At the same time, in line with the economic philosophy of the 1980s, the Tourist Boards have been required to be more financially self-supporting, depending increasingly on self-generated income from marketing and promotion activities and on the support of the tourist trade. Perhaps inevitably as a result of this policy, the Thames and Chiltern Tourist Board became a victim of the 1990s recession, closing in July 1992 with debts of over £300,000. Its area of operation was then divided between the East Anglia and Southern England Tourist Boards.

It is the policies and activities of the tourist authorities, however, that are of most relevance to countryside tourism and leisure. Indeed it was the question of a national *tourism policy*, as opposed to national *tourism administration*, that caused most controversy when the 1969 Act was introduced. Although the Act set up the mechanism of administration and promotion there was little or no indication of what the policies and objectives of the new authorities should be. In other words, despite the fact that tourism was a national industry of growing importance and value, there was no guidance from central government as to what direction the industry should be taking.

In the years since the Act a number of Reviews have tinkered with the administrative structure and have re-directed the emphasis of tourism development in line with prevailing economic strategies. A Review in 1974, for example, indicated that financial assistance should be directed to tourism projects in the less-favoured regional Development Areas whilst reducing promotional expenditure for the main tourist areas such as London. Later, in 1985, a report entitled *Pleasure, Leisure and Jobs - The Business of Tourism* was a firm statement of the Government's commitment to tourism, in particular because of the opportunities tourism offers for economic regeneration and job creation. However, as the tourism industry continues to argue, there is still no recognised national policy for tourism. Even the most recent policy statement, *Tourism: Competing with the Best* (Department of National Heritage 1995), refers to the Government's role as being *sponsorship* rather than direct control or intervention, and it contains no guidance or strategy for the tourism industry.

As will be seen in the next chapter tourism in the countryside is becoming an increasingly significant area of tourism promotional activity. At the same time the concept of sustainable tourism development has placed the need for conservation high on the agenda, linking tourism development policies with many of the provisions for landscape protection and enhancement found in the countryside legislation. Therefore the public sector of tourism administration has an important role to play in the future development of tourism and leisure in the countryside.

SUMMARY

The first and most far-reaching piece of legislation concerned directly with tourism and leisure in the countryside was the National Parks and Access to the Countryside Act 1949. It was introduced as a result of a coalition between the movements for access and conservation in the countryside and the political objective of creating a 'better' post-war Britain. Since 1949 a number of other legislative measures have been enacted which to a greater or lesser extent have had a bearing on countryside conservation and recreation. The provisions within the 1949 Act, however, remain largely intact. The important features of the legislation may be summarised as follows:

i The 1949 Act was based on assumptions about the volume and scope of countryside recreation that was to alter radically in the following years.

ii Throughout the legislation the rights of private landowners have remained dominant, resulting in a system of planning, management and recreation provision dependent on agreement and cooperation.

iii The farming and forestry industries have to a great extent been exempted from the planning process, arguably reducing the effectiveness of those organisations responsible for conservation and recreation provision.

iv Generally, countryside law has evolved in a piecemeal, haphazard fashion, reacting to demands and pressures rather than demonstrating a positive, proactive approach to the management of the countryside.

v An identifiable trend in the legislation has been towards conservation and containment as opposed to a policy of increasing opportunities for access to and enjoyment of the wider countryside.

In addition to creating new administrative organisations the legislation also brought widened duties and responsibilities to existing bodies and agencies. Therefore the next chapter examines the roles and activities of the diverse range of public and private organisations that are involved in countryside recreation and management.

Case Study: National Parks for Scotland?

Background
In England in 1947 the Hobhouse Committee published its Report on National Parks. This led directly, through the National Parks and Access to the Countryside Act 1949, to the designation of ten national parks in England and Wales. At the same time as Hobhouse the Ramsay Committee published its own recommendations for the creation of national parks in Scotland. Unlike Hobhouse, however, the Ramsay Report was rejected and thus legislation for Scottish national parks was never enacted.

The Ramsay Report recommended that five parks should be established, in the Cairngorms, Loch Lomond, Glencoe and Ben Nevis, Loch Torridon and Loch Maree, and Glen Affric. The failure to achieve designation for these areas, however, lay in the Report's acceptance of the concept that a national park should be truly national; that is, owned or controlled by the nation. Therefore the Report firmly recommended that the proposed areas in Scotland should be taken into public ownership, either by agreement or compulsorily. This radical proposal met with strong resistance from landowners and so the whole idea was dropped.

In the fifty years since then the arguments have continued as to whether or not national parks should be designated in Scotland. In 1991 a survey indicated that eighty per cent of Scottish people back the idea of national parks (Scotland on Sunday 1991), yet there is also a strong anti-parks lobby, including notably the Scottish Landowners Federation. Furthermore the debate has moved into the political arena with the Labour Party in Scotland supporting national park proposals but the Scottish National Party firmly opposed. Despite the efforts of the then Countryside Commission for Scotland, the latest proposals for national parks were once again rejected in 1991 by the Scottish Secretary of State.

Undoubtedly the debate will continue with the conservation/access lobby coming into conflict with the views of landowners and local authorities. The arguments for and against national parks in Scotland can be summarised as follows:

i For National Parks

The campaign for Scottish parks has been led by the Scottish Council for National Parks (the Scottish equivalent of the voluntary Council for National Parks in England) and the old Countryside Commission for Scotland which in 1990 proposed six areas for national park designation (see Figure 4.4.). Of these, four areas are seen to be in urgent need of protection, these being the most popular visitor destinations: Loch Lomond, the Cairngorms, Ben Nevis and Glencoe and, to a lesser extent, parts of Wester Ross. It is argued that the existing planning controls have failed to protect these areas from the increasing pressures of tourism and leisure, forestry and other developments and that the establishment of national parks, managed by independent authorities with a range of powers, is vital to protect these areas from further damage and inappropriate development. The proposals are supported by conservation organisations and access bodies such as the Ramblers Association. It is too early, however, to assess what the position of Scottish Natural Heritage will be regarding the question of Scottish parks.

ii Against National Parks

The principal argument against the designation of national parks is that it would heighten awareness of the proposed areas; the volume of visitors would further increase and tourist 'honeypots' would be created, putting yet more pressure on the landscape. This in turn, it is argued, would lead to the provision of more tourist facilities and attractions, further threatening the natural beauty and wilderness of the countryside. Additionally, the anti-lobby point to what are seen as the failings of the English and Welsh parks where designation did not halt, for example, the construction of oil refineries and major road building programmes. Opposition has also come from the local authorities in the proposed areas who envisage a loss of control to independent park authorities, from landowners fearing a tourist invasion and a loss of rights, and from the traditional Highland crofters who see national park designation as a further threat to their freedom and livelihood. Finally, it is argued that by ensuring public access as a right to the mountains and glens within the parks, landowners in other areas of Scotland would seize the opportunity to remove the traditional permissive rights of access, thereby limiting access to the countryside to areas within the parks.

THE FUTURE?

It is unlikely that national parks will be designated in Scotland in the foreseeable future; the strength of landowning interests and political factors will outweigh the perceived need for conservation and protection whilst the regional authorities are unlikely to surrender any power or control to new planning bodies. Nevertheless the campaigns for national parks are sure to continue and a close watch will be kept on the future developments in the national parks south of the border.

FIGURE 4.4. PROPOSED NATIONAL PARKS IN SCOTLAND

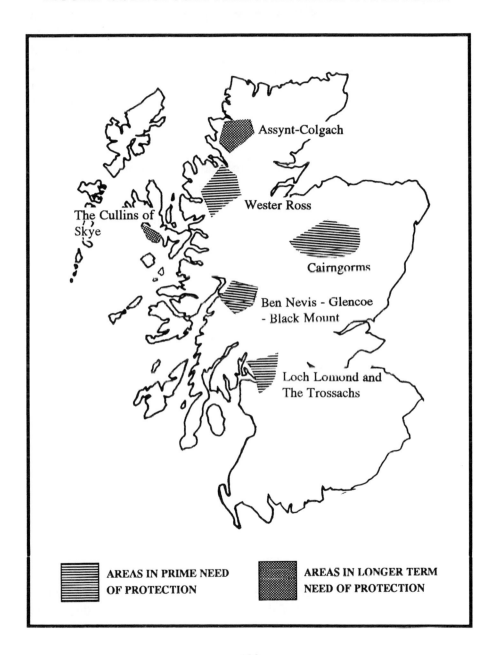

Assynt-Colgach

Wester Ross

The Cullins of Skye

Cairngorms

Ben Nevis - Glencoe - Black Mount

Loch Lomond and The Trossachs

AREAS IN PRIME NEED OF PROTECTION

AREAS IN LONGER TERM NEED OF PROTECTION

Chapter Five

Countryside Organisations

INTRODUCTION

A particular feature of countryside recreation is that it is inextricably linked with the overall planning and management of the countryside. Whilst recreation itself encompasses a wide and diverse range of activities it also invariably influences, and is influenced by, the other policies and demands related to the use of the countryside. At the same time, recreation provision is playing an increasingly important role in the economic survival of rural areas. As a result, there are a multitude of organisations involved to varying degrees in countryside recreation provision. Some of these have overlapping responsibilities whilst others appear to have conflicting policies and areas of activity. They can be broadly divided into public sector, private sector and voluntary organisations.

It would be impossible to list and describe every single organisation. The great majority are in the private, commercial sector, ranging from the large leisure organisations owning facilities such as Center Parcs down to individual farmers who supplement their incomes by offering bed and breakfast. The policies for recreation within overall countryside planning and management are, however, influenced most by a relatively small number of public sector organisations and agencies. It is these organisations that are the concern of this chapter.

Public sector organisations are to be found at both national and local level. At national level they are either directly or indirectly arms of central government. The former are actual government departments or ministries and specialised agencies or commissions created to funnel government grant-aid to particular areas of development. An example of this is the

Ministry of Agriculture, Fisheries and Food (MAFF). The latter are quasi-independent bodies, often created by Acts of Parliament, which enjoy relative autonomy yet are still funded by central government. Organisations such as the Countryside Commission fall into this second, indirect category.

At a local level it is local government in the form of county, district and parish councils that undertake the public sector administration of the countryside. Indeed, many of the statutory duties provided for in the legislation are the responsibility of local authorities. District councils, for example, are responsible for virtually all planning matters whilst county councils are responsible for all public rights of way (see Chapter Seven). There are also many local Countryside Project Groups, supported by both local and national funding, which make a significant contribution to the on the ground work at the local public sector level. One such group is the Luton and Dunstable Countryside Project (see Chapter Two: case study).

Apart from local authorities with their statutory powers and duties, a common thread links these diverse organisations inasmuch as they have limited, if any, power and authority. They rely primarily on agreement and co-operation for the implementation of their policies, a result of the underlying assumptions which, as we have seen, much of the legislation is based on. However, some organisations do in fact wield greater power than may be at first apparent, for the simple reason that money talks; that is, the advisory capacity of, for example, the Countryside Commission is greatly enhanced by its control of significant sums of grant funding from central government.

In addition to the public and private sectors, the voluntary sector also plays an important role in countryside conservation and recreation provision. The most notable organisation of this kind is the National Trust and its activities and policies are described later in the chapter.

THE COUNTRYSIDE COMMISSION
At the heart of countryside planning, policy-making and management at the national level is the Countryside Commission, the only organisation

entrusted with countryside conservation and recreation promotion as its prime functions. Its existence dates back to 1949 when, as the National Parks Commission, it was established to designate national parks and other areas worthy of protection. Under the Countryside Act 1968 it became the Countryside Commission with responsibilities for England and Wales whilst the Countryside Commission for Scotland was established by a separate Act a year earlier. For a number of years it was part of the Department of the Environment, an association which, in hindsight, diluted its effectiveness, but in 1982 it became an independent body although still grant-aided by the Department of the Environment. In 1993/94 this funding amounted to some £45 million, some 77 per cent of which spent on grants, advisory services and support of project work on the ground. Following the Environmental Protection Act 1990 the Countryside Commission's responsibilities in Wales were combined with those of the Nature Conservancy Council (NCC) forming the new Countryside Council for Wales. In Scotland a similar merging of responsibilities created Scottish Natural Heritage.

Now with its sphere of activity limited to England, the Countryside Commission has the two principal functions of conserving and enhancing the natural beauty of the countryside and improving the public's opportunity to enjoy and appreciate it. The work of the former NCC is still undertaken by a separate organisation, now called English Nature. The Commission itself owns no land in the countryside, nor is it responsible for the management of any recreational facilities such as country parks. Having few statutory powers it is an advisory and promotional organisation, relying on collaboration and co-operation, backed up by financial incentives, with a wide range of other organisations and individuals to achieve its aims and objectives. The Commission employs about 300 full-time staff, over half working at seven regional offices; members of the Commission (known as Commissioners) and the Chairman are appointed (and may be dismissed) by the Secretary of State for the Environment.

The Commission sees its twin aims of conservation and recreation as being mutually supportive. In other words, it believes that the English public has a *deep love for, and response to, the countryside* (Countryside Commission 1987) and that the public's enjoyment of the countryside can be harnessed to its conservation. This fundamental assumption about the importance of the countryside to the population of Britain is backed up by a recent survey (Countryside Commission 1996) which found that nine out of ten people feel that the countryside is an important part of the country's heritage and value it highly, even if they do not frequently visit rural areas. The survey also revealed that forty per cent of those questioned would be keen to be involved in protecting the countryside. However, this stated interest in conservation work is not mirrored in the numbers of people who actively participate in it (Ashcroft 1996).

This arguably idealistic approach may not, of course, always work in practice; the erosion problems caused by the popularity of walking in the Brecon Beacons, the fells of the Lake District and the Three Peaks area of the Pennines, for example, have simply increased the need for urgent conservation work. However, many of the Commission's policies and schemes are in fact geared towards involving the public in both enjoying the countryside and working towards its conservation.

Despite its stated objective of promoting countryside recreation and increasing opportunities for access to, and enjoyment of, the countryside, the overriding concern of the Countryside Commission is for the conservation of the countryside. Since 1968 there have been three distinct periods which have influenced the work and policy of the Commission:

i **1960s/early 1970s.** At the time the Commission was established in 1968 the major concern was for the environmental effects of increasing demands for countryside recreation resulting, in particular, from the dramatic increase in car ownership. The solution was seen in the provision of new facilities closer to centres of population to divert use away from the more traditional and fragile areas of countryside. With a prevailing fear of excessive access to the countryside the Commission's role, therefore, was to meet the demand for recreation and effectively contain it. In so doing it did, of course, create new opportunities for access (in particular Country Parks) but priority was undoubtedly given to conservation.

127

ii Mid 1970s/mid 1980s. The feared growth in the rate of increase in countryside recreation had failed to materialise and the Commission's attention shifted to the effects of intensive agricultural production, encouraged by EEC farming subsidies, on the landscape. It was during this period that many countryside management schemes were introduced with the aim of conserving and protecting the landscape.

iii Mid 1980s onwards. More recently there has, in effect, been a merging of rural and city life. With a move from manufacturing to high technology industries the population drift from the cities to the countryside has increased, placing new development pressures on the countryside. Furthermore, surplus food production has led to a reduction of land being used for agriculture whilst overall there has been dramatic increase in environmental awareness. Therefore the Commission's recent policies are directed at 'greening' the countryside as a whole through, for example, establishing new community forests. The opportunities for countryside recreation will be increased as part of these programmes but nevertheless it would seem that the conservation and protection of the countryside has taken precedence over the positive promotion of countryside recreation.

Today the Countryside Commission undertakes a wide range of activities. A number of these will be considered in detail in later chapters but in general the Commission has nine areas of work:

(a) Advising the government on matters related to the countryside.
(b) Introducing new approaches and schemes for the protection and enjoyment of the countryside.
(c) Undertaking research into landscape change and leisure patterns.
(d) Designating areas for protection and establishing national trails.
(e) Working with local planning authorities to secure strong policies for the countryside.
(f) Opposing potentially damaging development proposals.
(g) Providing technical advice on recreation and conservation to countryside managers.
(h) Providing grants for countryside conservation and access projects.

(i)   Promoting understanding of the countryside amongst the general
      public and countryside planners and managers.

Most of the activities within this wide remit are concerned to some extent
with the encouragement of countryside recreation. Within its advisory
and guidance role the Commission is unable, of course, to be directly
involved in the provision and promotion of tourism and leisure; rather, it
facilitates greater recreational use of the countryside by liaising with the
local authorities, other public organisations and the private sector.
Nevertheless the Commission is able, through its discretionary provision of
grant-aid, to exercise a degree of control and authority over the
organisations it supports, thereby ensuring that the management and
planning of countryside recreation falls within its own policy guidelines.

The Countryside Commission's most recent policy statements concerning
countryside recreation are *Policies for Enjoying the Countryside*
(Countryside Commission 1987a) and *Enjoying the Countryside: Policies
for People* (Countryside Commission 1992a). Together, they form the
basis for many of the schemes and activities currently being undertaken.
In recognising the growing importance of the countryside as a resource for
tourism and leisure, the Commission accepts that many of the long-
standing problems, particularly restrictions on access, conflicts of interest
between the different users of the countryside, and a lack of knowledge and
awareness on the part of countryside visitors, still need to be resolved. On
the other hand the changes in agricultural production and the
diversification in rural enterprise is seen as an opportunity for further
increasing recreational use of the countryside, with tourism and leisure
being the cash crops of the future.

The Commission's overall objective is to *improve and extend opportunities for
the public to enjoy the countryside. But in doing so, to re-emphasise the link
between the conservation of an attractive countryside and its enjoyment by
the public* (Countryside Commission, 1987a). To achieve this, its overall
policy is set out under two broad headings, namely People and Place.

As a result of surveys (see Table 5.1.), the Commission sees a great need to increase the general public's knowledge and confidence about the countryside. It therefore advocates that efforts should be made to improve the public's awareness of what the countryside has to offer while, at the same time, increasing both visitors' and landowners' understanding of the use of the countryside for recreation through the publication of booklets and Codes of Practice. In particular the research demonstrated that infrequent visitors lacked the necessary confidence to explore the countryside thus, in addition to improving access by providing more public transport, steps should also be taken satisfy this need.

TABLE 5.1. IMPROVEMENTS CONSIDERED IMPORTANT BY COUNTRYSIDE VISITORS

Improvement	% Rating very important
More information on where to go and what to do	72
Better kept public paths	67
Better public transport to the countryside	65
More safe, enclosed spaces with facilities	63
More public footpaths to the countryside	59
More open access to the countryside	58
More rivers/lakes open to the public	54

Source: Countryside Commission 1987a

Under the Place heading, the Commission proposes a broader approach to the provision of recreation, moving away from its earlier policy of developing specific facilities such as country parks. It suggests that access should be increased in a number of ways, in particular with improvements to the public rights of way network, opening more long distance footpaths (national trails) and affording greater access to open countryside (see Chapter Seven). Nevertheless, managed recreation sites such as country parks should continue to be provided but with a better definition of their purpose. The 1987 policy document also suggests that rural communities should take an active role in developing recreational facilities for the public in order to enhance their own social and economic life, whilst the recreation policy for protected, designated areas (national parks, AONBs, for example) should give priority to those types of recreation which are compatible with, or appropriate to, the character of the area.

The achievement of all these objectives is seen to lie primarily in the adoption of countryside management schemes and initiatives, most of which are centred upon a need to sustain and enhance the beauty of the countryside. The Commission envisages that the best way forward is through partnerships between local authorities, voluntary groups and landowners which work towards the protection and care of the countryside and making it more accessible for the general public. Recent schemes include Community Forests, Countryside Stewardship and the Parish Paths Partnership, initiatives which are considered in Chapters Seven and Eight. The overall aim of these policies would appear to be to encourage greater awareness of the countryside, greater public involvement in the care and conservation of the countryside, and forms of quiet, passive recreation that may be considered by some to be more appropriate to the rural environment.

More recently, the Countryside Commission published a policy agenda for the countryside as a whole (Countryside Commission 1991d). This document calls for a more strategic approach to the management of the countryside but throughout it is emphasised that, wherever conflict arises between different uses of the countryside, conservation should take precedence. It calls for a more sustainable approach to tourism and leisure development with recreation itself playing a role in supporting the conservation of the countryside. The future role of the Commission itself is set out in its latest consultation document, *Quality of Countryside: Quality of Life* (Countryside Commission 1995b), in which it sets itself five challenges for the twenty-first century:

(a) to conserve and enhance the quality and diversity of the countryside
(b) to secure balanced, multi-purpose farming and forestry
(c) to promote sustainable development in the planning and management of the countryside
(d) to improve and extend opportunities for people to enjoy the countryside
(e) to encourage understanding of the life and work of the countryside

Many of these challenges follow on from the Commission's current work and policies.

Thus, the Countryside Commission's overall policy gives a firm priority to the protection and conservation of the countryside, with the positive encouragement and promotion of recreation effectively taking a back seat. Undoubtedly this is a reflection of not only the wider national, and indeed international, concern for the environment but also of the trend towards sustainable development, a concept that will be expanded upon in Chapter Eight. In short, the Countryside Commission sees the provision and promotion of countryside recreation as a means to an end rather than an end in itself, as a tool that, effectively managed, can contribute to the well-being of the countryside and its communities.

Such a policy, it has been argued, fails to recognise many of the conflicts that occur in the countryside, both between different uses and between different forms of recreation. For example, the emphasis on quiet, passive recreation allows no space for more active or collective activities, whilst the initiatives to improve access to the countryside through existing mechanisms, such as the public rights of way network, ignores the calls for access to the wider countryside (see Clark *et al* 1994). It also brings the Commission into conflict with other organisations, such as the Sports Council, which support a broader approach to the use of the countryside for recreation.

Despite these criticisms and the fact that the lack of authority invested in the Commission and the wide-ranging (and sometimes conflicting) activities of other countryside organisations makes it more difficult for the Commission to implement its policies, it nevertheless plays a leading and vital role in the management of the countryside, a role that perhaps should be strengthened and more clearly defined through new legislation and guidance and greater resourcing.

THE FORESTRY COMMISSION
The Forestry Commission, which owns about 2.8 million acres of land (1,127,000 hectares), is not only the single largest landowner in the United

Kingdom but also one of the major providers of opportunities and facilities for countryside recreation. This, however, has not always been the case and the Commission is still probably better known for the controversy that has surrounded the planting of vast tracts of coniferous forests in upland areas, covering hillsides in regimented blankets of trees.

Now responsible to the Minister for Agriculture, Fisheries and Food and, in Scotland and Wales, the respective Secretary of State, the Forestry Commission was established by the Forestry Act 1919 with the primary purpose of replenishing the nation's stock of timber. Although it had been a desperate shortage of timber during the First World War that prompted the creation of the Forestry Commission, the history of the deforestation of the British countryside in fact dates back far longer. In some parts of the country, for example, evidence has been found of woodland that was cleared some four thousand years ago, starting a process that has continued through to modern times. By the beginning of the twentieth century forest and woodland covered less than five per cent of the land area of Britain. Concern for the deforestation of the countryside also dates back many years; during the sixteenth and seventeenth centuries many acres of oak trees were planted to supply timber for shipbuilding.

From 1919 through to the 1960s the main function of the Forestry Commission was the commercial development and management of the country's timber resources. This was achieved through acquiring existing woodland and other areas of land for afforestation and also by entering into agreements with private landowners for the dedication of their forests to timber production, supporting them with grants and technical help and advice. (In 1992/93, over 57,000 acres (23,300 hectares) of private forests were grant-aided by the Commission). It was because of this aim of building up stocks of timber that vast areas of land were planted with fast growing conifers; little attention was paid to the visual impact of these new forests on the landscape nor, as a rule, were the recreational opportunities offered by forests recognised. In the 1930s a small number of Forest Parks, such as the Forest of Dean, were designated (there are now fourteen Forest Parks in the UK) but it was not until the late 1960s that the Forestry Commission started to introduce recreational facilities in some of its forests. The Forestry Act 1967 recognised the increasing importance of forests for public recreation and gave the Commission the power to provide facilities such as camp sites, picnic places and visitor centres.

It was also during the 1960s that greater attention was paid to the visual effects of new forests. Newer planting has been more sensitive to the landscape whilst there has been a move away from dense conifer forests to a mixture of species of tree, giving a variety of colour. Furthermore, broad-leaved trees, such as beech, have been established around the original plantations, screening the dense conifers from view. A 1985 amendment to the Wildlife and Countryside Act further required the Forestry Commission to balance the requirements of timber production with the conservation of both natural beauty and woodland flora and fauna.

In a sense, the Forestry Commission has always played a dual role. On the one hand, it has been responsible for timber production, the management of forests and, more recently, the provision of receational opportunities and, on the other hand, it has advised on and implemented national forestry policies. These two roles were formally recognised in April 1992 when the Commission was reorganised into two separate functions (Forestry Commission 1993):

(a) **Forest Authority**, responsible for the payment of grants for tree planting, for licensing forestry, for forestry research and for advising landowners, local authorities, woodland groups and other individuals and organisations.

(b) **Forest Enterprise**, responsible for the management of the Forestry Commission's forests and woodlands, to maintain and increase the productive potential of forests and to provide for both conservation and recreation within forests and woodland.

Based in Edinburgh, the Forestry Commission employs almost 4,400 staff and in 1993 received grant-in-aid of £97.5 million from the Government.

There has been a dramatic increase in the use of forests for recreation. Since facilities such as car parks, picnic sites and visitor centres were first introduced the usage of forests has grown to about one hundred million visits per year. Equally, the provision of facilities has increased rapidly (see table 5.2.). In addition to these specific facilities there are also 10,000 miles (16,000 km) of forest tracks, most of which are open to public access on foot.

The forests support a wide range of recreational activities, both for day visitors and for those who wish to camp or to stay in the cabins or cottages that are rented out by the Commission. In addition to walking there are facilities in many forests for field archery, horse riding and cycling whilst the streams and rivers running through the forests are used for fishing, canoeing and sailing. Orienteering is a common sport for which forests are ideally suited. Some of the more unusual activities include cross-country skiing and husky dog sled racing. Nature conservation is an increasingly important area of activity; from over 340 SSSIs on Forestry Commission property, some forty six Forest Nature Reserves have been opened to public access in forests all around the UK (see Figure 5.1.). The Commission's forests are also used extensively for car rallying, from small local events to the annual RAC Lombard rally.

TABLE 5.2. FORESTRY COMMISSION RECREATION FACILITIES

Waymarked Trails and Paths	700
Picnic Sites	650
Holiday Cabins and Cottages	194
Camp sites	32
Forest Gardens	21
Visitor Centres	19
Forest Drives	10
Car Parking Spaces	20000

Source: Forestry Commission 1989

FIGURE 5.1. FOREST NATURE RESERVES

Source: Forestry Commission

1	Eilean Ruairidh Mor (Rory's Island)	24	Afon Gamlan Wetlands
2	Culbin Forest	25	Foel Friog Oakwood
3	Kylerhea	26	Pembrey
4	Glen Affric	27	Coed-Y-Rhaiadr
5	Ryvoan Pass	28	Dyffryn Crawnon
6	Leiterfearn	29	Cae Pwtto
7	Black Wood of Rannoch	30	Wyndcliff Wood
8	Glen Nant	31	Stoneybrook Pools
9	Dalavich Oakwood	32	Wyre Forest
10	Loch Lomond Oakwood	33	Haugh Wood
11	Redmyre	34	Cannop Valley Oakwoods
12	Glenan	35	Leigh Woods
13	Starr Forest	36	Ashclyst
14	Knockman Wood	37	Haldon Power Line
15	Retreat Wood	38	Ramsdown Hill
16	Lochaber Loch	39	Chambers Farm Woods
17	Back Burn	40	Bedford Purlieus
18	Holystone	41	Santon Valley
19	Deepdale	42	Salcey Forest
20	Raindale	43	Bernwood
21	Ransbarrow	44	Chalkney Wood
22	Hamsterley	45	West Walk
23	Coed-Y-Brenin	46	Whiteley Pastures

In future years the Forestry Commission is likely to direct more attention towards policies for conservation and recreation provision and away from the purely commercial aspects of forestry. As with the Countryside Commission, it sees the involvement of local groups and individuals as an essential ingredient in the future planning and use of forests for recreation and education. In 1992 the Forestry and the Countryside Commissions joined forces in the development of the new National Forest and twelve regional Community Forests, working in partnership with local authorities and voluntary groups (see Chapter Eight). However, following a government directive in 1989 the Commission has also been selling off its holdings to the private sector at the rate of about 24,700 acres (10,000 hectares) a year. It has been pointed out (Ramblers Association 1992) that this has led to a reduction in access to forests and woodlands, mainly as a result of local authorities having insufficient resources to enter into access agreements with the new private owners. More recently, the decision to effectively privatise the Forestry Commission has been reversed; however, the existing programme for selling off some of its property continues, albeit with increased provisions for maintaining access to any forest or woodland transferred to the private sector.

BRITISH WATERWAYS BOARD

The inland waterway system (navigable canals and rivers as distinct from lakes and reservoirs) is one of the most important resources for water based countryside recreation in the UK (see McCormack 1994). Not only does it support traditional activities such as fishing, sailing, cruising and canoeing but also canal towpaths and riverbanks which are popular locations for walking, cycling and other informal activities.

As with the public rights of way network the use of canals, in particular, for recreation and leisure is a far cry from their original purpose. Most of the canal system in the UK was built between 1757 at the start of the Industrial Revolution and the 1830s; in the days before steam, an efficient means of transporting goods between the new industrial centres was needed and the solution was to build a comprehensive network of canals. Thus they were in effect the arteries of the new industrial Britain.

The first canal to be built in this period was the Sankey Brook (St. Helen's Canal), which opened in 1757, followed by the Bridgewater Canal in 1761 which was built to carry coal between Worsley and Manchester. Over the next sixty years a large number of canals were built and at their peak about 4,250 miles (6,850 km) of navigable rivers and canals carried some thirty million tons of goods each year. In the early days cargoes were normally carried in horse-drawn craft. In the 1830s about two thirds of the waterway maintenance bill went on repairing and maintaining the towpaths rather than the canals themselves. Gradually steam driven craft took over to be replaced eventually by the diesel engine.

It was the arrival of the railways that revolutionised transport. The canals were unable to compete and, as their profitability dropped, their use began to decline. Many became overgrown or silted up and canal tunnels collapsed. Some survived into the twentieth century until motorways finally took over as the primary means of transport. Even today a significant amount of freight is carried on the canals; almost 4.7 million tonnes were moved by water in 1990.

On January 1st, 1963 the British Waterways Board was established and became the owners or managers of about 2,000 miles (3,200 km) of navigable rivers and canals. The first purpose of the Board was to ensure the safe, efficient and economical use of the waterways and to put forward proposals for the use of those which were no longer financially self-supportive. This led to the Transport Act 1968 which recognised the potential of the canal system for leisure and tourism and to this end gave the Board specific powers and duties. In particular the Act classified the waterways under the control of the Board, highlighting their value as a recreational asset.

Commercial Waterways (340 miles/544 km):
 to be principally available for the carriage of freight.

Cruising Waterways (1,100 miles/1760 km):
 to be principally available for cruising, fishing and other recreational purposes.

FIGURE 5.2. THE WATERWAYS NETWORK

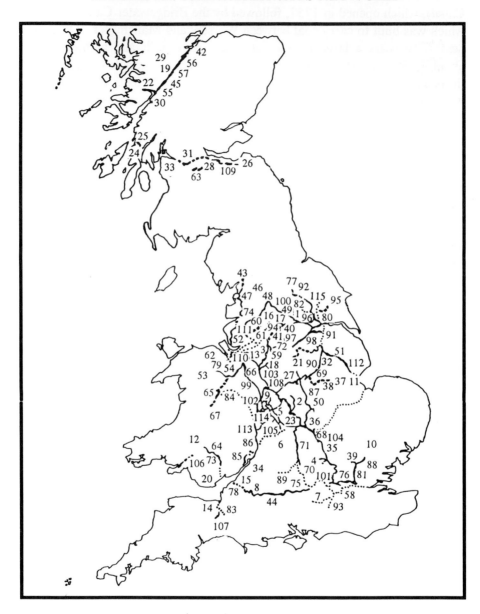

Source: British Waterways Board

1	Aire & Calder N	40	Huddersfield Broad C	79	R. Dee
2	Ashby C	41	Huddersfield Narrow C	80	R. Derwent
3	Ashton C	42	Inverness	81	R. Lee N
4	Aylesbury	43	Kendal	82	R. Ouse
5	Birmingham & Fazeley C	44	Kennet & Avon C	83	R. Parrett
6	Banbury	45	Laggan	84	R. Severn
7	Basingstoke C	46	Lancaster	85	R. Severn
8	Bath	47	Lancaster C	86	R. Severn N
9	Birm C N	48	Leeds & Liverpool C	87	R. Soar N
10	Bishops Stortford	49	Leeds C	88	R. Stort N
11	Boston	50	Leicester	89	R. Thames
12	Brecon	51	Lincoln	90	R. Trent N
13	Bridgewater	52	Liverpool	91	R. Trent
14	Bridgewater & Taunton C	53	Llangollen	92	R. Ure N
15	Bristol	54	Llangollen C	93	R. Wey
16	Burnley	55	Loch Lochy	94	Rochdale C
17	Calder & Hebble N	56	Loch Ness	95	Rocklington C
18	Caldon C	57	Loch Oich	96	Selby C
19	Caledonian C	58	London	97	Sheffield
20	Cardiff	59	Macclesfield C	98	Sheffield South York N
21	Chesterfield C	60	Man/Bolt/Bury C	99	Shropshire Union C
22	Corpach	61	Manchester	100	Skipton
23	Coventry Grand Union C	62	Manchester Ship C	101	Slough
24	Crinan	63	Monkland C	102	Staffs & Worcs C
25	Crinan C	64	Monmouth/Brecon C	103	Stoke-on-Trent
26	Edinburgh	65	Montgomery C	104	Stoke Bruerne C Mus
27	Erewash C	66	Nantwich	105	Stratford C
28	Falkirk	67	Newtown	106	Swansea
29	Fort Augustus	68	Northampton	107	Taunton
30	Fort William	69	Nottingham	108	Trent & Mersey C
31	Forth & Clyde C	70	Oxford	109	Union C
32	Fossdyke N	71	Oxford C	110	Weaver N
33	Glasgow	72	Peak Forest Canal	111	Wigan
34	Glouc/Sharp C	73	Pontypool	112	Witham N
35	Grand Union C	74	Preston	113	Worcester
36	Grand Union C	75	Reading	114	Worcs & Birm.
37	Grantham	76	Regent's C	115	York
38	Grantham C	77	Ripon C		
39	Hertford	78	R. Avon		

Key: C = canal, N = navigation, R = river

141

The Remainder (540 miles/864 km):
   to be dealt with in the most economical manner possible, consistent
   with the requirements of public health and the preservation of amenity
   and safety.

During the 1960s only 1700 miles (2720 km) of waterways under the
control of the British Waterways Board were actually navigable. The
Board does not have the statutory power to fund restoration work but, by
agreement with local authorities and local voluntary groups, some 190
miles (304 km) have been restored to navigation, 80 miles (128 km) of
which were reclassified from Remainder to Cruising status under the
British Waterways Act 1983.

Today the British Waterways Board is responsible to the Department of
the Environment and comprises a Chairman, Vice Chairman and between
four and nine members, all appointed by the Secretary of State. The
Executive Group undertake the day-to-day management with six regional
managers reporting to the Chief Executive. The waterways themselves are
also managed by region (see Table 5.3. and Figure 5.2.).

TABLE 5.3. LENGTH OF BWB WATERWAYS BY REGION

Region	Miles	Kilometres
Midlands and South West	631.08	1,009.72
North East	433.74	693.98
North West	472.48	755.96
South East	296.8	474.9
Scotland	145.0	232.0
Total	1,979.1	3,166.56

Source: British Waterways Board 1992

In addition to the navigable canals and rivers the Board owns and
manages, it also owns 89 reservoirs covering a total area of 4,065 acres
(1645 hectares). Furthermore, an impressive number of buildings and
structures are under the Board's ownership, including 4,763 bridges, 60
tunnels, 397 aqueducts, 1,549 locks, and 1,036 dwellings.

However, it is the Board's role in the provision of recreational facilities that is of most importance and, to an extent, the British Waterways Board could be described as the unsung hero of countryside recreation provision. Each year, for example, the public pay for about 20 million days out on the Board's canals, rivers and reservoirs, more than the number of visitors to either National Trust or English Heritage properties. Additionally, the potential volume of recreational use of the Board's facilities is enormous; almost 47 per cent of the population of Great Britain live within five miles (eight km) of one of its waterways. Indeed a total of 158 million visits of all kinds were made to the waterways in 1989 and it is estimated that one in six of the population use the boards facilities during the course of a year. Table 5.4. details the number of annual visitors categorised by activity.

TABLE 5.4. NUMBER OF VISITORS USING BWB FACILITIES

Activity	Number
Informal Users (Adults and Children)	7,280,000
Private Pleasure Boaters	570,000
Holiday Hire Boaters	370,000
Pleasure Trip Boaters	620,000
Anglers (Adults)	980,000

Source: British Waterways Board 1992

Equally impressive are the numbers of boats that are licensed or registered by the Board (see Table 5.5.).

TABLE 5.5. BOATS REGISTERED AND LICENSED IN ENGLAND AND WALES

Privately owned powered boats	25,121
Powered self-drive holiday hire boats	1,206
Powered self-drive day-hire boats	111
Day-trip and restaurant boats	120
Cruising hotel boats	22
Passage licences on Highland canals	1,213

Source: British Waterways Board 1992

The income that the British Waterways Board derived directly from leisure uses of the waterways in 1991 amounted to 36 per cent of its earned income, but less than ten per cent of its total income of almost £80 million (64 per cent of which was made up from government grants). In 1992/93, BWBs total income was £86.2 million. Of this, £8.6 million was earned from tourism and leisure activities, representing 25 per cent of earned income. Thus there is no doubt that the inland waterways owned and managed by the British Waterways Board are an important addition to the overall stock of countryside recreation facilities whilst recreation itself provides a significant source of income for the Board.

This importance of recreation is reflected in the Board's policy for tourism and leisure. Its mission is *to expand business on the waterways by pursuing a commercial approach, providing a safe and high quality environment for customers, staff and local communities...The waterways heritage and environment will be conserved, enhanced and made viable for future generations.* In effect, the Board is taking a sustainable approach to achieving its statutory duty of managing its waterways imaginatively for the purpose of leisure, recreation, amenity and conservation. That is, it is using the development of leisure and recreation to conserve and enhance the character of the waterways thereby attracting greater recreational use and hence increased income. This policy is supported by surveys which have shown that it is the environmental image of the canals and rivers that is their most highly valued quality.

Therefore the British Waterways Board's tourism and leisure strategy is to increase the recreational use of its rivers and canals. In particular it seeks to expand and develop profitable activities in conjunction with the private sector, thereby making the waterways more self-supportive and allowing the Board to achieve its primary function of maintaining and conserving the character and quality of the waterways' natural and built heritage.

WATER COMPANIES
Prior to 1989 the supply of water to domestic, industrial and commercial users, the collection and treatment of sewage, and the prevention of pollution in inland and coastal waters were the responsibility of the ten

regional water authorities of England and Wales. The Water Act 1989 divided these responsibilities with the new, privatised water companies inheriting the utility (water supply and sewage) functions whilst the responsibility for pollution control, flood defence, water resource management, fisheries and navigation was given to the new National Rivers Authority (NRA).

Responsible, like the British Waterways Board, to the Department of the Environment, the NRA is essentially the water industry's watchdog and environmental officer. Its involvement with recreation provision is therefore limited mainly to issuing fishing rights and managing fisheries although a small number of recreational facilities are under its control. The 1989 Act conferred on the NRA the duty, to *such extent it considers desirable*, to promote the conservation of the natural beauty and the flora and fauna of coastal and inland waters and their use for recreational purposes. However, less than one per cent of the NRA's 1989 budget of £355 million was spent on recreation and conservation, indicating the importance of the agency's other functions. In 1996, the NRA is to be merged into the new Environment Agency.

At the time of the creation of the new water companies there was much concern among both conservation and amenity groups that public access to land and water previously owned by the regional authorities would be curtailed. Many reservoirs had been opened for fishing and sailing and the surrounding land used for walking, horse-riding and so on and it was feared that either these opportunities would be lost, that access would be charged for or that the land would be sold off. The fact that over forty per cent of the land involved is within national parks or AONBs indicates its recreational value. Because of this concern, the 1989 Act imposed duties on the new water companies to have regard for the desirability of maintaining public access to open country or to buildings or sites of historic interest coming into their ownership. Furthermore, any of the companies intending to sell land is empowered to enter into a covenant with the Secretary of State for the Environment, accepting obligations with respect to public access to that land. This covenant is then binding on any future owners of the land.

To date, the creation of the water companies has had little impact on access for recreation. Despite no legal requirement to do so, the regional water companies have continued to offer recreational opportunities on their property and the greatest controversy, particularly during the drought in the summer of 1995, has resulted from many of the companies' alleged lack of investment and their failure to reduce leakages from water mains.

RURAL DEVELOPMENT COMMISSION

Although farming uses by far the greatest proportion of land in the countryside only ten per cent of the rural population is directly involved in agriculture, a percentage that is continuing to fall as the pressure increases to reduce agricultural production. Between 1986 and 1988, for example, the number of people working in farming fell 3.25 per cent, from 492,000 to 476,000. Therefore there is a continuing need to maintain rural services, to create new job opportunities and to support and encourage the large proportion of rural-based people working in non-agricultural businesses.

The national agency responsible for this task is the Rural Development Commission. Established in 1909 with a statutory duty to advise the government on all matters which affect the economic and social development of England's rural areas, the Commission's principal function is to encourage the creation of new jobs outside the agricultural sector. The purpose of this, in addition to replacing lost jobs, is to diversify the economic base of rural areas, thereby reducing their dependence on a single, declining industry and to encourage the creation of more skilled, higher paid jobs.

One of its prime areas of activity is in the provision of premises for small businesses, either by building new units or converting old, redundant buildings such as barns, stables, schools and even chapels. In some cases these may be funded entirely by the Commission, although owing to its limited budget (£37 million in 1990/91) its main approach is to work in partnership with the private sector, other government departments, local authorities and voluntary organisations. Also owing to its limited resources the Commission has identified 27 priority areas, known as Rural

146

FIGURE 5.3. RURAL DEVELOPMENT AREAS

Source: Rural Development Commission

Development Areas (RDAs), which are in greatest need of help (see Figure 5.3.). In each RDA a Rural Development Programme Committee prepares an annual submission for funds from the Commission to assist in overcoming local problems. These Committees are made up of local people including members of local authorities and also representatives of the Regional Tourist Board.

The Rural Development Commission has also recognised the present and potential value of tourism and leisure as a vehicle for the economic regeneration of the countryside. It sees tourism as being *a potent means* for diversifying the rural economy, providing new job opportunities as well as supporting local services. It is for this reason that it supports schemes such as the Cumbria Farm Tourism Initiative (see Chapter Three). However, it is also mindful of the potentially harmful impacts of unplanned tourism development in the countryside, impacts that the Commission itself could increase through its support of new tourism projects. Therefore the Commission has defined its role in the development of rural tourism and leisure (Rural Development Commission 1992) as:

i   promoting the importance of tourism in assisting the economic and community development of rural areas.
ii   taking an active and constructive part in the debate about tourism's future role and scope in the countryside.
iii supporting tourism development provided it is in the interests of the local economy and community and is not detrimental to the environment.
iv   providing direct assistance through its own programmes and advisory services to tourism projects which meet the above criteria and would not proceed without such help.

In other words the Rural Development Commission's policy for tourism and leisure in the countryside is to promote them as a tool for regenerating and diversifying rural economies, supporting projects that provide new job opportunities and bringing social and economic benefits to rural communities. At the same time, the development of tourism and leisure

148

should not pose a threat to the physical and cultural rural environment. As we shall see, this policy is in accordance with both the tourism industry's overall development policy and also the current emphasis on the sustainable management of the countryside.

LOCAL AUTHORITIES
As was mentioned at the beginning of this chapter, much of the responsibility for the planning and management of the countryside lies with local authorities.   Outside London there are three levels of local government, namely county councils, of which there are 44 in England and Wales, district councils (about 450) and parish councils, of which there are several thousand.   County councils are the highway authorities and also prepare structure plans for the county.   These may include plans for the county-wide development of recreation.   District councils are the local planning authority and parish councils, whilst having limited powers, are the most localised form of democratic government.

The co-operation and support of local authorities is essential to the work of many of the national agencies described above and they also own and manage many recreational facilities.   A complete description of their functions and policies is beyond the scope of this chapter but owing to their central role in the provision of countryside recreation many of their activities and duties are explained throughout the book.   However, it is important to note that, in addition to the range of statutory duties and functions undertaken by local authorities, they also play a significant role in the promotion and marketing of tourism and leisure. In England, for example, there are about 560 Tourist Information Centres, 75 per cent of which are financed and run by district councils.

TOURIST BOARDS
So far we have looked at organisations which include the provision or promotion of tourism and leisure as part of their overall field of activity. In contrast, the Tourist Boards' sole function is the development and promotion of tourism.   The statutory Tourist Boards were established under the Development of Tourism Act 1969 with The British Tourist Authority (BTA) responsible for promoting Britain overseas and the

national English, Wales and Scottish Tourists Boards responsible for domestic tourism. From 1984 the Scottish Tourist Board (STB) was also empowered to market and promote Scotland overseas. Tourism promotion on a regional basis is undertaken by the Regional Tourist Boards of England and Wales and the Scottish Area Tourist Boards.

The main reasoning behind the creation of the Boards was tourism's foreign earnings potential and thus they were originally responsible to, and funded by, the Department of Trade. However, following the publication of a report *Pleasure, Leisure and Jobs - The Business of Tourism* (HMSO 1985), the importance of tourism to the British economy, in particular to job creation, was given a higher profile and responsibility for the Tourist Boards was transferred to the Department of Employment.

During the 1980s much of the emphasis of tourism development was focused on those areas of the country which were suffering from economic decline and high unemployment, in particular the run-down inner city areas, with tourism seen as a means of complementing the government's urban regeneration schemes. In 1980, for example, Bradford started to promote itself as a short-break tourism destination, basing its attraction on its rich industrial heritage, the literary associations of nearby Howarth and its proximity to the Yorkshire countryside. By 1990 the rate of unemployment in Bradford had halved and some six million visitors annually were generating about £56 million. Following Bradford's lead, many other cities, including Manchester, Bristol, Portsmouth and Sheffield, have set up tourism development programmes.

The English Tourist Board (ETB) backed many such tourism development schemes with financial support under what was known as Section 4 funding (after Section 4 of the Development of Tourism Act). Additionally the ETB introduced a number of Tourism Development Action Programmes (TDAPs). These are short term schemes, usually lasting two to three years, and are partnerships between the ETB, local authorities, other public agencies such as the Rural Development Commission, and the private sector. Their purpose is to harness a wide range of research, marketing and development skills for the rapid implementation of tourism projects, financed as far as possible by the private sector. Indeed from 1989 no further grant-aid or loans were available in England under Section 4 funding (although the system continues in Wales and Scotland), limiting the ETB's involvement in TDAPs to an advisory, marketing and co-ordination role. This move was symptomatic of the government's policy of increasingly reducing public sector financial support of the tourism industry.

Towards the end of the 1980s the ETB switched its attention towards the economic development potential of tourism in the countryside. A number of TDAPs were set up in rural areas, including Exmoor, Kielder, the Forest of Dean, the Eden Valley in Cumbria and, more recently, in the North Pennines. Furthermore, one of the ETB's last grants under Section 4, and its largest ever, was the £1.5 million it put towards the first Center Parcs development in Sherwood Forest near Nottingham.

In 1988 the ETB announced its policy and strategy for the development of tourism in the countryside. Its overall aim was to enhance the contribution of tourism and leisure to the economy and prosperity of the countryside by encouraging greater levels of spending by visitors to rural areas. At the same time, the objective of the strategy was to conserve and enhance the countryside and to increase the range of amenities and facilities to improve visitors' enjoyment. In short, the ETB's strategy was designed to increase both the numbers of visitors to the countryside and also the amount of money and time spent in the countryside.

The ETB adopted an area approach; some rural areas are better suited than others to tourism development and some already have an established tourism and leisure industry. Thus in areas such as the Lake District the emphasis should be on increasing expenditure from existing visitors whilst in less popular or traditional areas greater attention should be paid to attracting more visitors through regional marketing and promotion and the development of new attractions and accommodation. As a result of this strategy there have been special regional marketing campaigns for areas such as the English Marches and also a number of local development initiatives, including the TDAPs mentioned above.

The ETB has also recognised the need for effective countryside conservation policies, although it might be argued that this stance is based more on commercial realism than on genuine environmental concerns. In other words, a more attractive countryside will attract more visitors thereby helping the ETB to achieve its statutory duties. Furthermore, both the ETB and the Regional Tourist Boards in particular are becoming increasingly dependent on financial support from the tourism industry and on income from their own commercial activities. It is therefore likely that the interests of the tourism industry take priority over wider environmental policies. In 1989 the ETB, in conjunction with the Countryside Commission, published its *Principles for Tourism in the Countryside* (see Figure. 5.4.). which stressed the need for balancing the recreational use of the countryside with the protection of both the landscape and local communities.

Since then the ETB has been paying increasing attention to environmental issues related to both countryside recreation and to tourism and leisure more generally. In 1990 the Shades of Green conference, sponsored by the ETB, the Rural Development Commission and the Countryside Commission, explored ways in which environmentally friendly rural tourism and leisure, or Green Tourism, could be developed and promoted. More recently the ETB pulished the findings of the Tourism and the Environment Task Force in a document entitled *Maintaining the Balance* (ETB 1991) which set out ways in which tourism and leisure can be developed in greater harmony with the environment.

In the same year it jointly published *Tourism in the National Parks - A Guide to Good Practice* and in 1992 *The Green Light*, a guide to taking a sustainable approach to tourism development, was published jointly by the ETB, the Rural Development Commission and the Countryside Commission. The principles and guidelines outlined in these publications are examined in Chapter Nine, but they are a manifestation of the ETB's growing involvement with environmental issues and increasing co-operation between the national agencies concerned with countryside conservation and recreation. A more detailed analysis of the role of the ETB within the context of countryside recreation can be found in Clark *et al* 1994.

FIGURE 5.4. PRINCIPLES FOR TOURISM IN THE COUNTRYSIDE

ENJOYMENT: The promotion of tourist enjoyment of the countryside should be primarily aimed at those activities which draw on the character of the countryside itself, its beauty, culture, history and wildlife.

DEVELOPMENT: Tourism development in the countryside should assist the purposes of conservation and recreation. It can, for example, bring new uses to historic houses, supplement usage and incomes to farms, aid the reclamation of derilict land and open up new opportunities for access to the countryside.

DESIGN: The planning. siting and management of new tourism developments should be in keeping with the landscape and wherever possible should seek to enhance it.

RURAL ECONOMY: Investment in tourism should support the rural economy, but should seek a wider geographical spread and more off peak visiting both to avoid congestion and damage to the resource through erosion and over use, and to spread the economic and other benefits.

CONSERVATION: Those who benefit from tourism in the countryside should contribute to the conservation and enhancement of its most valuable asset, the countryside, through political and practical support for conservation and recreational policies and programmes.

MARKETING: Publicity, information and marketing initiatives of the tourism industry should endeavour to deepen people's understanding of and concern for the countryside leading to fuller appreciation and enjoyment.

Source: ETB / Countryside Commission 1989

153

THE SPORTS COUNCIL

Traditionally the term countryside sport has been taken as referring to the narrow category of hunting, shooting and fishing with its associated class connotations. However, many of the countryside activities that are grouped under the general heading of tourism and leisure can be more accurately or specifically defined as countryside sports. Indeed there are some thirty or so different sports that may be categorised as countryside leisure activities, ranging from angling, rambling and caving to ballooning, hang-gliding and motorsports.

The national agency responsible for sport in Britain is the Sports Council. It was originally established in 1965 as the Advisory Sports Council (ADC) with the principal function, as its name implied, of advising government in the planning and development of sport and recreation. Its main role was to encourage local authorities to expand the provision of sporting facilities in line with increasing public demand. In 1972 the (GB) Executive Sports Council was established by Royal Charter as a quasi-independent organisation, replacing the ADC and taking on a broader role in sports provision and promotion. Despite its overall responsibility for British sport there are also separate Sports Councils for Wales, Scotland and Northern Ireland. The Sports Council's government grant for 1992/93 was almost £49 million, a sum that in real terms (allowing for inflation) demonstrates a reduction in financial support for the Council. However, the Council established itself as a trading company in 1987 and its income from its various activities in the 1990/91 period amounted to £5.5 million.

The Sports Council has four main aims as set out in its Royal Charter:

i   to increase participation in sport and physical recreation.

ii   to increase the quantity and quality of facilities for sport and recreation.

iii to raise standards of performance for all those taking part.

iv   to provide information for and about physical recreation activities.

Since it was established the Sports Council's policies have shifted away from the formal provision of sporting facilities and developing an overall policy for sport towards promoting the role of sport in society as a means of overcoming social and economic inequality, particularly in urban and inner-city areas. Within its programmes to develop mass participation in sport, such as the Sport for All campaigns, the Council targets particular groups such as women, ethnic minorities and younger people. In 1990/91, for example, over 40 per cent of regional projects financially supported by the Council were concerned with young people. Nevertheless, the Council directed almost £21 million in grant aid to national sports centres, sports' governing bodies and other national sports organisations and services in the same year (Sports Council 1991).

Inevitably, then, much of the Sports Council's work is directed towards the urban environment. However, the Council has also recognised that, whilst participation in sporting activities generally is on the increase, one of the main growth areas is participation in countryside sports. In 1992/93, it gave grants totalling more than £4 million to countryside sports. At the same time it acknowledges that other demands on the countryside and the awareness of environmental issues are also both on the increase and therefore a clear and effective policy is required for the future development of sport in the countryside.

The basis of the Sports Council's policy for sport in the countryside is sustainable promotion. It believes that the future of countryside sport is dependent on safeguarding the environment on which it is based at the same time as co-operating with the other users of the countryside to ensure the best multiple use of the countryside resource. Additionally the Council believes that *participation in countryside activities can encourage an understanding and responsible attitude towards the natural environment and the other uses of the countryside* (Sports Council 1991).

Owing to the diversity of countryside sporting activities the Council proposed in a consultancy document (Sports Council 1991) that planning for environmentally sustainable future increases in participation should be based on a system of category assessment. The characteristics of the activity, the capacity and suitability of the site and potential conflicts with other uses of the site should all be assessed. Furthermore, the Council also suggested four sporting land-use categories which could be used as a guide for planning the provision of countryside sport:

(a) Robust Areas where most countryside activities can be increased whilst improving the quality of the environment and remaining in harmony with other interests.

(b) Resilient Areas where the development of most activities would be environmentally sustainable, where long-term effects on the natural environment would be minimal and where the only conflict would be with other users or activities.

(c) Stable Areas where it is possible to maintain or gradually increase current levels of use through improved management or appropriate new facilities and where conservation of the environment is a primary interest.

(d) Sensitive Areas where there is currently excessive use causing serious conflicts or damage which cannot be resolved by improved management and therefore where there is a need to provide alternative sites.

The Council also proposed that, in order to safeguard areas of the countryside for sport and recreation, Outdoor Areas of Special Importance for Sport (OASIS) should be designated. However, many of these proposals were either diluted or dropped in the resulting policy document, *A Countryside for Sport*, published in 1992 (Sports Council 1992).

In that document, the Sports Council defines countryside recreation primarily in terms of active, formal or competitive activities, ignoring informal and quiet forms of activity which, as was shown in Chapter Three, account for the greater proportion of all countryside recreation activities. Furthermore, in applying its principle of 'Sport for All', the Council sees its role as promoting countryside activities to all who wish to participate. In terms of the sustainable use of the countryside, the onus is fimly placed on the governing bodies of various sports to ensure that types of activity or levels of participation are appropriate to different areas of countryside, the main form of regulation being through Codes of Conduct. The Council also states that *over most of the countryside, activities can be further developed sustainably and in harmony with other uses* (Sports

Council 1992: 13) and that involvement in these activities is likely to foster a greater understanding of the countryside and a commitment to conservation.

In short, although the Sports Council believes in principle that countryside activities should be matched to their location, echoing the policies of the Countryside Commission, the National Parks, the Rural Development Commission and many others, its actual policies appear to conflict with those of other countryside organisations. It sees the way forward as being through partnerships and greater co-operation between the various agencies concerned, yet its overriding policy supports the promotion of active sport in the countryside, opposing *the loss of existing access to natural resources for countryside activities, except in exceptional circumstances* (Sports Council 1992: 12). Therefore, it is perhaps not surprising that the Council was the only national body to oppose the proposed reduction in the speed limit on Lake Windermere at the public enquiry in 1994/95. At the same time, within the context of sustainable use and development, the Council places the emphasis firmly on self-regulation and codes of conduct. Thus, the Sports Council's policy is likely to result in less, rather than greater, harmony between the diverse recreational demands placed on the countryside resource.

ENGLISH HERITAGE

English Heritage (The Historic Buildings and Monuments Commission) was established under the National Heritage Act 1983. It is responsible to, and funded by, the Department of the Environment and currently has a permanent staff of about 1300, almost half of whom are directly involved in looking after the buildings in its care. By 1994 it had a membership of some 310,000. The primary functions of English Heritage are to advise the government on matters concerning the conservation of historic buildings and ancient monuments and to carry out its statutory duty of protecting and conserving England's architectural and archaeological heritage. It is also the major source of public funding for conservation schemes, repairs to historic buildings and monuments and for rescue archaeology.

English Heritage undertakes its duties either through statutory protective measures or custodianship. Historic buildings of national importance or interest are listed, either Grade I if of exceptional interest or Grade II if of special architectural or historic interest. Once a building has been listed the owners must obtain consent before undertaking any alteration, extension or demolition work, and any such work may be subject to conditions attached to the consent. There are about 435,000 listed buildings in England. The equivalent statutory protection for ancient monuments is known as scheduling.

It is English Heritage's custodianship of some 400 historic properties, a great number of which are in rural locations, that is of importance to countryside recreation. Most are open to the public and the 140 that charge an admission fee attracted five million visitors in 1990/91 (see Table 5.6.) Thus English Heritage plays an important role not only in conservation but also in the provision of leisure and tourism facilities and attractions.

TABLE 5.6. MOST VISITED ENGLISH HERITAGE SITES 1993/94

Stonehenge	672,065
Dover Castle	309,610
Osborne House	177,386
Tintagel Castle	155,914
Battle Abbey	149,249
Clifford's Tower	149,099
Housesteads Roman Fort	131,375
Kenwood House	111,428
Carisbrooke Castle	109,371
Whitby Abbey	107,343

THE NATIONAL TRUST
The National Trust for Places of Historic Interest and Natural Beauty, more popularly known as simply the National Trust, is the third largest landowner in the country after the Forestry Commission and the Ministry of Defence and hence the largest private landowner. It was founded in

1895 by Robert Hunter, a solicitor, Octavia Hill, a prominent campaigner for housing reform, and Harwicke Rawnsley, the Canon of Carlisle, who for many years had been actively campaigning for the protection of the Lake District. Their primary aim in forming the Trust was to preserve both buildings and countryside that were of historic interest and natural beauty for the enjoyment of the nation. They believed that the most effective way of achieving this was through the aquisition of property; the Trust's first property was the gift of 4.5 acres (1.8 hectares) of land at Dinas Oleu in North Wales. The Trust today owns over 590,000 acres (238,950 hectares) of countryside in England, Wales and Northern Ireland.

In 1907 the National Trust was incorporated by the National Trust Act. One of the most important provisions in the legislation was that the Trust was empowered to declare its properties *inalienable*; that is, the Trust cannot sell or mortgage its properties, nor can they be bought under a compulsory purchase order, without the consent of parliament. This was to ensure that the Trust would fulfil its role of protecting important buildings and landscapes for all time, although undoubtedly in some cases this has put an unwelcome strain on the Trust's finances. However, the Trust is able to lease its properties and almost half of its land holdings consist of tenanted farms to which the public are not afforded free access.

Over the hundred years of its existence the Trust has grown into the largest charitable body in Britain and the largest conservation organisation in Europe. Its headquarters are in London and its policy is decided by a Council of fifty-two members, half of whom are elected by Trust members and half nominated by national organisations who share an interest in the Trust's work, such as the British Museum and the Ramblers Association. Its membership has increased rapidly in recent years; between 1979 and 1989 it increased by over one million and in 1994/95 the Trust's 2.2 million members, through their subscriptions, provided 29 per cent of the Trust's £143 million income. Another important source of income for the Trust are legacies; in 1994/95, £25 million, representing eighteen per cent of the Trust's income, was received from this source. However, despite its important work in preserving the nation's heritage, the Trust does not receive any government grant-aid and is therefore heavily dependent on donations from various organisations and its special appeals for particular projects. In 1988, for example, there were nineteen such appeals running concurrently. Funding is occasionally made available through English Heritage for the conservation or restoration of particular properties and a significant amount of money is generated through the commercial operations of National Trust Enterprises which is responsible for the Trust's on-site shops and catering facilities.

In addition to its extensive land holdings, 7.5 per cent of which falls within national parks (in particular the Lake District where almost 25 per cent of the land is under its ownership), the Trust also owns some 547 miles (880 km) of coastline. Following a survey of the British coasts in the early 1960s the Trust concluded that up to one third of the total length of coast was worthy of protection and therefore in 1965 it launched Enterprise Neptune to raise the necessary funds. The campaign continues today with one sixth of the coastline under the Trust's ownership.

It is perhaps as the owner of stately homes and country gardens that the National Trust is best known. In its early years the Trust was mainly concerned with acquiring land but during the 1930s an increasing number of country houses and estates were threatened by spiralling maintenance costs and inheritance tax. Therefore, in 1937, the Country House Scheme was established whereby the Trust accepted properties and their contents as donations from the owners who nevertheless continued to live in the houses. Public access was allowed in return for the Trust's support. One effect of this scheme was that the Trust's image was altered and indeed it attracted much criticism, for the Trust was seen in some quarters to be perpetuating an out-dated and class dominated system of property ownership.

The Trust now owns over 400 properties which are open to the public and where entry charges are levied. Of these, 88 are large country houses and castles and another forty are associated with famous people, such as Rudyard Kipling and Beatrix Potter. There are also 163 gardens in the Trust's care. The Trust is also responsible for fifty villages and hamlets. Over ten million people visited the Trust's properties in 1994, demonstrating its important role in recreation provision, yet this popularity

160

is a double-edged sword. While the income received from visitors is vital to the Trust's continuing work the increasing numbers of visitors threaten to spoil the quality and character of the properties the Trust endeavours to protect. Bateman's, for example, a seventeenth century manor house in East Sussex where Rudyard Kipling once lived, receives about 80,000 visitors a year and as a direct result one floor has already collapsed.

To resolve the conflict between access and preservation the Trust limits rather than prevents access. At Sissinghurst Gardens in Kent, for example, time tickets are issued so that no more than 120 visitors are allowed in at any one time. Another policy has been to stop advertising and promoting the most popular sites, in effect de-marketing the properties, in an attempt to limit or reduce visitor numbers. A similar policy has been adopted by the National Trust for Scotland for three popular locations. Unfortunately, though, the Trust cannot prevent other organisations, such as tour companies and local authorities, from continuing to advertise their properties. Most recently, the Trust has also adopted the policy of reducing car usage at its properties by sixty per cent over the next thirty years. One of the first new sites to benefit will Prior Park near Bath, due to open in mid-1996, where there is no provision for parking and visitors will be encouraged to use ther frequent bus service from the railway station one mile away.

Thus the problems of access and conservation faced by the National Trust are similar to those faced by countryside organisations as a whole. At the same time, as the country's largest conservation organisation, it is also inevitable, perhaps, the National Trust has been criticised over some of its policies, in particular the emphasis placed on the preservation of country houses (see Weideger 1994). Nevertheless, the Trust appears to be fulfilling the objectives set by its founders although it is likely that, in the future, further limits may be placed on public access to Trust properties whilst a re-assessment of some of its policies may be necessary.

OTHER ORGANISATIONS
There is an almost incalculable number of other national and local groups involved in countryside conservation and recreation. In 1983, for example,

it was estimated that one in ten of the adult population belonged to an environmental group. Some groups are primarily concerned with conservation, such as Friends of the Earth and the Council for the Protection of Rural England, whilst others, such as the Ramblers Association, are pressure groups campaigning for greater access. A third category are those organisations that play a dual role, such as the Royal Society for the Protection of Birds and the Council for the National Parks, supporting both conservation and recreation. One organisation, the British Trust for Conservation Volunteers (BTCV) provides the most direct link between conservation and recreation by organising holidays and short breaks working on conservation projects. Furthermore, most countryside sports and activities are represented by national governing bodies, whilst both landowners and farmers have a national voice through the Country Landowners Association and the National Farmers Union. It is therefore inevitable that a great number of conflicts arise in the management and use of the countryside. Some have suggested that many of these conflicts could be resolved to some extent by the establishment of a single organisation with sufficient authority and resourcing. Whilst this is unlikely to occur, there is little doubt that a broad national policy, clarifying and guiding the functions of present rural orgnaisations, would be welcomed in many quarters.

SUMMARY
The management, planning, provision and promotion of tourism and leisure in the countryside is notable for the number of organisations that play a role in it. These organisations operate at both a national and local level and in both the public and private sectors. In many cases these organisations appear to have conflicting policies and objectives although there is a growing trend towards the adoption of measures for sustainable development. Despite the different objectives of the Countryside Commission, the Rural Development Commission, the Tourist Boards, the Sports Council and so on they are united in their recognition of the need to conserve and protect the countryside and the contribution that tourism and leisure can make to the protection and enhancement of the countryside resource. Nevertheless the logical conclusion is that there is a need for a more co-ordinated and well defined national policy for the management of the countryside.

Case Study: Countryside Organisations in the Lake District

The Lake District National Park, covering an area of 880 square miles (2280 sq km), falls entirely in the county of Cumbria in north west England. It is the largest national park in England and Wales and one of the most popular countryside tourism destinations with at least 12 million visitors each year. Over three quarters of these are day visitors and 80per cent travel to the Lake District by car. Not surprisingly, tourism is the mainstay of the local economy; in 1989 tourism spending in Cumbria as a whole was almost £300 million and it has been estimated that over one third of all employment in the national park is directly and indirectly dependent on tourism.

Owing to its popularity the Lake District also suffers from a number of adverse impacts. There are traffic related problems of congestion (on one day in 1989 the police found it necessary to prevent access to the Lake District at the southern junction on the M6 motorway), parking and pollution. Many paths are seriously eroded and not only are around sixteen per cent of all dwellings in national park either second or holiday homes but also in 1987 house prices in the popular areas were 25 per cent above the national average.

The organisation responsible for the management of the national park is the Lake District Special Planning Board which carries out all the planning functions that would otherwise be undertaken by the county and district councils. It also provides accommodation, information and education services, car parks and toilets and a ranger service. A number of other oganisations are involved in the administration of the area. Cumbria County Council is the highway authority and also prepares the Structure Plan for the county. Four district councils fall within the boundaries of the national park, namely Eden, Allerdale, Copeland and South Lakeland. Each of these have their own tourism strategy, with the Eden Tourism Action Programme and the West Cumbria Strategic Development Initiative in particular having a bearing on tourism within the national park. The District Councils also provide information services whilst tourism promotion as a whole is the reponsibility of the Cumbria Tourist Board.

The administration of the Lake District is also related to the pattern of land ownership. The National Trust owns almost a quarter of the land area, over eighty farms and 250 cottages and is also involved in conservation work and the provision of access and car parks. The Forestry Commission and North West Water between them own over twelve per cent of the land area. Both the Rural Development Commission and the Ministry of Agriculture, Fisheries and Food play a significant role in the development of the Lake District, with the Countryside Commission overseeing the activities of the Special Planning Board.

A number of voluntary organisations are involved in the protection and conservation of the Lakes. The Friends of the Lake District is the most influencial organisation and the RSPB and the Cumbria Wildlife Trust also work and advise on conservation projects. Furthermore the British Trust for Conservation Volunteers is very active in the; in 1988 the BTCV arranged 3266 working days on dry-stone walling, tree planting and footpath repair in the Lake District. There are additionally four National Nature Reserves and seventy-nine Sites of Special Scientific Interest within the national park.

Chapter Six

Land Designation in the Countryside

INTRODUCTION

Land designation in the countryside began in earnest with the National Parks and Access to the Countryside Act 1949. This was the first piece of legislation concerned with both conserving the countryside and promoting its enjoyment by the public. The Act's principal function was to single out the more beautiful and environmentally sensitive areas of the countryside for protection and recreation provision. These areas were then designated into different categories worthy of varying degrees of protection, such as national parks, Areas of Outstanding Natural Beauty (AONBs) and National Nature Reserves (NNRs). Since 1949, as the demands and pressures on the countryside have changed and increased, further measures for its protection have been introduced to the extent that, if all categories of designation are included, almost half of the rural land area of England and Wales is now covered by at least one designation. It is also feasible for some areas to be multi-designated; many nature reserves, for example, fall within national parks.

In general the designation of countryside areas is designed to conserve wildlife and scenic quality, to provide for recreation and leisure, or a combination of the two. The overall purpose is to afford greater protection against unsuitable or potentially damaging use. In practice, however, measures to protect designated areas rely on the same planning mechanism that applies to the rest of the countryside. Thus farmers, for example, continue to enjoy relative freedom from planning controls even if their land falls within a national park or an AONB. For this reason the effectiveness of land designation, although the primary means for balancing the varying and conflicting demands on the countryside, has been the subject of much debate.

This chapter examines the various categories of land designation, with particular respect to the provision of tourism and leisure, and considers how far they have achieved their objectives. Firstly, however, it is useful to look briefly in a general sense at the aims and objectives of land designation as a planning and management tool.

THE PURPOSE OF LAND DESIGNATION

Land designation is a method by which governments try to intervene in or influence the use of a particular area of land which, certainly in the case of Britain, they do not own. The overall purpose of designating land and imposing stricter controls over its use is to try to reconcile the needs of the landowner with the broader needs of society as a whole. For example, a farmer might find it economically beneficial to create a 'prairie' farm by clearing large tracts of land suitable for the use of large machinery but the resulting destruction of woodland, hedgerows and wildlife may be considered a loss to the country. In this case, financial incentives might persuade the farmer to retain or adopt more traditional farming practices. The Countryside Commission's Countryside Stewardship scheme is an example of this. Control is also sought through the imposition of stricter planning regulations or, in the extreme, compulsory purchase, although the latter is rarely used in the UK.

In Britain, land designation has been introduced primarily for the purpose of conservation. Of course in many areas the provision of recreation is a further objective and an increase in leisure and tourism is often a by-product of designation. Yet even where a dual conservation/recreation purpose exists, as in the case of the national parks, conservation normally takes precedence. One of the problems, however, is that conservation is a broad term that covers a number of different specific objectives, and it is therefore necessary to define what is actually meant by conservation in relation to land designation.

In its most literal sense, conservation generally refers to conserving, or saving, increasingly scarce resources. Common examples of this are the recycling of paper to limit the destruction of forests and the development of smaller, more efficient car engines to reduce the consumption of oil.

166

Thus, at a practical level, the purpose of conservation is the more efficient use of limited resources, saving them for future use. The conservation of the countryside can be viewed in the same way. The avoidance of farming and forestry methods that eventualy exhaust or destroy the land will ensure that the resource is preserved for future use. At the same time, the major pull or attraction of the countryside as the basic resource for tourism and leisure is its scenic character and quality. A conserved countryside, in an aesthetic sense, is essential for the future prosperity of the tourism and leisure industry and of those communities that depend on tourism.

In short, conservation is often motivated by practical, economic reasons. On the other hand, it is frequently based on moral or ethical grounds rather than purely practical objectives. In other words, it is concerned with people's relationship with the natural environment and the extent to which, rather than how, the environment should be used or adapted. The conservation of the natural beauty of the landscape, as is the case with the designation of AONBs and national parks, is therefore based on the perceived intrinsic value of the landscape rather than on any potential practical use. Likewise, nature conservation is based on the moral or ethical objective of protecting wildlife from destruction. Furthermore, conservation motivated by ethics is likely to be dependent to a great extent on value judgements and, in the absence of clearly defined objectives, this can lead to conflicts of use within designated areas. The landscape of the British countryside, for example, is in fact the artificial result of man's activities over thousands of years; the decision to conserve it at its present stage of evolution is therefore to make a value judgement over the extent to which it should be further developed and one which may not coincide with the needs of those who live and work in the countryside.

Land designation for conservation and the provision of recreation is therefore based on both practical and ethical grounds. A conserved landscape will continue to attract and support tourism and leisure at the same time as fulfilling the social objective of providing greater opportunities for recreation. At the same time the desire to conserve and protect the landscape for its own sake is motivated by the uniquely British relationship with the countryside. However, against the background of private land ownership, increasing demands for leisure and recreation and a system of planning and management that relies on agreement and co-operation, designated land areas have not always enjoyed the degree of protection that was originally envisaged.

COUNTRYSIDE LAND DESIGNATIONS

There are six main categories of land designation in England and Wales which have been established for the purposes of conservation and/or recreation provision. These are National Parks, Areas of Outstanding Natural Beauty, Heritage Coasts, Country Parks, Nature Reserves and Sites of Special Scientific Interest. Whilst the purpose of some designations is primarily for landscape or nature conservation they nevertheless form an important part of the countryside recreation resource.

i National Parks

The single most important event in the history of countryside recreation provision was undoubtedly the creation of the national parks in England and Wales. For the first time, through the 1949 Act, statutory procedures for the protection and promotion of specific areas the countryside were implemented, establishing a planning and management framework that to this day remains largely unaltered. Almost from the start, however, questions were raised about the potential effectiveness of the national parks in resolving the many and various pressures and demands placed on them, in particular with respect to the degree of control and authority invested in the bodies entrusted with the management of the parks. Therefore, we shall consider the development of the national park system and how far it has been able to achieve its original objectives. (For a detailed and complete appraisal of the national parks see MacEwan and MacEwan 1982 and 1987).

The events leading up to the National Parks and Access to the Countryside Act 1949 are described in Chapter Four. As a result of the Act a total of ten national parks were designated; the Peak District, the Lake District, Dartmoor and Snowdonia were all designated in 1951 with the remaining six being established in the years following (see Figure 6.1.). The last to be designated was the Brecon Beacons National Park in 1957. Since that time no other areas have been designated as national parks although the Norfolk Broads gained the equivalent of national park status in 1989 followed by an announcement in 1992 (rescinded in 1994) that the New Forest would also be accorded similar protection.

It is not the actual designated areas, however, that have been one cause of controversy and criticism. Rather it is the term national park itself that is thought by some to be both inappropriate and misleading, for in a literal sense they are neither national nor parks. The internationally accepted definition of a national park, as proposed by the International Union for the Conservation of Nature and Natural Resources (IUCN), is an area which has not been *materially altered by human exploitation and occupation*, where the government of the country *has taken steps to prevent or eliminate as soon as possible exploitation or occupation* and where *visitors are allowed to enter, under special conditions, for inspirational, cultural and recreative purposes* (IUCN 1975). In other words, a national park should be an area of natural wilderness that is either owned or managed by the government, a definition to which many national parks in the United States conform to.

Clearly, however, the same cannot be said for the national parks of England and Wales. Firstly, the great majority of the land within the parks is under private ownership and therefore it cannot truly be described as national. In fact the Countryside Commission states that the parks are national only in the vague sense that they are of special importance to the whole nation. Overall, if the landholdings of the Forestry Commission, the National Trust and the Ministry of Defence are included, less than 23 per cent of the total land area of the national parks is under public or semi-public ownership. Of this, just 2.3 per cent is owned by the National Park Authorities (Eade 1987).

The actual pattern of land ownership varies between individual parks; the National Trust, for example, owns 24 per cent of the land within the Lake District but less than one per cent of the Northumberland National Park. Conversely publicly owned land accounts for some 45 per cent of Northumberland but less than two per cent of the Yorkshire Dales. The

Ministry of Defence owns half of the publicly held land in Northumbria, with important implications for access for recreation, whilst almost a third of Dartmoor is owned by the Duchy of Cornwall. The dominance of private land ownership within the national parks has meant that from the outset the national management of the parks has been severely constrained. Also, the administration of the parks has been largely influenced by local needs and decision-making, thereby further reducing the national character of the parks.

Secondly, the word park is usually applied to an area that is enclosed and used for a specific purpose such as recreation or nature conservation. The national parks, on the other hand, are extensive areas of open country in which over a quarter of a million people live and work. Furthermore the 'natural' beauty that national park status seeks to preserve is anything but natural; it is the artificial result of centuries of human habitation and influence on the landscape. In comparison, one of the first policies of the American National Park Service (NPS) following its formation in 1916 was to work towards the removal of all inappropriate or unnecessary developments or commercial enterprises within the national parks (Albright and Cahn 1985). Thus, in effect, the national parks of England and Wales have been mis-designated both in a literal sense and also according to the IUCN definition, and as a result none are included in the list of internationally recognised national parks.

Along with the actual term used to describe the designated areas, there has also been much controversy surrounding the actual management and administration of the national parks. The Dower and Hobhouse Reports had recommended that a central body should be established to manage the parks within the national interest. The 1949 Act, however, gave the National Parks Commission a purely advisory role in designating the parks whilst their administration became the responsibility of local organisations. These were intended to be Joint Boards, independent of the counties in which the parks fell although two-thirds of their members would come from local authorities with the remaining third being nominated by the Secretary of State. It was envisaged that the Boards would bill their constituent counties and that they would employ their own staff.

FIGURE 6.1. NATIONAL PARKS AND AREAS OF OUTSTANDING NATIONAL BEAUTY

Source: Countryside Commission 1989

In practice only the first two parks to be designated, the Peak District and the Lake District, were given their own independent boards. Due to resistance from local authorities the other eight parks came under the administration of committees made up almost entirely of members of the county councils covered by the parks. (From 1968 both the boards and the committees were required to have at least one third of their membership made up of nationally appointed representatives). This inevitably meant that from the outset the majority of the national parks were managed in respect of local rather than national interests and that little money was earmarked for the running of the parks as the costs had to be covered entirely by local rates. In fact by 1971 the total annual expenditure of all the parks was just £1.2 million, half of which was spent by the Peak District and Lake District Boards.

In 1974, following the reorganisation of local government, the administration of the parks was altered slightly and central government agreed to pay 75 per cent of the administrative costs of all the parks. The two original boards became Joint Boards with greater planning powers whilst new National Park Committees (or Joint Committees where a park straddled county boundaries) were established to administer the other eight parks. Each park authority had to appoint a national park officer and furthermore each park was required to prepare a national park plan, setting out their objectives and the means of achieving them. Nevertheless, the new Committees were still effectively arms of the local councils which set budgets, employed the staff and provided legal, financial and administrative services. However, in 1991, following the publication of the Report of the National Parks Review Panel (the Edwards Report, or *Fit for the Future*) it was announced that all National Park Authorities would become 'stand alone' planning authorities, independent from local authority control. The relevent legislation enabling this reorganisation was included in the Environment Act 1995 and it is envisaged that the new authorities will be in place by 1997. The *Fit for the Future* report also recommended that many of the functions of other organisations, such as nature conservation, should be delegated to the park authorities, but this was not provided for in the 1995 legislation. However, forty years after the first parks were designated the system of administration is finally approaching that envisaged in the 1949 Act, although the Council for National Parks (a voluntary organisation supporting national parks) still favours a single, national body to administer the national parks in the national interest.

The actual responsibilities and functions of the park authorities fall into two broad areas, namely planning and management. With respect to planning, the authorities undertake the duties normally exercised by district and county councils, such as considering planning applications, controlling mineral extraction and so on, but generally applying stricter control than in other areas. Some authorities also act as highway authorities, with particular respect to footpaths. In addition to preparing a national park plan, the management functions of the authorities include the provision of car parks, refreshment facilities, accommmodation, and education and information services. Furthermore, they can appoint wardens and enter into both conservation and access agreements with local landowners.

The national parks as a whole support a wide and diverse range of uses and face an equally wide range of development pressures. However, in the context of this book it is important to consider how successful the national parks have been in achieving their original objectives, particularly with respect to the provision and promotion of recreation. The statutory duties of the parks, as set out in the 1949 Act, are the preservation and enhancement of the natural beauty of the designated areas and their promotion for public enjoyment. The conservation aim has certainly not always been achieved and, paradoxically, it has been the government which in some cases has been the culprit. The Okehampton by-pass in Dartmoor and the widening of the A66 through the northern Lake District were both controversial road development schemes, whilst the Milford Haven oil refineries on the Pembrokeshire Coast, the nuclear power station at Trawsfynydd in Snowdonia and the Fylingdales early warning station on the North York Moors are famous examples of large scale developments in national parks. On a more local level the park authorities have been hampered by the relative freedom of farming and forestry from planning control and the lack of independence from local authorities. On the other hand, a large number of inappropriate developments have not been allowed.

The promotion of recreation in the national parks was, at the time the parks

173

were designated, seen to be compatible with the conservation aim. However, the unforeseen and dramatic increase in countryside tourism and leisure from the 1960s onwards has increasingly brought the two purposes of the national parks into conflict. As early as 1966 the Lake District national park authority recognised that the numbers of visitors at popular times of the year might need to be controlled to avoid both the landscape and the enjoyment of visitors being spoiled. In 1974 the first National Parks Review Committee (the Sandford Report) concluded that where conservation and recreation came into conflict then priority should be given to preserving the natural beauty of the landscape, a recommendation that was later accepted by the government. This view was endorsed by the 1991 *Fit for the Future* report which stated that the Principles for Tourism in the National Parks (see Figure 6.2.) should be included in the formal planning policy of the parks. The report also recommended that the purposes of the national parks should be redefined in a new National Parks Act as being:

(a) *to protect, maintain and enhance the scenic beauty, natural systems and land forms, and the wildlife and cultural heritage of the area.*

(b) *to promote the quiet enjoyment and understanding of the area, insofar as it is not in conflict with the primary purpose of conservation.*

It further proposed that the national park authorities should have regard to the social and economic well-being of the communities within the parks, suggesting that overall they should play a more positive and wider role in the planning and development of the national parks with conservation being the overriding concern. As a result of the reports proposals, the Environment Act 1995 redefined national parks as having the purpose of:

(a) *conserving and enhancing the natural beauty, wildlife and cultural heritage of the areas specified*

(b) *promoting opportunities for the understanding and enjoyment of the special qualities of those areas by the public*

This new definition of the purpose of national parks fell short of what many had hoped for, in particular with respect to the omission of the purpose of 'quiet enjoyment'. This omission resulted from strong lobbying in parliament by, amongst others, the motor sports lobby and the Sports Council.

FIGURE 6.2. PRINCIPLES FOR TOURISM IN NATIONAL PARKS

1. Conservation. The tourism industry can help to protect the distinctive landscapes and wildlife of national parks by supporting practical conservation measures. This can be achieved, for example, through joint initiatives involving the public, private and voluntary sectors.

2. Enjoyment. The activities and interests promoted by tourism should draw on the special character of the national parks, with their many opportunities for quiet open-air recreation and their distinctive beauty, culture, history and wildlife. Improved access for visitors should be sought where this is compatible with conservation requirements.

3. Rural Economy. The social and economic well-being of the residents of the national parks is an essential consideration in achieving the statutory objectives of national parks, and empoyment in the tourist and related service industries is an important part of the economy of the national parks. The tourism industry should support the economy of local communities through, for example, using employees, products and services from the locality and by supporting the skills and economic activities which are traditional to national parks.

4. Development. Appropriate facilities are needed to enable tourists to enjoy the national parks. All tourism development must respect the quality of the landscape and environment in national parks. Its scale, in particular, must always be appropriate to the setting. It should also recognise that some areas of national parks are valued for being wild and remote. Proposals for development should always be tempered by the capacity of the immediate site and surrounding landscape to absorb visitors. Development can asist the purposes of conservation and recreation by, for example, bringing sympathetic new uses to historic buildings and derelict sites and opening up new opportunities for quite open air recreation.

5. Design. The scale, siting, planning, design and management of new tourism developments should be in keeping with the landscape, and should seek to enhance it. The distinctive and highly valued character and landscapes od national parks will continue to evolve through small scale changes. Major alterations to the landscape are unacceptable.

6. Marketing. The tourism industry should use publicity, information and marketing opportunities to deepen people's enjoyment, appreciation, understanding and concern for national parks.

Source: Countryside Commission / ETB 1989

175

The continuing popularity of the national parks as a resource for tourism and leisure is undoubted. Together they attract over one hundred million visitors each year with the most popular parks, the Peak District and the Lake District, annually playing host to up to twenty million visitors. It is in the more popular parks, of course, that the impacts of tourism and leisure are most keenly felt, but despite the differences in the numbers of visitors and the physical characteristics of each park they all suffer from the same problems. These impacts include pollution, traffic jams and illegal parking, erosion of footpaths, the loss of local services and traditional shops, high costs of housing and land and an over-dependence on tourism as a source of income and employment.

The possible means of resolving some of these problems and conflicts are discussed in later chapters. However, it is perhaps inevitable that, given the level of demand for recreation in the parks and the resulting impacts, it has become impossible for the national park authorities to give equal attention to their original twin aims of conservation and recreation provision. The primary purpose of the national parks has become conservation, both of the landscape and of the parks' communities, with a greater emphasis being placed on the sustainable development and promotion of more traditional forms of countryside recreation. Recent publications such as *Tourism in the National Parks - A Guide to Good Practice* (Denman 1991) further assert the need for tourism and leisure to be developed in harmony with the environment and to contribute towards conservation.

In short, then, it may be argued that the national parks were hindered from the start by inherent weaknesses in the administrative system, a lack of authority and funding and perhaps even by being designated as national parks in the first place. Their two fundamental purposes have for a long time been in conflict and it is likely that the need for effective conservation will be seen to be an ever greater priority whilst their policy for recreation will shift towards the promotion of a higher quality (and hence more expensive) tourism utility to reap greater economic returns from a smaller number of visitors. It is feared by some that this would lead to the national parks becoming elitist and a radical departure from the original concept of the parks.

(a) The Norfolk Broads

The Norfolk Broads, consisting of about forty shallow lakes connected by waterways, were created by the flooding of medieval peat workings. With some 50,000 acres (20,234 hectares) of open water and almost one hundred miles of navigable channels they have for a long time been a valuable and popular recreational resource. They are also of vital importance as a wetland wildlife habitat.

Despite being included in the Hobhouse Committee's list of potential national parks, the Broads were not amongst the ten that were finally designated. In 1976 the Countryside Commission proposed that the Broads should be designated as a national park because, during the 1960s and 1970s, they had suffered from increasing damage from the drainage of wetlands, the erosion of banks and the pollution of the water from both motor vessels and agricultural fertiliser. The proposal was rejected, but in 1978 a joint planning committee of the local councils was established to take a more co-ordinated and strategic approach to the planning of the Broads. It was decided that, owing to the special characteristics of the area, it would be inappropriate to designate the Broads as a national park, but in 1988 the Norfolk and Suffolk Broads Act was passsed which led, in 1989, to the creation of the Broads Authority.

The Authority, consisting of a wide membership from both local councils and national bodies, has the same independence and duties as a national park Board. It receives 75 per cent of its financing from central government, it is the sole planning authority for the area and, within its duty of managing the Broads for both conservation and recreation, it is required to prepare a management plan outlining its policies and objectives. Thus, in effect, the creation of the Broads Authority established the eleventh national park in everything but name, although its main function is the preservation of the unique wetland landscape.

(b) The New Forest

The New Forest in Hampshire is a large open area of heath, grassland and woodland. Not only is it an important wildlife habitat but it has also long been a popular recreation destination. Each year the Forest plays host to

177

some seven million visitors, spending about £66 million. Over seventy per cent of spending is accounted for by overnight stays, although less than forty per cent of visits are overnight. In February 1992 it was announced that the New Forest was to be given the equivalent of national park status under a system similar to that established for the Norfolk Broads. The New Forest has, in fact, been a protected area for over nine hundred years. In 1079, William I created a royal hunting preserve over an area of woodland and heath, known as the New Forest and since that time a number of Acts of Parliament, including the New Forest Act 1877, have ensured that a balance has been maintained between the production of wood, the rights of commoners, the preservation of the natural beauty of the area and its enjoyment by the public.

There are four different definitions of what constitutes the New Forest (see Figure 6.3.). The central core area of some 66,690 acres (26,988 hectares) is Crown Land which is managed by the Forestry Commission. Secondly the wider *Perambulation*, as defined by the 1964 New Forest Act, includes both the Crown Land and other private land. The New Forest Heritage Area, adopted by the New Forest District Council in 1985, includes all the surrounding countryside which has visual and historical links with the Forest. Finally there is the New Forest District as established by the 1974 Local Government Act. The administration of the area is shared between the Forestry Commission, which has statutory duties related to both conservation and recreation provision, the District and County Councils, and a body known as the Verderers. The latter was established by statute in the mid nineteenth Century and is responsible for the management of grazing and commoners' rights within the Forest. Furthermore, a substantial section of the core area is an SSSI and the southern fringe of the Forest is an Area of Outstanding Natural Beauty.

In 1990 the non-statutory New Forest Committee was established to co-ordinate the activities of all the public organisations involved in the management of the forest. Following the recommendations of the *Fit for the Future* report, that the New Forest should be considered for designation as a national park, the government proposed in September 1992 that the Committee should form the basis of a new statutory body. The purposes of this body will be:

(a) *conserving and enhancing the natural beauty, flora, fauna and geological or physiographic features of special interest of the area.*

(b) *maintaining the grazing and management regime that so contributes to the New Forest's character.*

(c) *promoting the quite enjoyment and understanding of the area by the public.*

However, despite the support of many local and national organisations, including English Nature, the Countryside Commission, the CPRE, the relevant county, district and parish councils and 65 per cent of local inhabitants, the proposed establishment of a statutory New Forest Committee was reversed by the Government in 1994. Although no official reason has been given, a number of factors may have influenced this decision. Some organisations, such as the Ramblers Association, felt that only full national park status would solve many of the problems and challenges facing the Forest, whilst others saw the propsed new authority simply as an extra and unnecessary layer of bureaucracy. The potential erosion of the rights of commoners was also a major stumbling block, indicating that the future administration of the New Forest has been influenced more by short term political constraints rather than longer term environmental considerations.

ii Areas of Outstanding Natural Beauty

When John Dower recommended in his 1945 report that national parks should be established in England and Wales he also listed over thirty other areas which, due to their special scenic quality, he believed should be protected. The Hobhouse Committee accepted this proposal and recommended that 52 areas should be designated as Conservation Areas. Thus, alongside the provisions enabling the creation of national parks, the National Parks and Access to the Countryside Act 1949 also gave the National Parks Commission the power to designate parts of the countryside as Areas of Outstanding Natural Beauty (AONBs). These were to be areas which, whilst lacking the extensive areas of open country which would make them suitable for national park status (and hence suitable for the positive promotion of recreation), were nevertheless of an equally high landscape quality worthy of protection. At the same time, although the provision of recreation was not a formal objective, the need to allow for public access was also emphasised. Since 1956 a total of 41 AONBs, covering 20,297 square kilometers, or almost 15 per cent, of the countryside have been designated in England and Wales (see Table 6.1. and Figure 6.1.).

The process of AONB designation is continual; after a lengthy consultation period, Nidderdale in North Yorkshire was designated as an AONB in 1994, whilst the Tamar and Tavy valleys and the Berwyn Mountains are amongst areas being considered for future designation. As can be seen in Table 6.1, AONBs vary enormously in size and geographical location. The North Pennines, the North Wessex Downs and the Cotswolds AONBs are all larger than most of the national parks, whilst the Scilly Isles AONB covers just 6.2 square miles (16 square km). Some are coastal areas, some are chalk downland and others are farmland. However, they all share the same objective, which is to conserve and enhance the natural beauty of the landscape. A secondary purpose of AONBs is the provision of quiet enjoyment of the countryside.

The responsibility for the management of AONBs lies with local authorities working within the existing planning system. The local authorities are also empowered to appoint wardens for AONBs and they are encouraged, although it is not a statutory requirement, to nominate an officer to co-ordinate strategic and management plans. In the absence of extra planning and development powers, the most significant effect of AONB designation is that it strengthens the position of the local planning authority in rejecting inappropriate proposals, and it indicates that the area is of national importance in terms of its environmental quality. In effect, it is a warning that stricter planning guidelines will be applied although, generally, AONB designation affords no extra statutory protection. A study of the effectiveness of AONB designation in East Devon found that more planning applications were refused outside the AONB than within it.

FIGURE 6.3. THE NEW FOREST

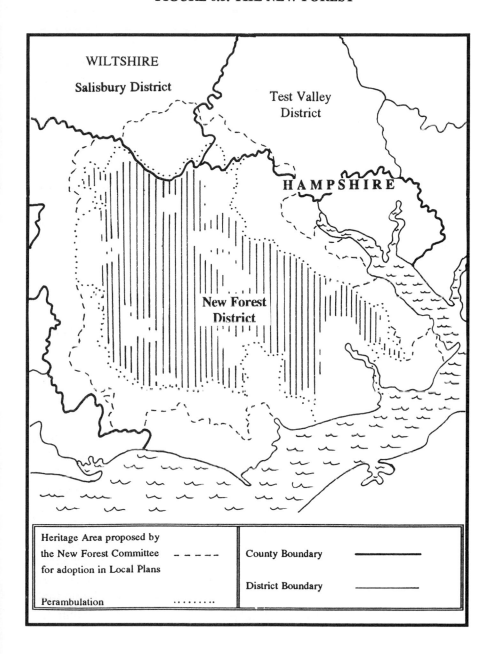

WILTSHIRE

Salisbury District

Test Valley
District

HAMPSHIRE

New Forest
District

| Heritage Area proposed by the New Forest Committee for adoption in Local Plans | – – – – – | County Boundary | ——— |
| Perambulation | ········· | District Boundary | ——— |

TABLE 6.1. AREAS OF OUTSTANDING NATURAL BEAUTY

Area	Date of Designation	Area (sq. km)
Gower	1956	189
Quantock Hills	1957	99
Lleyn	1957	155
Northumberland Coast	1958	129
Surrey Hills	1958	414
Cannock Chase	1958	68
Shropshire Hills	1959	777
Dorset	1959	1,036
Malvern Hills	1959	104
Cornwall	1959	932
Extension to Cornwall	1983	25
North Devon	1960	171
South Devon	1960	332
East Hampshire	1962	391
East Devon	1963	267
Isle of Wight	1963	189
Chichester Harbour	1964	75
Forest of Bowland	1964	803
Solway Coast	1964	107
Chilterns	1965	800
Chilterns Variation	1990	33
Sussex Downs	1966	981
Cotswolds	1966	1,507
Anglesey	1967	215
South Hampshire Coast	1967	78
Norfolk Coast	1968	450
Kent Downs	1968	845
Suffolk Coast and Heaths	1970	391
Dedham Vale	1970	57
Dedham Vale Extension	1978	15
Wye Valley	1971	325
North Wessex Downs	1972	1,738
Mendip Hills	1972	202
Mendip Hills Variation	1989	4
Arnside and Silverdale	1972	75
Lincolnshire Wolds	1973	560
Isles of Scilly	1976	16
High Weald	1983	1,450
Cranbourne Chase and West Wiltshire Downs	1983	960
Clwydian Range	1985	156
Howardian Hills	1987	205
North Pennines	1988	1,998
Blackdown Hills	1991	370
Nidderdale	1994	603
Total		**20,297**

Source: Countryside Commission 1995

Despite the emphasis on conservation, many AONBs are important and popular destinations for visitors. The Wye Valley, the Quantocks, the North and South Downs, and Cannock Chase have for a long time supported a high level of recreation and many other AONBs are becoming increasingly popular. In the North Pennines AONB a tourism development partnership has been established to promote the area under the banner of *England's Last Wilderness*. While the development of tourism in the North Pennines is designed to reverse the area's economic decline it nevertheless seems to conflict directly with the original purpose of AONB designation. Indeed, AONB designation effectively advertises the existence of an area; there was concern amongst the inhabitants of Nidderdale that designation would result in a dramatic increase in recreation in the Dale, bringing with it many of the problems that are experienced in the neighbouring Yorkshire Dales National Park.

Therefore AONB designation can be a double-edged sword, increasing both protective measures and recreation and development pressures. Dependent as it is on existing planning control, the farming and forestry industries that account for a great majority of land use within AONBs can also have a significant effect on the landscape whilst being relatively immune from planning control. The Countryside Commission has recognised the failings of AONB designation and plan to identify priority areas where stronger local management arrangements will be implemented, whilst recreation management should feature more prominently in AONB management. However, the Environment Act 1995, which broadened and strengthened the role of national parks, made no reference to AONBs, thereby potentially diminishing their effectiveness in comparison to the national parks.

iii Heritage Coasts
Some of Britain's most dramatic and beautiful scenery is to be found along the coastal regions, as are many important wildlife and marine nature reserves. Equally, the coasts of Britain have for a long time played an important role in tourism and leisure provision. The development of the traditional seaside resorts from the early nineteenth Century onwards signified the beginning of what was to become mass tourism and up until

the 1950s the recreational use of the coast was limited to the resorts and purpose built holiday camps. Since then, however, increased mobility and improved road links have opened up most of the undeveloped coastline for recreation and leisure, bringing problems similar to those in other countryside areas. Furthermore, just as greater use has been made of the coasts, so too has the range of activities diversified. In addition to walking, swimming or visiting the beach people now participate in climbing, hang-gliding, sand yachting and a variety of water sports.

Recreation is not the only pressure on the coastline, although some of what are perhaps the most inappropriate developments, such as caravan sites and holiday villages, are a direct result of the spread of tourism and leisure along the coast. Its scenery and fragile eco-system have been facing ever increasing threats from industrial development, intensive farming methods, housing development and new marina developments. A further danger to the coastline, and indeed to those people who either live in or visit coastal regions, is the increasing level of litter and pollution both on the shoreline and in coastal waters.

Enterprise Neptune is a special appeal established by the National Trust in 1965 to raise funds for the purchase of valuable sections of the coast. In the following year the then National Parks Commission began a study of coastal preservation and development which culminated in 1970 with the publication by the Countryside Commission of two reports, *The Coastal Heritage* and *The Planning of the Coastline*. The main proposal of these reports was that selected stretches of undeveloped coastline should be designated as Heritage Coasts and afforded greater protection. In 1972 the government accepted this proposal and recommended that local authorities should identify areas of coastline worthy of designation and, in consultation with the Countryside Commission, prepare management plans for them. However, it was decided that heritage coasts should not be added to the list of statutory land designations. Since 1972 a total of 45 stretches of coast have been given heritage coast designation (see Table 6.2.); together they add up to 954 miles (1537 km), or about one third of the coastline of England and Wales.

The great majority of heritage coasts lie within national parks or AONBs; just seven stretches of coast fall outside previously designated areas. About half of all coastal Sites of Special Scientific Interest are contained within the heritage coasts and one third of the total designated coastline is under the ownership of the National Trust. However the overall purpose of designation is not simply to add a further layer of protective status but to highlight the special management needs of the coasts.

The original objectives of heritage coast designation, as set out in the 1970 proposals, were:

(a) to identify the finest stretches of undeveloped coast

(b) to conserve and manage them comprehensively

(c) to facilitate and enhance their their enjoyment by the public through the promotion and encouragement of recreational activities consistent with the conservation of their fine natural scenery and heritage features.

The planning and management of heritage coasts is the responsibility of local authorities working to a locally devised management plan. During the 1970s three successful pilot projects, largely funded by the Countryside Commission, demonstrated the importance of having a heritage coast officer to achieve an effective balance between conservation and recreation management and today three quarters of designated coasts have their own staff and rangers. A large number of authorities have yet to complete management plans, though, perhaps indicating a lack of commitment to what may be considered a further planning constraint. In 1988 the Countryside Commission set up the Heritage Coast Forum as a national body to promote the concept of heritage coasts and to be the focal point for all organisations involved in the management of heritage coasts.

TABLE 6.2. HERITAGE COASTS IN ENGLAND AND WALES

Coast	Date Defined	Length (km)
North Northumberland	1973	93
Sussex	1973	13
Gower	1973	55
North Anglesey	1973	29
Holyhead Mountain	1973	13
Aberffaw Bay	1973	8
Lleyn	1974	88
South Pembrokeshire	1974	66
Marloes and Dale	1974	43
St. Brides Bay	1974	8
St. David's Peninsula	1974	82
Dinas Head	1974	18
St. Dogmaels and Moylgrove	1974	23
Isles of Scilly	1974	64
North Norfolk	1975	63
South Foreland	1975	7
Dover-Folkstone	1975	7
Suffolk	1979	56
North Yorkshire and Cleveland	1981	55
Purbeck	1981	52
Ceredigon Coast	1982	34
West Dorset	1984	40
East Devon	1984	28
Hartland (Cornwall)	1986	11
Pentire Point-Widemouth	1986	54
Trevose Head	1986	4
St. Agnes	1986	11
Godrevy-Portreath	1986	10
Penwith	1986	55
The Lizard	1986	28
The Roseland	1986	54
Gribbin Head-Polpero	1986	24
Rame Head	1986	8
South Devon	1986	74
Spurn	1988	18
Hamstead	1988	11
Tennyson	1988	35
St. Bees Head	1989	6
Flamborough Headland	1989	19
Glamorgan	1989	27
Great Orme	1989	7
Hartland (Devon)	1990	47
Lundy	1990	18
Exmoor	1991	45
North Devon	1992	32

Source: Countryside Commission 1995

More recently a policy document published by the Countryside Commission in 1991 (*Heritage Coasts: Policies and Priorities*) broadened the objectives of heritage coast status to include nature, marine and built heritage conservation, the need to cater for a wider range of sporting and recreational activities, recognition of environmental health factors and to pay particular attention to the *social needs of the small communities on these coasts, through promoting sustainable forms of social and economic development, which in themselves conserve and enhance natural beauty and heritage features* (Countryside Commission 1991). As in most other areas of the Countryside Commission's work, the involvement of local groups and individuals is also seen as an essential ingredient to the overall management of the coasts.

The importance of these coasts for their natural and scenic quality and as a resource for recreation and leisure is undeniable. Yet, as we have seen, the stricter planning measures brought about by their designation has not rendered them completely unsusceptible to development. It may be concluded, therefore, that as most heritage coasts fall within existing designated areas, the need to single out the coasts for extra protection indicates a failing of the original land designation.

iv Country Parks
Within the context of this chapter country parks are the odd-man-out. Whereas most land designation in Britain is concerned with the protection of nature and landscape, and balancing the various demands in specific areas of the countryside, country parks are the result of a positive policy to provide wider opportunities for countryside recreation. Having said that, the creation of country parks was originally motivated by a perceived need to protect other areas and so the underlying purpose was still the conservation of threatened or fragile parts of the countryside.

As is described in Chapter Four, country parks have their origins in the 1966 White Paper *Leisure in the Countryside*. At that time there were fears that an ever increasing demand for leisure and recreation in the countryside would place an intolerable strain on traditional countryside destinations, in particular the national parks. The proposed solution was to syphon off some of this demand by creating counter-attractions closer to the main centres of population, in effect bringing the countryside closer to the people. Therefore the primary purpose of country parks was to act as a kind of safety valve, limiting the use of the more fragile areas of countryside as well as fulfilling the social role of improving the opportunities and accessibility of countryside recreation. Implicit in this policy were certain assumptions about the motivations and perceptions of countryside visitors, which have meant that country parks have not fully achieved their original objective.

The proposals outlined in *Leisure in the Countryside* were embodied in the Countryside Act 1968 and the Countryside (Scotland) Act 1967. Local authorities were empowered to purchase land for the purpose of establishing country parks and to provide necessary facilities such as car parks, toilets, picnic areas, visitor centres and restaurants. Additionally, private landowners were permitted to establish country parks on their land. The Countryside Commission was empowered to contribute to the costs of developing the parks, up to fifty per cent of the costs of local authorities and up to 75 per cent in the case of private landowners.

During the first few years of the scheme the designation of country parks progressed rapidly. By 1973 over one hundred parks had been approved, and the number increased to one hundred and fifty by 1978. In 1989 the total number of country parks exceeded 220 and yet more continue to be established. There are now roughly 300 country parks in the UK and, although no maximum number of parks has been set as a target or limit, it is likely that the number of new parks will reduce significantly in the future due to lack of both suitable locations and financial support.

In considering the creation of a country park, local authorities are required through the legislation to have regard to both the location of the park with respect to centres of population and the availability and suitability of existing facilities. There is no doubt that country parks have provided new opportunities and facilities for recreation close to major urban areas (see Table 6.3.).

TABLE 6.3. REGIONAL DISTRIBUTION OF COUNTRY PARKS (1989)

Northern	15
Yorkshire and Humberside	17
North West	24
Wales	23
Midlands	53
Eastern	18
South East	53
South West	17

Source: Countryside Commission 1989a

Nearly half the parks are located in the Midlands and the South East of the country, areas relatively distant from national parks. Whether these parks attract visitors who would have otherwise travelled to other countryside areas is a matter of debate.

The Countryside Commission's policy toward country parks was originally that they should be easily accessible to large numbers of people either by car or on foot, that they should offer a range of facilities with, as a minimum, parking and toilet facilities and that they should be managed by statutory or private organisations. More recently, the Commission broadened its policy towards the parks whilst at the same time re-emphasising their safety valve role. Country parks should:

(a) *take large numbers of visitors who want a convenient place in which to relax within reach of major centres of demand. This relieves the pressure of visitors on the surrounding countryside.*

(b) *be the venue for a range of sporting activities, especially water-based ones, which are enhanced by a countryside location. But sites must be large enough and managed so that sports activities do not interfere with more casual use and the quiet enjoyment of the countryside.*

(c)   *be the instrument for restoration of derelict land, and also for the*
continued maintenance of existing parkland, hence demonstrating
one link between conservation and recreation.

(d)   *be gateways from which the public can explore...the wider*
countryside beyond.

(Countryside Commission 1987a)

It is in fact impossible to determine how far country parks adhere to these policy objectives for they differ enormously in size, location and the range of facilities available. All have the minimum required facilities, such as car parks and toilets, but beyond that they vary to a great extent. Strathclyde Country Park, for example, is a large park near Glasgow which attracts over three million visitors annually. Its main focus is a water sports centre which offers sailing, water skiing and other sports and which hosted the Edinburgh Commonwealth Games rowing competition. A large number of events take place on the site each year.

On the other hand one of the more recently established parks, Riverside Park near Gillingham in Kent, covers just a few acres of land beside the Medway and offers opportunities for walking and bird-watching. Yet, although its facilities are limited to a small car park and visitor centre, and it is certainly unable to cater for large numbers of visitors, it nevertheless offers a more realistic countryside experience than many other parks. Indeed, many country parks are little more than outdoor activity centres, falling far short of the objective of bringing the countryside closer to the people. However, some country parks meet the criteria as set out by the Countryside Commission; one such park is the Rother Valley Country Park in South Yorkshire and it is described in detail in the case study at the end of this chapter.

It has been estimated that only ten per cent of all countryside visits are to country parks yet the cost of developing and maintaining them rests with the public sector. It is therefore important to ask how far they have achieved their original purpose of creating new opportunities for countryside recreation, thereby diverting demand away from other countryside areas.

Research has shown that in fact over sixty per cent of country parks now in existence already hosted some form of recreational use prior to designation. Thus not only was there a limited addition to the overall stock of countryside recreational facilities but also a significant sum of public money has been directed over the years to merely improving and upgrading existing facilities. Furthermore there was no national plan or strategy for a systematic spread of parks; they have been developed more as a result of opportunism on the part of local authorities and private landowners. As a result many parts of the country have less country parks than might be considered necessary, especially outside the Midlands and south-east urban centres.

Of most importance, it was perhaps idealistic to propose the creation of new 'countryside' closer to towns and cities. Many parks are undoubtedly already in countryside locations and are true countryside, such as Beacon Fell in Lancashire and Stockgrove Park in Bedfordshire. However, it is still enclosed, sanitised countryside, far removed from the relatively wild and open countryside of the national parks. It would be necessary to undertake research into the motivations of visitors to a broad spread of country parks to determine whether or not they are an effective alternative to traditional countryside. One survey carried out at Rufford Park in Nottinghamshire in 1981/82 found that ten per cent of visitors liked the forest, 27 per cent liked the walks, 15 per cent enjoyed the peace and quiet and 25 per cent liked the unspoilt natural character (Countryside Commission 1983). In other words, only a minority were attracted by its countryside characteristics.

It would therefore be safe to conclude that country parks cater for a wide range of outdoor activities and pursuits and have absorbed much of the increase in demand for non-traditional countryside activities and sports. They have also increased the opportunities for, and accessibility of, outdoor (but not necessarily countryside) recreation. They have not, however, achieved the original aim of reducing recreation demand in areas such as the national parks. Indeed, as the Countryside Commission has recognised, country parks can act as gateways to the wider countryside. That is, a visit to a country park can encourage people, or give them the confidence, to explore the wider countryside. This is a complete reversal of the policies of the 1970s.

v Nature Reserves

So far we have considered land designations which have as their principal aims the protection and enhancement of the landscape and the promotion of the public's enjoyment of the countryside. However, the Huxley Committee published its report in 1947 proposing that nature reserves should be established in England and Wales for the purpose of protecting and undertaking scientific research into natural wildlife habitats. An equivalent system was proposed for Scotland by the Ritchie Committee. Thus a dichotomy was established between the protection and conservation of the scenic and the natural qualities of the countryside which, at least in England, remains to this day.

The National Parks and Access to the Countryside Act 1949 empowered the then Nature Conservancy, or indeed any local authority, to establish both national and local nature reserves. A nature reserve is defined as an area of land managed for the protection of its flora and fauna and natural features, or for scientific study and research. Nature reserves can be established either by the land being purchased by agreement or through compulsory purchase powers, or by entering into a management agreement with the owner of the land in question. In the case of management agreements, the landowner is entitled to financial compensation for any restrictions imposed by the terms of the agreement. National Nature Reserves (NNRs) are those which are considered to be of national importance and are therefore owned or managed by the relevant national body, namely English Nature, the Countryside Council for Wales or Scottish Natural Heritage. Local Nature Reserves, on the other hand, are the responsibility of local authorities. Between 1949 and 1988 a total of 231 NNRs were established, covering 408,743 acres (165,412 hectares) or just over 0.7 per cent of the land area of the UK. Of these, 120 are in England, 67 in Scotland and 44 in Wales, with the great majority being either leased or under management agreement rather than owned outright. By 1988 there were also 154 Local Nature Reserves, though covering a much smaller total land area of 37,566 acres (15202 hectares).

Although the primary purpose of nature reserves is conservation and scientific research they are nevertheless an important addition to the stock of countryside recreational facilities. Public access may be restricted for the protection of natural habitats but in many cases the public are permitted to visit nature reserves as long as the overriding objective of conservation is not compromised.

In addition to NNRs and local reserves there are also numerous non-statutory nature reserves. These are reserves which are under the control of private organisations such as the Royal Society for the Protection of Birds, which owns over one hundred reserves extending over more than 125,000 acres (50,585 hectares). There are also some forty County Trusts for Nature Conservation which own over 1,300 reserves whilst the Woodland Trust, as its name suggests, purchases and manages threatened woodlands. In total the non-statutory reserves cover 7.7 per cent of the UK land area.

vi Sites of Special Scientific Interest

There are over 5,300 Sites of Special Scientific Interest (SSSIs) in the UK, extending to some seven per cent of the total land area. As with most other land designations, SSSIs have their origins in the National Parks and Access to the Countryside Act 1949 although, as is discussed in Chapter Four, the current law regarding their identification and designation is found in the Wildlife and Countryside Act 1981. SSSIs are areas of land which are outside nature reserves but nevertheless are considered worthy of protection due to their special flora and fauna. Once an SSSI has been designated the local planning authority, when considering any development proposals for the area, must consult the relevant national body, such as English Nature, before coming to a decision. The local authority is not obliged to follow advice but will usually do so.

The deficiences of the system of identification and designation of SSSIs are well documented. It is important to note, however, that once a site has been designated as an SSSI it is not necessarily guaranteed protection from harmful or inappropriate use or development. It simply means that the importance of a site has been officially recognised. This has meant that not only have landowners been able to damage or destroy SSSIs, but also the government has also been effectively breaking its own rules. In other words, where other needs are considered to be more important, such as road building, then conservation interests will be overridden. For example, the extension of the M3 across Twyford Down in Hampshire destroyed a number of SSSIs and important archaeological sites as it was decided that the extra cost involved in building a tunnel through the hillside outweighed the necessity to conserve the sites. Similarly, in 1996 the controversy surrounding the building of the Newbury bypass centred on the destruction of three SSSIs and other important wildlife habitats.

vii Other Designations

(a) Environmentally Sensitive Areas

The designation of Environmentally Sensitive Areas (ESAs) commenced in 1986 as a direct result of European Community policies for the protection of agricultutal land. There was increasing concern about the damaging effects of intensive farming practices such as the destruction of woodland and hedgerows and the draining of wetlands; Community funding was made available as an incentive to farmers to revert to more traditional farming methods. The Agriculture Act 1986 empowered the Ministry of Agriculture, Fisheries and Food (MAFF), in consultation with the Countryside Commission and the then Nature Conservancy Council, to designate ESAs to conserve the natural beauty, the flora and fauna and the built heritage of areas of special importance.

The first five ESAs were identified in 1986 and the schemes started in 1987. One of these areas was the Norfolk Broads where an experimental scheme had been established on the Halversgate Marshes in 1985. There, farmers had been paid to retain the land for grazing and conservation rather than draining the marshes for conversion to arable farming. By 1994 a total of 30 ESAs had been established. (see Table 6.4.)

TABLE 6.4. ENVIRONMENTALLY SENSITIVE AREAS

The Norfolk Broads	Mountains of Mourne
Somerset Levels	Stewartby of Kirkcudbright
South Downs	Uists
West Penwith	Whitlaw / Eildon
Breckland	Avon Valley
North Peak	Exmoor
Shropshire Borders	Lake District
Suffolk River Valleys	North West Kent Marshes
Pennine Dales	South Wessex Downs
Test Valley	South West Peak
Cambrian Mountains	Blackdown Hills
Lleyn Peninsula	Cotswold Hills
Loch Lomond	Dartmoor
Breadalbane	Essex Coast
Shropshire Hills	Upper Thames

(b) Green Belts

The original purpose of green belts surrounding major towns and cities was not to provide opportunities for leisure and recreation but to plan and regulate the expansion of urban centres. London was the first city to create its green belt in the 1940s and, since the 1955, a number of other towns and cities have adopted green belts. These areas offer enormous potential for recreation for urban populations whilst, following the contraction of manufacturing industries, many urban fringe areas contain derelict land that is suitable for reclamation and development for recreation and leisure.

The area of approved green belt land in England has doubled since the mid-1980s and now covers over ten per cent of the land area of England, or over 1,550,000 hectares (HMSO 1993). Green belts are not statutory designations, yet they are regarded as both a *cornerstone of planning policy and a key element of environmental policy* (CPRE 1994). They have five main purposes:

1   to check unrestricted urban sprawl
2   to safeguard surrounding countryside from further encroachment
3   to prevent neighbouring towns merging into one another
4   to preserve the character of historic towns
5   to assist in urban regeneration

Research has shown that these objectives have largely been achieved (HMSO 1993). However, in recent years there has been increasing pressure to develop green belt land for a variety of purposes including, of course, leisure and recreation. There are no increased rights of public access within green belts but, given their proximity to major centres of population, they are seen as a prime resource for increasing the accessibility of, and opportunities, for countryside recreation. In particular, there has been increasing pressure on green belts to provide for new and diverse forms of recreation, such as dry ski slopes or golf driving ranges. Such developments often require facilities such as club houses, refreshment areas and car parks and are, therefore, strongly opposed by those who consider that only quiet, appropriate forms of recreation should be promoted. At the same time, however, many parts of the urban fringe contain derelict industrial or agricultural land which represents a valuable potential addition to the 'stock' of rural recreation resources. A number of schemes, such as Community Forests, have been implemented to reclaim such areas for the purpose of both conservation and recreation, and these are considered in greater detail in Chapter Eight.

SUMMARY
The majority of statutory land designations date back to the National Parks and Access to the Countryside Act 1949 and, overall, their purpose has been the conservation of either the scenic quality of the landscape or of the nature and wildlife within the designated areas. National Parks were originally intended to serve the needs of both conservation and recreation provision but there has been increasing conflict between the two objectives. Today in national parks there is a presumption against further tourism development and against forms of recreation that are deemed to be inappropriate to the inherent character of the parks. Thus, with the

exception of Country Parks, which have only partly fulfilled their original objectives, there are a number of issues common to all land designations:

i   The effectiveness of land designation in the UK is weakened by both extensive private land ownership and the reliance on agreement and co-operation within existing planning regulations.

ii The relative immunity of farming and forestry from planning control has heightened the conflict between conservation and other land uses.

iii The provision of recreation is increasingly being seen as a means of supporting and contributing to conservation rather than as an end in itself.

iv Due to lack of statutory authority and government financing greater emphsasis is being placed on partnerships and community involvement in the management of designated areas.

v   Many areas are multi-designated, potentially reducing the impact and effectiveness of each category of designation.

The implication of these trends is that tourism and leisure in the countryside, although of vital economic importance to rural communities, will become secondary to the perceived need to protect the countryside and that what is perhaps needed is an overall national policy for the development and use of the countryside and the specific role that land designation can play.

Case Study: Rother Valley Country Park

The 740 acre (300 hectare) Rother Valley Country Park (RVCP) was opened in May 1983 after eight years of development work involving five different local authorities. Situated between Sheffield, Worksop and Chesterfield, it was established to cater for the recreational needs of an estimated three million people living within easy reach of the park and by the time the project is fully completed some £8 million will have been spent on the scheme.

With an expected increase in the local population resulting from housing developments, the RVCP was first proposed in the late 1960s. By the early 1970s Derbyshire County Council had adopted a policy of providing new recreational facilities to relieve pressure on the nearby Peak District National Park. A Joint Committee was formed to oversee the development of the park. However the chosen site in the Rother Valley, an area of low grade farmland which was susceptible to flooding, had also been earmarked by the National Coal Board for extensive open-cast mining. It was therefore decided that, working to a development plan, as each section of the area was mined it would be restored and landscaped.

The main feature of RVCP was to be the Rother Valley Lake, which would accommodate a variety of water sports. A further three smaller lakes, one of which was to be the centre of a nature reserve, were also included in the plans so that the river and lakes within the park would form an effective flood control system (see Figure 6.4.). The surrounding landscape was to be returned to its original form although extensive tree planting, with a variety of deciduous and conifer trees, would be undertaken. The aim was to create a countryside atmosphere with opportunities for education and nature walks.

Between 1978 and 1982 work on developing the park gradually progressed. As coal was extracted from each section of the site the area was landscaped, and by the time the park opened over 125,000 trees and shrubs had been planted, with further phases of planting planned for future years. The total today stands at 400,000 trees and shrubs. Additionally an old 17th century mill and farm complex, situated near to the main lake, was restored and converted into a visitor centre. This was designed to host exhibitions and displays of arts and crafts and to house facilities such as toilets, a shop and a cafe. The majority of financing (eighty per cent) for the development of RVCP was provided by South Yorkshire Metropolitan County Council and by 1984 the Countryside Commission had also provided over £1 million in grant aid.

Today RVCP attracts about 700,000 visitors a year, the majority of whom come from within a twenty mile radius of the park. Those visitors from farther afield tend to be attracted by special events such as water sports competitions. Many come to take advantage of the opportunities for water-based activities such as sailing, wind surfing, canoeing and the increasingly popular jet skiing. Indeed the parks single greatest source of earned income is from hire fees and charges for water sports. There are also cycling and horse riding routes through the park, facilities for grass skiing and guided nature walks throughout the summer months. Future plans include the development of an 18-hole golf course, an equestrian centre and a shooting and archery range.

Although recent surveys have shown that the majority of visitors are attracted to RVCP by its countryside atmosphere, the park's marketing strategy is largely based on events throughout the year. In 1991 these ranged from the Dragon Boat Regatta National Championships and Jet Ski Championships to hosting a section of the Lombard RAC Rally. Thus there appears to be a potential conflict between the quiet enjoyment of the park and the move towards an activity/events centre. The latter would appear to be motivated by a need for the park to be more self-supporting. Nevertheless RVCP is a major countryside recreation facility in the South Yorkshire/North East Derbyshire area and a prime example of how country parks can fulfil many of the objectives as set out by the Countryside Commission.

FIGURE 6.4. ROTHER VALLEY COUNTRY PARK

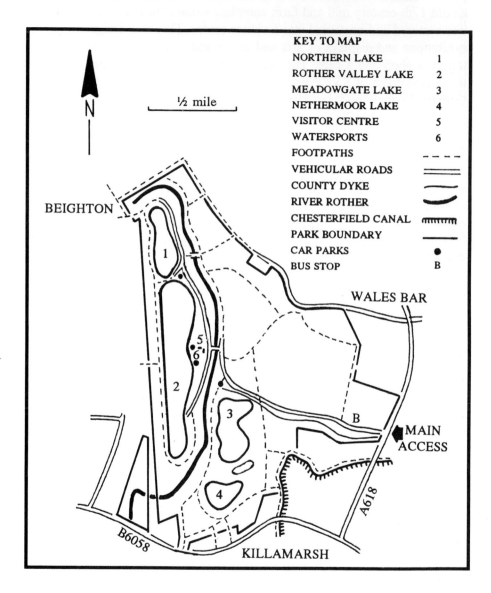

Chapter Seven

Access to the Countryside

INTRODUCTION

The wide range of activities and pursuits that constitute countryside leisure and tourism must, by definition, make use of and take place in the countryside. For the great majority of visitors this requires sufficient and suitable means of access both to and within the countryside; indeed, many activities such as walking, riding, climbing, fishing and so on are entirely dependent on access. Therefore it is immediately apparent that the question of access is of central importance to the provision and management of countryside tourism and leisure.

Two factors further heighten this importance. Firstly, England is a crowded nation. It is ten times more densely populated than the United States and, perhaps surprisingly, supports more people per square mile than Japan. Thus, as the population becomes ever more leisure orientated and is encouraged by organisations such as the Countryside Commission, the Sports Council and the Tourist Boards to visit and make use of the countryside, the capacity of the countryside resource to sustain all the demands placed on it is becoming overstretched. Secondly, most of the British countryside is privately owned land over which the public enjoy no general right of access whilst public landowners such as the Forestry Commission and the Ministry of Defence tend not to view recreation provision as a high priority. In fact, in law, any land owned by a public body is still deemed to be private land and private property rights are likely to dominate any question of access. Furthermore, as was shown in Chapter Four, the law concerning access in general to open countryside has, by relying on agreement and cooperation, come down firmly in favour of the rights of landowners.

In simple terms, the amount of countryside available for recreational use is in short supply. Some would argue there should be greater access to privately owned land; the freedom to roam campaign continues to this day, as witnessed by the Ramblers Association's Forbidden Britain days which emulate the mass trespasses of the 1930s, whilst others question the very basis of the British tradition of land ownership (see Shoard 1987).

On the other hand, a small but growing number of landowners are taking the initiative. They have increased access opportunities by introducing innovative pay-as-you-walk and pay-as-you-ride schemes on paths and bridleways across their land where walkers and riders pay a small fee for access to safe and well-maintained routes. For example, Eastern Toll Rides is a charitable organisation which, through agreements with farmers, has established a network of almost 200 miles of toll routes for horse riders through Surrey, Kent and Sussex. The farmers receive seventy per cent of the toll income and the remainder covers the costs of signposts, maps and administration. Such schemes, requiring payment for access to our land, do not of course meet with the approval of the access lobby yet nevertheless they have opened up more of the countryside for recreation.

Another less publicised scheme is where, in return for exemption from inheritance tax, landowners agree to open up part of their estates for public access. It is thought that over the last ten years some 330,000 acres (133,550 hectares) of private land, spread over about one hundred and fifty private estates, have been added to the stock of land available for countryside recreation.

Broadly speaking, the whole subject of countryside recreation is concerned with access. The purpose of this chapter, however, is to examine specifically the various rights of access to the countryside and the rights and responsibilities of both landowners and the public with respect to different categories of land and, in particular, the public rights of way network.

ACCESS OR ACCESSIBILITY?

Before looking at the various problems and practicalities concerned with countryside access is is important to define what is actually meant by the term *access*. In particular a distinction must be made between *access* and *accessibility*. The Countryside Commission (1986a) has summarised the difference as follows:

> *Access refers to certain rights of approach to entry; accessibility, on the other hand, refers to whether and how far these rights are recognised and can be exercised in a particular time and place.*

In other words, access is concerned with the mechanics of reaching and travelling around the countryside, whereas accessibility is concerned with the ability of the general public to gain access to the countryside. In short, although a right of access is necessary it does not always guarantee accessibility to the wider countryside. Thus the freedom to roam movement, for example, was concerned more with accessibility than with access whereas the legislation is primarily directed at affording rights of access. This distinction in turn highlights the contrast between the actual legal procedures for securing access and the moral or social right of the public to wander at will in the wider countryside. Whilst this chapter deals with the former, the issue of increasing accessibility for recreation is of central importance to the overall planning and management of the countryside and is discussed in Chapter Eight.

THE ACCESS STUDY

Except where a legal right exists, the accessibility of the countryside is generally dependent on agreements with landowners. Securing such permissive access therefore can be seen as the result of a kind of transaction between the landowner and the individual or group requesting access. The success of this transaction will be dependent on how far the attitudes and needs of the landowner match those of the recreationists, in particular attitudes concerning the use of the countryside and the appropriateness or acceptability of different pursuits or activities.

Between 1983 and 1985 the Countryside Commission and the Sports

Council jointly sponsored a major study into recreation and access in the countryside to determine how successfully this process of negotiation works in practice. Called simply *The Access Study* (Countryside Commission 1986b), it had four main aims:

(a) to assess the nature and scale of the demands for access to the countryside and how these related to access provision

(b) to develop a better understanding of the processes by which access is achieved

(c) to develop an understanding of the attitude taken by individuals, bodies and organisations involved in or affected by access

(d) to develop an understanding of a broad range of current access issues

A brief analysis of the study's main findings will provide a useful conceptual basis for the consideration of different types and categories of access later in this chapter.

The overall aim of the study was to determine why different individuals or groups seeking access to the countryside meet with either success or failure. It examined the various legal mechanisms for access, such as rights of way, and also the different strategies adopted by user groups in order to obtain access. Of most interest it compared the differing attitudes, approaches and needs of the two separate groups concerned with access, namely recreationists and what it termed the *resource controllers*, principally private farmers and landowners.

Overall the report concluded that the wide range of attitudes and opinions to the use of the countryside held by recreationists was opposed by a set of narrower, more traditional opinions on the part of farmers. Farmers, for example, were found generally to be opposed to greater public access to farmed land and resented the intrusion into their privacy threatened by public access. Those, however, who viewed farming as a business rather than a way of life, were more in favour of increased public access as long as any agreement was financially beneficial. This perhaps explains the success of the pay-as-you-walk schemes described earlier.

The inference of these results is that achieving access to the countryside by agreement is as much dependent on values as it is on the actual mechanism for doing so and that groups representing traditional and so called acceptable countryside activities, taking a cooperative as opposed to principled approach, are most likely to be successful in gaining access. On the other hand, newer forms of countryside sport and leisure, particularly motorised sports, are less likely to be acceptable and therefore may require the intervention and support of public authorities for the provision of suitable land. With the rapid increase in the range of, and participation in, such activities there are serious implications for future access arrangements.

ACCESS AND THE CLA

The Country Landowners Association (CLA) is the major national organisation representing the rights of landowners in England and Wales. In a policy statement published in 1991, *Recreation and Access in the Countryside: A Better Way Forward* (Country Landowners Association 1991), it makes a number of recommendations for resolving the conflicts between the needs of landowners and the increasing demands for access to the countryside. The CLA is not necessarily representative of the views of all landowners, of course; the Moorland Association, for example, is a smaller group of landowners firmly opposed to allowing wider public access to the countryside. Nevertheless, the CLA's statement is a useful reference point against which the current mechanism for access can be balanced.

A basic assumption underlying the CLA's policy reinforces both *The Access Study*'s findings concerning landowners' attitudes and also the precedence given to the rights of landowners inherent in the legislation. That is, the rights of landowners to privacy and to use and manage their land should be respected. At the same time the CLA states that, faced with problems such as trespass, vandalism, sheep-worrying, poaching and so on, many landowners are justifiably wary of attempts to increase access to their property. However, it also recognises that there are increasing public demands for attractive landscapes, conservation and leisure facilities, and that with recent changes in agricultural policies such demands in fact present new opportunities for landowners.

Therefore, the CLA believes that a new atmosphere of communication and cooperation is required between landowners, local authorities, statutory agencies and countryside recreation organisations working, albeit, within the existing legislative framework. Its recommendations fall into two broad areas:

i Statutory Duties
Landowners should honour their legal duties regarding public rights of way and should work together with local highway authorities to ensure that all rights of way are open, well-maintained and signposted as required by law. At the same time, highway authorities should respond by producing complete and accurate definitive maps, with no outstanding claims, by the end of the century. In short, many of the present problems and conflicts would be resolved by the existence of a recognised, accepted, well-maintained and legally defined rights of way network.

ii Access to Wider Countryside
Calls for a universal freedom to roam should be resisted by the Government and the onus should not fall on landowners to show why public access should not be provided. Local authorities should, on the other hand, make greater use of existing powers to enter into access agreements with landowners where a genuine need exists whilst landowners should recognise opportunities for making agreements with user groups, such as riding or motorbike scrambling clubs, on a commercial basis.

To secure effective action, the CLA recommends that Countryside Recreation and Access Groups, bringing together landowners, user groups, statutory agencies and local authorities should be established in each county to address local problems and opportunities. Essentially then, the way forward is seen by the CLA as being an enforcement of existing statutory obligations, rather than a fundamental alteration of the laws of access, combined with greater communication, cooperation and, implicitly, compromise between all parties. Whether or not a closer matching of the often disparate values and attitudes of recreationists and resource controllers can be achieved remains to be seen.

COUNTRYSIDE ACCESS: RIGHTS AND PROVISIONS

Generally speaking, public access to the countryside is afforded by one of two means, namely access or use as of legal right (known as *de jure* access) or by permissive access or use (i.e. with the express permission of the landowner). Public rights of way fall into the first category whilst free access onto National Trust property is an example of the second. In some cases, access is also afforded on private land where the public is uninvited but tolerated (*de facto* access). In other words access is with the implied, as opposed to the actual, permission of the landowner. This is most likely to occur on remote, unenclosed private land where it is impractical or unnecessary to try to prevent access.

As has been stressed earlier, the rights of way network, including National Trails, is the single most important resource for countryside recreation and therefore it is necessary to examine the rights and duties of landowners, users and the highway authorities with respect to rights of way in some detail.

Confusion can arise as to the rights of access to particular types of land. There is, for example, no general right of access to open countryside as defined in the legislation, nor is there a common right of access to, or common (public) ownership of, common land. For the purposes of this chapter, therefore, it will be useful to examine the various rights of access, and the process of securing access, from the point of view of different categories of land. Specifically, consideration will be given to the following:

(a) Open Country (section iv).
(b) Lakes, Rivers and Canals (section v).
(c) Beaches and Foreshores (section vi).
(d) Common Land (section vii).

i Trespass

It is, of course, possible to gain access to land without a legal or permissive right; anyone who enters land which does not belong to them against the wishes of the owner is committing the offence of trespass. Likewise, straying off a right of way, either knowingly or unknowingly (ignorance is not a defence) onto private land is trespass and, perhaps most interestingly, doing things that are not reasonably incidental to passage along a right of way also constitutes trespass. Thus, stopping to have a rest or to admire a view would be incidental to the use of a public footpath whereas pitching a tent, for example, would not.

Contrary to what most signs on private land state, trespassers cannot be prosecuted; trespass is a civil offence and not a crime. The exception to this rule is land owned by either British Rail or the Ministry of Defence where trespass is a criminal offence. A landowner is, however, entitled to ask a trespasser to leave, to remove him or her with the minimum force required when necessary and to sue the trespasser for damages. Conversely, if a landowner threatens a trespasser with a shotgun then the landowner is committing a criminal offence.

As a result of the well-publicised problems of New Age Travellers camping illegally on farms and other concerns, such as unlicensed rave parties on private land, new legislation concerning trespass was introduced in the Criminal Justice Act 1994. Under this Act, groups of more than two people trespassing on private land, or even on rights of way, are liable to prosecution, but only if their behaviour is with the intent to disrupt the legal use of that land. Therefore, normal recreational activities are unlikely to be affected by this legislation.

ii Public Rights of Way

The public rights of way network is the single most important asset in terms of recreation in the countryside. Its 140,000 miles (224,000 km) of footpaths, tracks and roads are invaluable in affording the general public the means of enjoying the countryside as of right. Equally the definition, classification, maintenance and promotion of public rights of way is one of the areas of greatest activity within the planning and management of countryside recreation. The purpose of this section, therefore, is to examine the rights and duties of landowners, local authorities and users with respect to rights of way and in particular to consider the current policies and schemes designed to open up, maintain and promote the use of the rights of way network (details may be found in Countryside Commission 1994a).

(a) What is a Public Right of Way?
Essentially it is precisely what the words imply; it is a route or way along which members of the public have a legal right to pass and repass. In so doing they are not committing trespass against the owner of the land over which the route passes. In exercising their right, the public are also able to do things which would normally be considered as reasonably incidental, such as stopping to rest or to look at a view. Any activity that is deemed not to be incidental to the use of a right of way, hence interfering with the landowners use of the land, is trespass. A famous example of this is where a sports journalist stood on a footpath making notes near to where some racehorses were training and was found to be committing trespass.

(b) Categories of Public Rights of Way
The term public right of way is usually applied to paths, tracks and unmetalled roads such as green lanes (although roads and motorways, legally defined as carriageways, are of course also public rights of way). There are several categories of ways over which the public have a right of passage, collectively known as highways. These categories reflect the public rights which exist on them, in particular with regard to the type of traffic that may use each category of way:

Footpath A highway over which the public may pass only on foot. The footpath is the entire highway, as distinct from the pavement alongside a road which is known as a footway.

Bridleway A highway over which the public may pass on foot, on horseback, or leading a horse on foot. Since 1968 the riding of bicycles has also been permitted on bridleways although bicycles must give precedence to both pedestrians and horse riders. Furthermore, highway authorities need only maintain the surface of a bridleway in a condition suitable for walking or riding. The popularity of all-terrain mountain bikes in recent years has, however, increased the use of bridleways for cycling.

Byway Open to all Traffic (BOAT) A highway over which the public have a right to use wheeled vehicles of all kinds, including horse-drawn vehicles, but one which is used mainly for the same purposes as footpaths and bridleways.

Road Used as a Public Path (RUPP) The right of passage over a RUPP is rather ambiguous, though it is usually used as a footpath or bridleway. To avoid confusion, Section 54 of the Wildlife and Countryside Act 1981 has required all RUPPs to be reclassified as footpaths, bridleways or byways, although this task is far from complete.

(c)   Historical Development

The evolution of public rights of way is steeped in history and many have existed for for centuries. The oldest highway in Britain is said to be the Great Ridgeway, an ancient route crossing the downs of Berkshire and on down into Dorset. It is thought to date from neolithic times and today the Ridgeway long distance path (national trail) follows part of the original route.

The role of public rights of way in catering for the recreation and leisure needs of countryside visitors is, of course, very different from their original use. Many were created in medieval times by people walking from village to village, going to church or to market, or, in the case of some longer distance routes such as drove roads, by farmers driving their cattle from the countryside to major towns and cities. From these earliest times routes were established as rights of passage across private land and, in law, that right of passage exists for all time. In other words, once a right of way has been created then, even if it is no longer used or the land over which it passes is ploughed over, it remains a right of way. Only in certain circumstances can a statutory order be made to either divert or extinguish a right of way.

Thus the great majority of public rights of way originated out of necessity over the centuries. Indeed, in more recent times, as they have become used more for pleasure than as a means of travelling from one place to another, a greater number of previously existing public rights of way have probably been lost than new ones have been created. This has resulted from changes in agricultural land use, urban and road development, or simply becoming overgrown through lack of use. Furthermore, prior to 1949 there was no legal requirement for highway authorities to record and preserve public rights of way (although the Rights of Way Act 1932, since repealed, enabled landowners to deposit with the highway authority maps and statements of dedicated ways over their land). It is for this reason that, although legal procedures exist for the creation of new rights of way, much of the law and also much of the work undertaken now by highway authorities is concerned with the protection, definition and maintenance of public rights of way.

(d) Creation of Public Rights of Way

Public rights of way can be created in law by one of two means, either by the traditional common law method of dedication or through statutory powers. (See Highways Act 1980).

Firstly, if a way has been used as of right and without interruption by the general public for a period of twenty years then it may be considered to have been dedicated as a public right of way. Two phrases are important, namely *as of right* and *without interruption*. As of right implies that the landowner approved of the use of the way without giving express permission, thereby dedicating the route a public right of way. If, on the other hand, the landowner makes it known that the use is permissive, then no right has been exercised. Likewise, if a route is closed for just one day each year during the twenty year period then it cannot be dedicated as a public right of way. In addition to this implied dedication, a landowner may also expressly dedicate a route as a public right of way. Most highway authorities today have a backlog of claims for the dedication of public rights of way, usually based on the twenty years' use rule.

Secondly, county and district councils are empowered through the

211

Highways Act 1980 to create footpaths or bridleways either compulsorily or with the agreement of landowners. These Public Path Creation Orders would normally be made when a new path would be of substantial benefit to the public; in practice, these powers are rarely used.

(e)   Duties of Highway Authorities
The duties of highway authorities with respect to public rights of way result from the various pieces of legislation described in Chapter Four. These duties fall into three broad areas, namely, completing and updating the definitive map, maintaining the condition of a right of way with respect to its use, and signposting and waymarking routes. Additionally, highway authorities are required to protect and assert the public's right to use rights of way and are empowered under the Rights of Way Act 1990 to bring criminal proceedings against landowners who have, by whatever means, made it difficult or impossible for the public to exercise their right of access. The maintenance duty can be delegated to district and parish councils who may reclaim any expenses incurred from the highway authority.

Many highway authorities appear to be failing in their duty to assert the public's right of access. In August 1992 the Ramblers Association listed sixteen counties where many rights of way were still blocked or obstructed because the authorities had not taken action against offending landowners. The problem is seen to be compounded by the lack of completed definitive maps, thereby allowing landowners to dispute the existence of public rights of way. A further three counties were pointed out by the Ramblers Association for failing to complete their definitive maps.

Part of the problem has undoubtedly been the low priority given to public rights of way in terms of manpower, time and funding relative to the provision of all leisure and recreation services and facilities. It has been estimated that local authorities spend £1000 million annually on leisure and sports facilities whilst just £21 million annually would be required over the next ten years to bring the public rights of way network up to standard. This would mean that the cost to an authority of a long walk in the countryside would be about 9p per person as opposed to £1 per person for a visit to a sports hall (Countryside Commission 1989b). Given the domination of walking as the most popular outdoor activity, it is therefore not difficult to justify the calls for greater public expenditure on maintaining rights of way. Current national policy is giving a high priority to the public rights of way network.

(f) Duties of Landowners

The principal duty of landowners is to maintain the public rights of way crossing their land so that the general public are able to exercise their right of passage. One of the most common areas of conflict in the past has been where a right of way crosses a field and is either covered by crops or ploughed over. The Rights of Way Act 1990, however, went a long way to clarifying the duties of farmers; it is now illegal to plough over a right of way that goes round a field, and a right of way crossing a field, if ploughed over, must normally be restored within 24 hours of ploughing. Additionally, the line of a right of way must be kept apparent, to specified widths, through crops.

(g) Policies for Rights of Way

In the mid-1980s surveys of leisure activities revealed that the majority of walkers in the countryside stayed on metalled roads, less than one third used public rights of way at all and only twelve per cent used paths that were not fully waymarked (see Table 7.1.). The implication of these findings was that the public were unable, either through obstructions or lack of knowledge or directions, to take advantage of the rights of way network.

TABLE 7.1. WALKING IN THE COUNTRYSIDE

Type of surface used on last walk in the Countryside	Walkers (per cent)
Country lanes and roads used by cars	22
Pavements on side of roads	6
Roads through villages	5
Beaches, commons, moorland	19
Farmland with no path	5
Signposted paths or trails	22
Non-signposted paths	12
Can't remember	8

Source: Countryside Commission 1987a

As a result of these surveys, the Countryside Commission stated in its policy document for public rights of way that the entire network should be *legally defined, maintained and available for use by the end of the century* (Countryside Commission 1987a). This is echoed by the Ramblers Association who have set the same target date for all paths to be signposted, well maintained and free of obstructions. The 1990 White Paper on the Environment, *This Common Inheritance*, recognised the importance of the rights of way network to countryside access and stated the government's support for the Commission's objective.

The basis of this policy is that the rights of way network should

(a) provide the public with readily accessible routes close to centres of population
(b) be easy to use
(c) provide a variety of opportunities ranging from short, local walks to longer journeys through wilder, more remote areas.

To satisfy these three criteria the Countryside Commission suggested that rights of way should categorised by the requirements of the potential users:

Parish Paths and Community Paths Whilst signposted and marked on maps, these are primarily intended for use by those who wish to find their own way in, or to discover, the countryside and therefore are not promoted.

Local Walks and Rides Paths which are signposted, waymarked and promoted for popular local use.

Regional Routes Longer, named paths, based perhaps on a theme or feature and offering tourism potential.

National Trails Paths that allow extended journeys on foot, horseback or bicycle and which appeal to both domestic and international visitors.

In 1988 a further survey was carried out to assess the actual condition of rights of way. It estimated the total length of the network by category (see Table 7.2.), but it was the condition of rights of way that gave some indication of the enormity of the task facing highway authorities if they are to meet the policy deadline.

TABLE 7.2. THE PUBLIC RIGHTS OF WAY NETWORK

Category	Length: (miles)	(km)	Per Cent of Total
Footpaths	106,000	170,000	76
Bridleways	28,000	45,000	20
BOAT's/RUPP's	6000	10,000	4
	140,000	**225,000**	

The overall aim of the 1988 survey was to determine how easy it was to make use of the country's rights of way. It found that even though twenty years had passed since it had become the statutory duty of highway authorities to signpost rights of way where they left a metalled road only 32 per cent had in fact been signposted, leaving a further 280,000 signposts to be put in place. Of the remainder, over one third were difficult to find. Less than half of the footpaths surveyed could be followed without the use of a map, and seventeen per cent of all footpaths were difficult to follow even with the benefit of a map. Generally, however, most paths were in a satisfactory condition for walking, although 21 per cent by length were found to be unusable. Put another way, a staggering 22,000 miles (35,200 km) of public footpaths were impassable. The overall conclusion of the survey was that over one half of all rights of way were unusable to those without map-reading skills and that on an average two mile walk in the countryside there was just a one-in-three chance of completing the walk without encountering an obstruction.

There are some, however, who would argue that signposts and waymarks are an intrusion and, to an extent, sanitise the countryside. In other words, they believe that, by having clearly marked routes, the experience and challenge of exploring and discovering the countryside is diminished. Such a viewpoint may of course be described as elitist and it certainly contradicts the policy of the Countryside Commission.

The results of this survey would indicate that the statutory duties of highway authorities had been sadly neglected. The Countryside Commission urged that greater resources should be directed towards achieving the year 2000 objective and that, as the CLA policy document also suggested, greater cooperation should be sought between the authorities, landowners and the users of rights of way, in particular enlisting the help and support of local communities and voluntary groups. The case study at the end of this chapter describes what one highway authority, Kent County Council, is doing to comply with the Countryside Commission's policy and objectives.

iii National Trails
Long distance footpaths, or national trails as they were renamed in 1989, are the flagship of the rights of way network. The legal provision for their creation dates back to the National Parks and Access to the Countryside Act 1949 under which the Countryside Commission (then the National Parks Commission) was empowered to propose a number of long distance routes through the countryside. Based as far as possible on existing rights of way, their purpose is to allow for either short or extended journeys on foot, bicycle or horseback along routes *which, by virtue of their character and quality, are national, reflecting the grandest, wildest and most beautiful landscapes the nation has to offer and also the most characteristic* (Countryside Commission 1990).

The first, and undoubtedly now the most popular and heavily used, national trail was the Pennine Way. Following the spine of England along the Pennines for over 250 miles (402 km) from Edale in Derbyshire to Kirk Yetholm on the Scottish borders, it was first approved in 1951 and finally opened in 1965. (See Figure 7.1). This time-span of fourteen years is indicative of the lengthy and often difficult process involved in creating a national trail, in particular with regard to negotiations with individual landowners. The need to create new rights of way to link existing paths can often lead to long delays and in some cases has resulted in the failure to establish a trail. For example, after ten years of negotiations the plans for the Cambrian Way through central Wales finally had to be dropped owing to the opposition of landowners and local authorities. Nevertheless, since 1951 a total of eleven national (including the Thames Path, to be opened during the summer of 1996) trails have been created in England and Wales, with a total length of 1452 miles (2336 km) (see Table 7.3.). The Hadrian's Wall Path and Pennine Bridleway were both approved in 1995; it is likely to be some years before either route is officially opened.

There are also three official long distance routes in Scotland. The West Highland Way is 95 miles (152 km) long and was opened in 1980, the Speyside Way is 48 miles (77 km) and was opened in 1981 and the Southern Upland Way, which stretches for 212 miles (340 km) right across southern Scotland from coast to coast, was the last to be opened in 1984.

TABLE 7.3. NATIONAL TRAILS IN ENGLAND AND WALES

	Approved	Opened	Length (km)
Pennine Way	1951	1965	402
Cleveland Way	1965	1969	150
Pembrokeshire Coast Path	1953	1970	299
Offa's Dyke Path	1963	1971	270
South Downs Way	1963	1972	129
Extension	1988	-	42
South West Coast Path:			
Cornwall (North)	1952	1973	431
Cornwall (South)	1954	1973	
South Devon	1959	1974	155
Somerset & North Devon	1961	1978	168
Dorset	1963	1974	116
Ridgeway	1972	1973	137
North Downs Way	1969	1978	227
Wolds Way	1977	1982	127
Peddars Way & Norfolk Coast Path	1982	1986	150
Thames Path	1989	1996	344
Total			**3147**

Source: Countryside Commission 1995

FIGURE 7.1. NATIONAL TRAILS IN ENGLAND AND WALES

Source: Countryside Commission 1990a

In addition to these official national trails a number of other long distance routes are popular. Some of these have been established by local authorities and others by writers. Perhaps the best known of these is the Coast to Coast Walk from St. Bees in Cumbria to Robin Hood's Bay in North Yorkshire; such is its popularity that one company offers package holidays, booking accommodation and transporting their customers' luggage by van along each daily section of the Walk!

Owing to the national importance and character of the national trails the responsibility for their selection and supervision lies with the Countryside Commission. Once a proposal for the designation of a long distance route as a national trail has been approved by the Secretary of State, the county councils through which the route passes take over the work of negotiating with landowners, creating new rights of way where necessary to link existing ones, signposting and waymarking, and undertaking the day-to-day maintenance and promotion. Thus the Countryside Commission fulfils its responsibilities mainly through the provision of funding to the relevant local authorities, covering the full cost of establishing a national trail and thereafter up to 75 per cent of its management.

In addition to the national trails already in existence a number of other long distance routes are in preparation (See Figure 7.1.). As already mentioned, the Hadrian's Wall Path and the Pennine Bridleway have both been recently approved. The latter is a somewhat controversial proposal due to the popularity and erosion problems on the existing Pennine Way. Furthermore, both a Cotswolds Way running 100 miles (160 km) along the crest of the Cotswolds and a 120 mile (192 km) semi-circular route in central Wales (Glyndwr's Way) are presently under consideration. One of the longer term aims of the Commission is that all the long distance routes should be linked to local and regional paths, thereby creating a truly national, inter-linking rights of way network.

In considering new national trails a number of criteria are used to judge the suitability of a proposal (Countryside Commission 1990a). Each trail should:

219

(a) pass through areas attractive for long distance journeys
(b) show evidence of potential demand
(c) be based on existing rights of way capable of improvement both for the route and associated shorter links
(d) have tourist potential and be capable of bringing economic benefits to the area
(e) be supported by local authorities responsible for the areas through which it passes

The implication of these criteria is that, for any new route to be considered, there must be evidence of potential recreational demand and that the economic benefits resulting from the opening of a particular trail would justify the costs of its creation. In other words, despite the recognised importance and popularity of national trails, the Countryside Commission would appear to be adopting a market-led approach to the provision of access in the countryside or, in simple terms, putting a price on countryside recreation. This view is supported by the fact that the Commission has emphasised the desirability of obtaining commercial sponsorship to meet the costs of establishing new trails (as with the Thames Path). Furthermore, in 1992 it commissioned a study into the local economic benefits of national trails and the current 75 per cent funding arrangement, effectively to assess whether national trails presented value for money.

It could be argued that such an approach goes against the spirit, if not the letter, of the Countryside Commission's duties in terms of the promotion of tourism and leisure in the countryside. There is no doubt that some, if not all, of the existing national trails are becoming victims of their own success. The problems of erosion on the most popular and vulnerable sections of the Pennine Way, for example, have been well publicised and it has been estimated that the total repair bill could exceed £5 million. The question to be asked is, should it be the Countryside Commission and local authorities who foot the bill for the repairs or should it be the visitor who pays?

It has been proposed by some that recreation in the countryside, in an economic sense, should be viewed like any other leisure activity; that is, it makes use of certain resources and facilities that should be paid for by the user. The arguments for and against the concept of charging for countryside recreation are examined in Chapter Nine. However, a 1990 survey of the use of the Pennine Way produced some interesting results (Countryside Commission 1992).

From the survey it was estimated that, between April and October, a total of 163,000 people walked on the Pennine Way. Of this total, just 10,000 people, roughly six per cent, were long-distance walkers and only forty per cent of them, 2.5 per cent of the total, were walking the entire length. On the other hand, some 104,000 people, or 64 per cent, were on a short walk of two miles or less or walking for part of a day. Furthermore it was estimated that the total spending of all walkers whilst on the Pennine Way generated an income of £423,400 for local businesses with long-distance walkers spending on average about twice as much per day as day-walkers.

Two important points emerged from the survey. Firstly, the great majority of users of the Pennine Way do not use it as a long distance route but as an ordinaryright of way. Secondly, the economic benefit to the local community, whilst not insignificant, is outweighed by the potential maintenance costs. Therefore, although it would be wrong to make generalised assumptions based on a single survey, it is nevertheless safe to conclude that in the future alternative sources of funding may be sought to maintain the national trail network. It is also certain that national trails will continue to play a vital role in maintaining and increasing access to the countryside.

iv Open Countryside

Open countryside was defined in the National Parks and Access to the Countryside Act 1949 as being areas of mountain, moor, heath, down, cliff or foreshore, a list added to by the Countryside Act 1968 with the inclusion of woodland, canals, rivers and lakes. In effect, open countryside today is any area outside centres of population other than enclosed agricultural farmland. Access to open countryside is, therefore, concerned with other than rights of way which are routes through the countryside with a right of passage.

Most open country is privately owned yet very often access to such countryside is without any formal arrangement or agreement with the landowner. In some cases access may be allowed through custom; that is, although the landowner has never given formal permission for access people have nevertheless enjoyed a freedom of access for a long time. Therefore permissive access is allowed through tradition and custom and is most likely to occur either where the use of the land by the public is at no disadvantage or cost to the landowner or where it is impractical to prevent or control access. Access to much of the Scottish Highlands, for example, is on this basis.

On the other hand, access to open countryside can also be with the express permission of the landowner subject to any conditions laid down. The National Trust, for example, owns much open country, especially in the Lake District and along the coast (see Chapter Five) and it is the Trust's policy to permit public access to their open land. Likewise many Forestry Commission holdings and woods owned by the Woodland Trust are open to the public for both recreational and educational purposes.

A third means of permitting access is through Access Agreements, particularly in those areas of open country which are popular with countryside visitors. Such agreements are made between the landowner and the local authority, are legally binding and allow the public to walk within the area covered by the agreement for the purposes of quiet enjoyment. As part of the agreement the local authority may pay the landowner an annual sum in compensation for the access and it is also able to issue bylaws relating to the use of the area. In practice, relatively few Access Agreements have been entered into.

Similarly a landowner can enter into a Management Agreement with a local authority as permitted in the Wildlife and Countryside Act 1981. The purpose of such an agreement is for *conserving or enhancing the natural beauty or amenity of any land which is in the countryside ... or promoting its enjoyment by the public* (Section 39). Access is therefore an objective of management agreements although their overriding concern is with conservation.

v Lakes, Rivers and Canals
Many countryside recreation activities are dependent on access to or along inland water areas, such as rivers, canals, lakes and reservoirs. Rivers and natural lakes (as opposed to reservoirs) are classified as open country and indeed are part of the land on which they occur. Although there may be a right of way alongside a river, the river itself (or to midstream if the river forms the boundary between two different properties) and the adjacent land belongs to the landowner. Access to the riverbank, therefore, does not mean there is a right to fish in the river. Similarly, access to the land surrounding a lake does not necessarily mean there is access to the lake itself. Reservoirs, and the land surrounding them, are owned by water companies, British Waterways or sometimes by private industries. Again there is no general right of access although access may be permitted and facilities provided for recreational purposes. Such access is entirely dependent on the owners of the property; access has never been allowed on Thirlmere in the Lake District, for example, whilst a variety of activities are permitted on and around the Kielder Reservoir in Northumberland.

With regard to canals and navigable rivers, the towpath or bank is legally part of the waterway and hence owned by the canal or river owner. Many canal towpaths, although originally used for just that, have become rights of way over time and in practice most other towpaths and riverbanks have a permissive right of access. Access *along* a waterway, for canoeing, sailing, rowing and so on, is dependent on a right of navigation which, like access to land, can be either statutory or permissive. In practice statutory navigation rights are relatively rare, and most categories of pleasure boats used on rivers and canals must be licensed or registered. Access along a waterway does not mean there is a right of access to the adjacent land.

vi Beaches and Foreshores
Beaches are owned land and generally the public enjoys a right of access

to them. Many beaches are in local authority ownership and are dedicated to public use. Similarly the extensive areas of coastline owned by the National Trust are open to the public.

On the other hand there is, at least technically, no general right of access to the foreshore. The foreshore is the area which lies between the high and low tide lines and is in fact shown on Ordnance maps. This piece of land is owned by the Crown although on particular parts of the coast it may have been sold. Thus there is the odd situation that there is an absolute right of navigation on the water when the tide is in but no right of access on foot when the tide is out. In other words, to go swimming in the sea at low tide necessitates committing trespass!

vii Common Land

Common land, once described as *the last reserve of uncommitted land in England and Wales* embraces a huge variety of landscape. Commons can be found in areas as far apart as the uplands of Dartmoor, the fells of the Lake District, Epping Forest, Port Meadow in Oxford and the New Forest in Hampshire. The urban commons in London, such as Clapham and Wimbledon, are also common land.

It has been estimated that in the mid-seventeenth century about half the land area of England and Wales was common land. Today there are a total of 8675 commons covering an area of 1.37 million acres (0.55 million hectares), roughly equivalent to the combined area of Surrey, Berkshire and Oxfordshire. (See Table 7.4.).

They are a *unique collection of green places of every size, shape and description* (Countryside Commission 1989c) and are often to be found in the more remote and wild parts of the countryside. It is perhaps no coincidence that 45 per cent of common land is to be found in the national parks, a further 25 per cent are within areas of outstanding natural beauty and in some counties up to seventy per cent of commons have been designated as SSSIs.

TABLE 7.4. COMMON LAND IN ENGLAND AND WALES

Region	Number of Commons	Acres	Hectares
South-east	2,238	75,257	30,455
South-west	1,172	158,422	64,111
East	844	19,041	7,705
Midlands	813	29,500	11,938
North	851	375,612	152,004
North-west	275	25,593	10,357
Yorks & Humbs	859	227,824	92,197
Total England	**7,052**	**911,249**	**368,767**
Wales	**1,623**	**457,767**	**185,252**
	8,675	**1,369,016**	**554,019**

Source: Countryside Commission 1989c

Presented with these facts it would be logical to assume that, in addition to being a valuable part of the countryside resource, common land plays an important role in the provision of recreation. On the contrary, there is a legal right of access to less than one fifth of common land. Firstly, it is important to define what commons are are what rights of use are attached to them.

Common land does not refer to common ownership but to common rights of usage, a principle that dates back many centuries. What this means, in effect, is that certain people, usually *commoners*, but not the general public, share a right to use the land in common with the owner of that land. In the years following the Norman Conquest much of the land was owned by the Lord of the Manor. Not all the manorial land was suitable for agriculture and so the tenant farmers, or commoners, were given certain rights to use this manorial waste. This, in part, explains why many commons today are to be found in relatively wild and barren parts of the countryside. The rights of usage to this land were as diverse as the type of land itself; they included the right to pasture animals, to cut peat or to collect wood for fuel.

This system continued until the middle of the eighteenth century when advances in agricultural techniques meant that the medieval open-field system was no longer suitable. Therefore parcels of land were enclosed by hedgerows, fences and walls (many of today's hedgerows date from this period), excluding commoners from the exercise of their rights. The next hundred years or so saw the enclosure of millions of acres of agricultural land and commons, although some areas suffered more than others. The Midlands, for example, were particularly hard hit so that today there are just 36 commons in Northamptonshire, almost all of which are smaller than one acre.

By the 1850s there was increasing alarm over the loss of common land, with the area covered having been reduced to some 2.5 million acres (one million hectares). This concern led to the establishment of the Commons, Open Spaces and Footpaths Preservation Society (now the Open Spaces Society) which campaigned both through the courts and by taking more direct action against the often unlawful enclosure of common land. Epping Forest, for example, was saved by the actions of the Society. Soon legislation was enacted to preserve common land and to increase public rights of access. The Metropolitan Act 1866 provided for public access to commons within London, a provision extended to a few regional urban commons under the Commons Act 1876. In 1899 a second Commons Act empowered district councils to provide public access to commons in their area and the Law of Property Act 1925 gave the public rights of access for air and exercise to all common land falling within either the Greater London area or in other boroughs or urban districts as they were before the 1974 reorganisation of local government. This, of course, applied to only a small proportion of all commons hence the limited overall right of access to common land mentioned earlier. The situation is alleviated to an extent, however, as the National Trust owns over 200 commons.

More recently the Commons Registration Act 1965 required that all common land and claims of right in common (with the exception of certain areas such as the Forest of Dean and the Stray in Harrogate) should be registered. The Act, however, did not include the provision recommended by a 1955 Royal Commission that all commons should be open to public access of right. Nor was it completely successful; many commons were

226

not be registered, losing their protection and status, and other areas of land were wrongly registered. Accordingly the Countryside Commission set up the Common Land Forum in 1984 which made a large number of proposals. Most importantly, with respect to public access, it recommended that within a five year period owners, commoners and local authorities should set up a management association for each and every common to balance the needs of agriculture, conservation and access. At the end of the five years, all commons would become open to public access though only for quiet enjoyment on foot.

Initially the Government supported these proposals. However, a more recent statement seemed to favour the opposing view, put forward by the Moorland Association, that public access to common land, in particular heather moorland common, should be restricted to designated footpaths. Until any new legislation is introduced the future protection of the commons lies in the hands of the owners and local authorities whilst the question of access is firmly embroiled in the access to wider countryside debate.

SUMMARY
Many of the recreational activities that take place in the countryside are dependent on sufficient and appropriate means of access. The pattern of land ownership, the wide variety of demands placed on the countryside, changes in agricultural techniques and, not least, the relatively limited amount of countryside available for recreation have all resulted in difficulties in maintaining, as well as increasing, opportunities for access to the countryside. Therefore the issue of providing well-maintained, varied, sufficient and defined access routes is central to the planning and management of tourism and leisure in the countryside.

The most valuable asset in terms of access is the public rights of way network along which the public enjoy a legal right of passage. At the pinnacle of the network are the national trails, although their popularity is causing problems of erosion through over use. The potential of future national trails is likely to be assessed on their financial viability and the availability of commercial sponsorship. More generally, recent studies have shown that the statutory duties of the definition, maintenance, signposting and waymarking of rights of way are far from complete. Therefore, to achieve the Countryside Commission's objective of a fully open, accessible and usable network by the end of the century will require a significant increase in resources directed towards these tasks.

Permissive or traditional access to open countryside is to a great extent reliant on the goodwill of landowners. With reductions in agricultural production it is likely that more land will become available for recreation; the development of improved understanding and cooperation between users and land resource controllers is seen as the way forward to securing greater access to the countryside.

This chapter has examined the mechanisms of countryside access. Equally important is the question of accessibility; that is, the ability of the public to make use of the means of access or, in a broader sense, to exercise their social or moral right to enjoy and explore the countryside. This issue is discussed in Chapter Eight.

Case Study: Rights of Way in Kent

Lying in the south-east corner of the country, Kent is known as the Garden of England. Its fertile land and mild climate are an ideal combination for agriculture, in particular for the traditional industry of hop-growing. Indeed, until mechanisation took over, many Londoners annually migrated to Kent to spend their summers hop picking. The landscape is still dotted with the unique Kentish oast houses used for drying the hops. Today the county is also home to the small but expanding wine making industry.

In addition to a rich historical past Kent is blessed with a wide variety of landscapes. The North Downs stretch across the county from Dover to the north east and on into Surrey whilst the coastline changes from rugged cliffs at Dover to the flat Thames Marshes. Furthermore, despite its proximity to London and an extensive network of motorways and other major roads, Kent has managed to retain its essentially English character of rolling farmland and traditional country villages.

Given its agricultural and historical background it is perhaps not surprising that Kent has a wide and varied public rights of way network. At present there are a total of 4188 miles (6740 km) of rights of way shown on its definitive map, comprising some 43 per cent of all highways in the county and three per cent of the national rights of way network. One national trail crosses the county (the North Downs Way) and a further seven named long-distance routes are promoted (see Table 7.5. and Figure 7.2.). Other counties in the south-east region have an average of only 2000 miles (3200 km) of rights of way making Kent's network of both regional and national importance.

TABLE 7.5. LONG DISTANCE FOOTPATHS IN KENT

Route	Length:(miles)	(km)
North Downs Way (Kent and Surrey)	140	224
Saxon Shore Way	140	224
Greensand Way	105	168
Wealdway	80	128
Stour Valley Walk	35	56
Darent Valley Path	15	24
Eden Valley Walk	15	24
Wantsum Walks	8	13

Source: *Kent for Walking*, KCC 1992

Whilst these figures show that opportunities for access to the countryside in Kent are twice those in other counties in the region, they also imply that the task of defining, maintaining, signposting and promoting the rights of way network is also twice as great! Overall responsibility for the network lies, of course, with Kent County Council (KCC), and their key objective is:

> *...to improve access to the countryside by developing and promoting recreation routes and to define, protect and maintain the Public Rights of Way network in accordance with the County Councils's statutory duties as both Highway and Surveying authority.*

(KCC 1992)

The Council has identified five strategic aims for the achievement of its overall policy objective (KCC 1992):

(a) **The Definition Aim** To ensure that all public rights of way have their status and route clearly recorded as soon as possible.
(b) **The Protection Aim** To provide an accessible public right of way network free from obstruction and interference.
(c) **The Management and Maintenance Aim** To provide a well maintained public rights of way network througout Kent.
(d) **The Development Aim** To provide a network of high quality and varied recreation routes easily accessible from centres of population and to accommodate demand for countryside access.
(e) **The Promotion Aim** To develop awareness of recreation routes to allow people to enjoy, understand, value and respect the countryside.

These strategic aims appear to fall into two distinct categories, namely, undertaking statutory definition and maintenance duties (aims (a), (b) and (c)) and increasing and promoting the accessibility of the countryside (aims (d)and (e)). These two categories of work are in fact split, perhaps illogically, between two separate council departments, the first being undertaken by the Public Rights of Way Unit in the Highways and Transportation Department and the second by the Countryside Group which forms part of the Planning Department.

FIGURE 7.2. LONG DISTANCE FOOTPATHS IN KENT

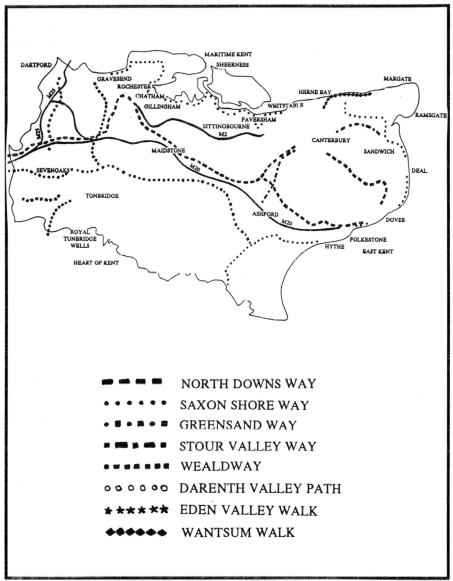

Source: *Kent For Walking*, Kent County Council 1992

The Countryside Group's activities are centred around a recreation routes programme, inspecting, promoting and marketing the major routes in the county and considering further ways of improving accessibility either in particular areas or for particular user groups such as the disabled. Their promotional work includes publishing guides, writing features for the local press and producing information sheets. A total of 81 different guided walks, with volunteer leaders, are also arranged on one or more occasions throughout the year.

It is the activities of the Public Rights of Way Unit, however, that are of greater interest in the context of this chapter. Working within the Unit are a National Trails Officer (responsible for the North Downs Way) who works closely with his counterpart in the Planning Department, a Rights of Way Enforcement Officer who works and liaises with landowners, and a Public Rights of Way Maintenance Officer who oversees the maintenance of the network by enlisting the support of volunteer organisations or contracting work out to private companies when necessary.

An example of maintenance work is the Bridge Kit Initiative. Volunteers supervised by Council staff replace or build new bridges where rights of way cross rivers or streams. Often a bridge is simply two or three railway sleepers laid across a ditch but for wider streams or rivers bridges, supplied literally in kit-form, are constructed. This is probably the single greatest cause of confrontation with landowners; not only do they often object to the presence of a bridge on their land, but it also means that walkers start to use a right of way that may have been impassable for many years.

There are also two Rights of Way Officers working on the updating of the definitive map and four Rights of Way staff coordinating and implementing the new Parish Paths Programme. Around the county are six Divisional and fourteen District Public Rights of Way Officers, the latter having ultimate responsibility for rights of way in their local area.

All members of the Unit are involved in working towards the achievement of the Countryside Commission's year 2000 objective in addition to their specific responsibilities. The task facing them is enormous. More than 320 RUPPs have to be re-classified and in 1992 there were a total of 58 outstanding claims for the creation of public rights of way. This alone will take many man-years to complete. Furthermore, about 75 per cent of rights of way have yet to be signposted as legally required and it is estimated that over 500 bridges need to be installed.

The financial implications are considerable. Although an extra budget of some £290,000 was allocated to Public Rights of Way for 1992/93, the completion of the necessary work within a reasonable timescale will be dependent to a large extent on the commitment of volunteer groups and additional external funding. The cost of maintenance along the North Downs Way is already supported by the Countryside Commission (currently 75 per cent of costs although this may be reduced in future years). The Commission also supports the new Parish Paths Programme, which, along with a varient scheme, is sharing the responsibility for public rights of way with local user groups and individuals.

i The Parish Paths Programme
In simple terms the Parish Paths Programme (PPP) is a project designed to ensure the maintenance and promotion of public rights of way at a local, parish level. It is based on community action with the participation of local people, including walkers and landowners. Although the initial impetus and guidance comes from the PPP staff in the Public Rights of Way Unit the ultimate responsibility for the success of the project lies with the local community working with their District Officer.

The PPP involves a series of four stages after which all the rights of way in a parish should be clearly defined, well maintained, promoted and cared for. The four stages are:

(a) Survey
Organised by a local volunteer coordinator, the first stage of the project is to undertake a survey of the rights of way in the parish.

(b) Maintenance
Under the guidance of a Parish Paths Programme Officer local volunteers, including landowners, undertake necessary maintenance work identified by the survey.

(c) Promotion
Once the maintenance work has been completed, the local rights of way network should be promoted. The PPP supplies a parish map, positioned in a prominent position, highlighting the rights of way in the parish and local people are encouraged to organise guided walks, for example.

(d) Adopt-a-Path
Following a successful and innovative scheme set up in South Yorkshire in 1980, the final stage of the project is a stewardship scheme. Local people are invited to adopt a path and to walk it three or four times a year, reporting any problems or obsructions to the District Rights of Way Officer.

The main involvement of the PPP is with the first two stages; when these have been completed parishioners are expected to take an active interest in their own rights of way, liaising as required with their District Rights of Way Officer. By involving the local community it is hoped that people will take greater care of their paths and that landowners will recognise their responsibilites. In Kent, where the Countryside Commission covers 25 per cent of the costs of the programme, it was expected that twenty parishes would reach the adoption stage by the end of 1992/93.

ii The Parish Paths Partnership
Kent is one of the first counties to participate in a new national scheme called the Parish Paths Partnership. From 1992 a total of £3.75 million from central government has been made available over three years to selected highway authorities to initiate the scheme which, like the Parish Paths Programme is designed to further increase the involvement of local communities in the maintenance and promotion of the rights of way in their parish.

It is in fact very similar to the Parish Paths Programme, except that, under the terms of an agreement with the KCC Rights of Way Partnership Officer, local groups are given grants of an agreed amount per mile (1.6 km) to undertake survey, maintenance and promotion work themselves without the supervision and guidance of the highway authority. With the same overall objectives as the Parish Paths Programme, the Partnership scheme is designed to harness the skills and commitment of interested local groups and individuals whilst the highway authority only becomes actively involved if, for example, a legal problem needs resolving. It is expected that the first parishes in Kent to participate will be those that have worked successfully under the Parish Paths Programme.

Overall, then, the KCC Rights of Way Unit is working to complete its statutory definition and maintenance duties within the aims and objectives of the national policies for public rights of way. Faced with inadequate resources, as indeed are all highway authorities, it is taking a leading role in involving local communities in the care and protection of its rights of way network with schemes that are likely to be adopted more widely in other parts of the country.

Chapter Eight

Countryside Planning
and Management

INTRODUCTION

The planning and management of the countryside as a resource for recreation has traditionally been a *reactive* process. Most of the countryside legislation enacted since 1949 has been in response to increasing demands and pressures on the countryside whilst, similarly, the policies and activities of many countryside organisations have been designed to manage and contain recreation. In recent years, however, there has been a move towards *proactive* countryside recreation planning. That is, national and local countryside organisations are now adopting a more positive, strategic approach to conservation and recreation provision.

This change in emphasis has come about for a number of reasons. Firstly, as a result of surplus production, the dominance of farming and agriculture as a major land use is declining. Significant areas of the countryside are now becoming available for alternative uses, including recreation, and there has been a radical shift in government policy towards the conservation of farmland. Thus, as the countryside becomes more multi-purpose there is a greater need for positive planning and management policies. Secondly, tourism and leisure are playing an increasingly important role in rural economies. Rather than being something to be managed and contained, recreation is now positively promoted as a source of income and employment and as a means of encouraging and supporting conservation. Thirdly, the urban/rural population shift and the diversification of industry in the countryside has reduced the distinction between city and rural life. Policies for housing, economic development, conservation and recreation provision have, therefore, become integrated and inter-dependent. Fourthly, the increasing concern for the environment in general, and the recognition that the countryside is a finite and fragile resource in particular, have led to the introduction of broader, sustainable development policies. Finally and, perhaps, most importantly, the expansion of tourism and leisure in the countryside has resulted in an equally large growth in the number of businesses involved in rural recreation. Most of these are more concerned with shorter term profit rather than longer term environmental concerns and there has been a need, therefore, to positively plan and control the development of such facilities and attractions in rural areas.

This chapter considers the various ways in which positive, integrated policies for countryside recreation and conservation are being implemented within the context of the planning and management of the wider countryside. It examines policies and schemes that conform to the concept of sustainable development and highlights, in particular, the important issues of the development of the urban/rural fringe for recreation and the need for effective and sustainable transport in the countryside.

THE NEED FOR PLANNING AND MANAGEMENT
At first sight, the overall planning and management of tourism and leisure in the countryside would appear to be a complex, if not impossible, task. The range of activities in which visitors to the countryside participate is enormous and, as is shown in Chapter Three, the demand for countryside recreation is largely spontaneous, informal, and motivated by a variety of social and economic factors. The provision, or supply, of countryside recreation is determined by the diverse elements of the tourism and leisure industry. Natural or man-made attractions, facilities, such as accommodation, food, drink and retail outlets, marketing and information services, and transport, whether organised or private, all combine to create the countryside recreation product, yet the majority of suppliers are small, private sector businesses. Furthermore, the countryside is almost entirely privately owned; the provision of access for recreation is largely dependent on co-operation and agreement rather than statutory requirements (see Chapters Four and Seven) and, therefore, individual

landowners' interests are likely to take precedence over local or national planning policies. In short, a notable feature of countryside recreation is the diverse and fragmented nature of both demand and supply which could, justifiably, defy attempts to introduce overall planning and management policies.

Nevertheless, as has been emphasised throughout this book, the countryside is the basic resource that attracts visitors and, in turn, supports the tourism and leisure industry. At the same time, the physical and social environment of the countryside is dependent, to an extent, on the income from visitors. Without an attractive countryside there would be no visitors, without visitors there would be no industry, and without visitors and the industry the countryside would suffer. Thus, despite the diversity and scale of recreational activities and the tourism and leisure industry there is an interdependence between the components of countryside recreation, and a common interest in the effective management and planning of the countryside

If the development of tourism and leisure in the countryside brought only benefits or positive impacts there would be little or no need for planning and management. Quite the opposite is true, however. The countryside is both finite and fragile, and there is a limit to the type and scale of recreation that any particular rural area can absorb depending on its physical, geographical and social characteristics. Recreation can lead to serious negative impacts on the environment which can outweigh any economic benefits (see Chapter Two). There is, therefore, a need to plan and manage tourism and leisure to minimise these impacts, thereby maintaining the character and quality of the environment that attracts visitors, and to optimise the benefits to visitors, the industry and local communities. In other words, there is a need to strike a balance between the development and promotion of countryside recreation and the maintenance of the resource that supports it. The method of achieving this balance is seen to be through the development of sustainable tourism and leisure.

SUSTAINABLE TOURISM AND LEISURE DEVELOPMENT

i   Alternative Tourism vs. Mass Tourism

Tourism has been frequently hailed as the economic success story of the second half of the twentieth century. Internationally it is fast becoming the world's largest industry and in the UK alone it employs around 1.5 million people directly and indirectly and annually generates some £30 billion. In many countryside areas, in particular the national parks, it has become the dominant source of income and employment. Furthermore, tourism has often been called the industry without chimneys, that is, a relatively environmentally friendly industry, and, in the words of the World Tourism Organisation, *a positive and ever present factor in promoting mutual knowledge and understanding...among all the people of the world* (WTO 1980).

Even by the early 1970s, however, concern was beginning to increase about the growth of tourism and its effects on the environment. Most attention was directed towards the problems associated with international mass tourism and its impacts on the environment, society and culture of destination countries. The solution was seen to lie in the development of alternative forms of tourism that were less environmentally damaging and more sensitive to the needs of the destination. It was even suggested that main cause of the problem was not tourism itself but the need of increasing numbers of people to escape from their home and work environments. The answer, it was proposed, was to reduce the people's need to go on holiday by improving their day to day quality of life (see Krippendorf 1984).

These new approaches to tourism development have variously been termed appropriate tourism, soft tourism, alternative tourism, responsible tourism, eco-tourism, and green tourism. The terminology itself can be confusing; green tourism, for example, can refer to either a green, or environmentally friendly, approach to tourism in general or to specific tourism activities that take place in a green, or rural, environment. Thus, for example, walking in the countryside may be described as a form of green tourism or leisure but, as is described in Chapter Two, the popularity of walking and rambling has led to serious erosion problems. Nevertheless, a feature common to all these approaches is that they are proposed as an alternative, rather than a solution, to large scale, mass tourism.

The basis of alternative tourism development policies as opposed to mass tourism can be seen in Figure 8.1.

The major weakness of alternative tourism development is that it proposes a localised, small scale solution to what is a large scale problem. It ignores the fact that tourism is a widespread, mass activity and that, even in the context of recreation in the countryside, visitors have a variety of objectives and motivations. Furthermore, it implies that tourism should only be available to those who wish to understand and experience the host environment whilst, in economic terms, small scale tourism is expensive tourism. Thus, it is, perhaps, inevitable that alternative tourism has been described as elitist and middle class (Wheeller 1991).

FIGURE 8.1. ALTERNATIVE vs. MASS TOURISM

Mass Tourism	Alternative Tourism
Large Scale	Small Scale
Large Volume of Tourists	Small Volume of Tourists
Short Term Development	Long Term Development
Environmentally Unsensitive	Environmentally Sensitive
Rapid Development	Slow Development
Requires New Developments	Litte or No New Development
Imports Labour and Resources	Uses Local Labour and Resources
Price Concious	Quality Concious
Dominant Economic Activity	Contributes to a Mixed Economy
Outside Control	Local Community Control
Tourists' Interests	Total Interests

Some newer innovations in the supply of countryside recreation certainly conform to the principles of alternative tourism. The concept of Country Village Weekend Breaks, for example (see Chapter Three), was based on existing local resources and the involvement of local people. A small number of visitors experienced rural life and culture in a natural setting and as a result the negative impacts on the environment were minimal whilst the benefits to both the visitors and their hosts were optimised. The Center Parcs developments have also been described as being environmentally friendly, although to what extent is a matter of debate, and conservation holidays are probably the most environmentally friendly, green form of countryside recreation. These types of activity, however, attract a relatively small number of people. The majority of visitors in the countryside participate in informal, unplanned activities away from managed sites and attractions and, therefore, the implementation of alternative tourism policies has little bearing on the planning and management of overall countryside recreation. Nevertheless, despite the criticisms of alternative tourism, it provides a useful basis for broader policies related to the sustainable use of the countryside as a resource for tourism and leisure.

ii Sustainable Development: Tourism and Leisure

As concern for the environment in general has increased the concept of sustainable development has become more widely accepted; indeed, sustainability has become the buzz word of the 1990s. However, the notion of sustainable development emerged during the 1980s as concern about the exploitation of the world's natural resources entered the mainstream of international politics (Yearley 1991). For example, a number of international commissions and conferences, such as the 1980 Brandt Commission and the 1987 World Commission on Environment and Development (the Brundtland Commission), published reports which highlighted the need to conserve natural, non-renewable resources, whilst the Green Parties became also active in politics. The most recent conference was the Earth Summit at Rio de Janiero in 1992; following this, the UK signed up to *Agenda 21*, committing itself to the implementation of sustainable development strategies. It was also during the 1980s that pressure groups, such as Greenpeace and Friends of the Earth, gained increasing international support and influence. As a result, environmental issues were placed high on the political agenda and it became increasingly widely recognised that a new approach to the use and exploitation of natural resources was required. This new approach became known as sustainable development.

One of the problems concerning sustainable development is that it means different things to different people. There are innumerable definitions of sustainability (see Pearce *et al* 1989) yet at the core of sustainable development is the fundamental requirement that, for any activity to be maintained over time, the resource that supports that activity must also be maintained. Thus, one of the clearest and simplest ways of describing sustainability is *the capacity for continuance* (Porritt 1995).

There are three principles of sustainable development. Firstly, any economic activity, including tourism and leisure, should put greater emphasis on the conservation of the natural, man-made and cultural *environment*. Secondly, the concept of *futurity* requires that sustainable development should be based on long term planning and, thirdly, any form of development should place an emphasis on providing for the needs of the least advantaged in society, both in the present and the future. This is referred to as intra- and inter-generational *equity*. These three principles are embodied in the most widely quoted definition of sustainable development:

> ...*development that meets the needs of the present without compromising the ability of future generations to meet their own needs.*
>
> (Brundtland 1987)

If the concept of sustainable development is applied to the countryside it means that the present demands made upon the countryside as a resource for recreation should not reduce its ability to support a thriving tourism and leisure industry in the future. At the same time, the benefits to both visitors and local communities should be optimised. The sustainable recreational use of the countryside is dependent, therefore, on maintaining a balanced relationship between visitors, local communities and the countryside.

There are a number of problems inherent in the adoption of such an approach.

(a) Virtually every recreational activity will have some effect on the environment and the impacts of visitor pressure can be cumulative over time. Thus, a degree of compromise is necessary in achieving the desired balance because, in the extreme, the only form of sustainable tourism is no tourism.

(b) The demands on the countryside change and evolve as the needs of society change and develop. Therefore the relationship between visitors, communities and the countryside must be flexible in time and place. In some areas recreation must be adapted to the environment, in others the environment may be adapted to the needs of recreation.

(c) The tourism and leisure industry comprises a large number of small, private businesses. It is likely than many will be influenced more by individual short term financial goals rather than longer term environmental concern.

(d) In some areas the sheer volume of numbers may need to be strictly controlled to ensure the maintenance of sustainable countryside use.

(e) Countryside recreation is synonymous with transport, in particular the use of cars. The success of the sustainable development of countryside recreation is, therefore, dependent on national transport policies. This issue is considered later in this chapter.

(f) The sustainable use of the countryside is, ultimately, dependent on the activities and behaviour of those who participate in countryside recreation. Appropriate planning and management measures will, therefore, be relatively ineffective without the co-operation and support of visitors to the countryside.

In 1990 the government set up a Task Force to consider the environmental impacts of tourism and to suggest ways in which tourism could be developed in a more sustainable manner. In its 1991 report, *Tourism and the Environment: Maintaining the Balance*, the Task Force suggested seven principles to guide the planning for sustainable tourism development which, although directed towards the tourism industry as a whole, are of particular relevance to countryside recreation development and planning (see Figure 8.2.).

The Task Force also proposed seven practical means of achieving sustainable development.

(a) Assessment of Capacity Determining the capacity of a destination is crucial to its sustainable use (see Chapter Two). Where the capacity is exceeded then appropriate steps should be taken to control visitor numbers. This, of course, is easier to achieve at managed sites than in the wider countryside.

(b) Transport Management There is no greater impact on the countryside than that caused by cars. This impact can be limited by effective transport policies, management and, where necessary, regulation.

(c) Marketing and Information It is possible to influence the timing and destination of visits to the countryside through effective marketing. Demand can be directed away from popular attractions by de-marketing whilst visitor behaviour in the countryside can be influenced by information, such as signposting.

(d) Conservation and Adaption Countryside destinations may become more sustainable through practical work, such as repairing and reinforcing footpaths.

(e) Design and Control of Development The careful location and design of new buildings and the re-use of redundant buildings, such as barns, can minimise the visual impact on the rural environment as well as contributing to conservation.

(f) Community Involvement The involvement of local people in the planning and development of tourism and leisure is of prime importance in maintaining the balance between the needs of visitors, local communities and the countryside. Yet whilst it is a desirable aim, it is probably the most difficult to achieve.

FIGURE 8.2. PRINCIPLES FOR SUSTAINABLE TOURISM

i   The environment has an intrinsic value which outweighs its value as a tourism asset. Its enjoyment by future generations and its long term survival must not be prejudiced by short term considerations.

ii Tourism should be recognised as a positive activity with the potential to benefit the community and the place as well as the visitor.

iii The relationship between tourism and the environment must be managed so that the environment is sustainable in the long term. Tourism must not be allowed to damage the resource, prejudice its future employment or bring unacceptabel impacts.

iv Tourism activities and developments should respect the scale, nature and character of the place in which they are sited.

v   In any location, harmony must be sought between the needs of the visitor, the place and the host community.

vi In a dynamic world some change is inevitable and change can often be beneficial. Adaption to change, however, should not be at the expense of any of these principles.

vii The tourism industry, local authorities and environmental agencies all have a duty to respect the above principles and to work together to achieve their practical realisation.

Source: ETB/Employment Department 1991

The Task Force concluded that sustainable development can only be achieved through greater co-operation and co-ordination between the organisations involved in the provision of recreation, working to a local or regional strategy. It recommended, in particular, that a partnership approach should be adopted as the most effective way of avoiding conflicts, harnessing resources, and working towards a common, sustainable goal.

In 1994, the Government published *Sustainable Development - The UK Strategy*, which included a chapter on tourism and leisure and, more recently, the Countryside Commission produced an advisory booklet, *Sustainable Rural Tourism: opportunities for local action* (Countryside Commission 1995c). In this, the Commission suggests that sustainable rural tourism is dependent on sustaining each element (the environment, the host community and the visitor) and that action is needed at both the local and the national level, with the full co-operation of national agencies and the tourism and leisure industries, for sustainable tourism to become focused and relevant. The booklet also includes details of 21 case studies of local sustainable tourism and leisure projects, some of which are referred to below. An evaluation of these projects found that there has been increasing support for sustainable tourism, that new approaches have been tried and tested and that, in many areas, progress has been made. However, it was also found that many tourism and leisure businesses do not consider sustainable development to be a priority, that only some visitors are receptive to it and that consultation and involvement, a cornerstone of sustainable tourism and leisure development, is not easy to achieve. Nevertheless, as with the Task Force, developing effective partnerships is considered to be the first essential approach.

THE PARTNERSHIP APPROACH
The planning and management of countryside recreation involves a large number of organisations from both the public and the private sector. The public sector is normally concerned with the provision of services and resolving conflicts over land use whilst the private sector's aim is financial gain and job creation from the promotion of tourism and leisure. Together they are concerned with the efficient use and management of the countryside resource to the benefit of local communities, visitors and the countryside itself.

In order to avoid potential conflicts between the different organisations and to ensure that they work together towards a common goal, a public-private sector partnership approach to the development of tourism and leisure has been adopted in many areas of the countryside. The first such partnerships evolved in the early 1980s. The English Tourist Board (ETB), offering advice and limited financial support, set up three-year Tourism Development Action Plans (TDAPs). These were designed to bring together private and public sector organisations, forming a partnership to encourage private investment in the proactive development of tourism. By 1990 a total of twenty TDAPs had been established, many of which were in industrial or heritage towns, such as Bradford, Lancaster, Portsmouth, Carlisle and Norwich. Partnerships have also been set up in rural areas; Exmoor, Kielder, East Kent, and Cornwall, for example, have all enjoyed TDAP status although, since the abolition of Section 4 funding in 1989, ETB input has been limited to guidance and advice. One of the main advantages of a TDAP is that, in addition to working to a common plan, tourism and leisure businesses contribute to overall marketing and promotion strategies that, individually, they would not be able to afford.

Many TDAPs have run their course, successfully establishing the development of tourism and leisure in particular towns or regions. However, a more recent and large scale countryside scheme was set up in October 1990 in the North Pennines Area of Outstanding Natural Beauty. The traditional industries in the region, including lead and zinc mining, have disappeared and the local agriculture and hill farming industries have also suffered in recent years. In response the North Pennines Tourism Partnership was established to promote and develop tourism under the banner of *England's Last Wilderness*, at the same time as working towards the conservation of the landscape.

The Partnership comprises nine district planning authorities, the regional tourist boards, the Countryside Commission, the Rural Development Commission, and representatives of local private businesses and voluntary conservation organisations. It was founded on the belief that sensitively developed tourism can contribute to the economic and social well-being of the region as well as enabling both visitors and local people to enjoy the particular qualities of the countryside. Despite its stated recognition of the need to conserve and protect the countryside the overall aim of the Partnership is *to provide an effective mechanism for the promtion and development of tourism in the North Pennines to bring economic, social and environmental benefits to the area* (NPTP 1991). The emphasis on tourism promotion is also demonstrated by the fact that the Partnership Officer is employed by the Cumbria Tourist Board and so it remains to be seen what balance is achieved between conservation and recreation provision. However, the original three year 'life' of the partnership has been extended until 1996 and it is felt that the NPTP has successfully undertaken a marketing, development and training role, although it has been difficult to quantify increases in tourism directly resulting from the Partnership's activities (Countryside Commission 1995c: 76).

Parnerships have also been established on a more local basis, with local authorities working with their regional tourist board to boost tourism in their areas. For example, Eden, in Cumbria, set up a three-year Tourism Action Plan (TAP) in 1988. Eden District Council provided the majority of the funding whilst the Cumbria Tourist Board undertook the co-ordination of the plan, offering advice and employing a Project Manager. The Rural Development Commission was also involved, providing an office for the manager and promoting sources of finance. The main aims of the plan were to extend the visitor season, increase visitors' length of stay and spending, and to ensure a spread of visitors throughout the district. Following the initial success of the TAP it was extended to a fourth year.

A similar scheme is the Tarka Project in North Devon. Named after the book *Tarka the Otter*, the project is an integrated conservation and recreation strategy which aims to develop small scale tourism and leisure activity in the area, but with landscape conservation and enhancement a prime objective. The project is funded by the County Council, the four district councils and the Countryside Commission and its initiatives include the development of a disused railway line into a 180 mile (290 km) long distance walking route (the Tarka Trail), conservation work, and the production of brochures and information leaflets. Other partnership projects include the Peak Tourism Partnership and the Dartmoor Area Tourism Initiative, both of which are described in *Sustainable Rural Tourism*.

Perhaps the main drawback of the partnership approach is the extent to which a true partnership is established. That is, sustainable recreation development requires the involvement of local communities and, therefore, questions must be raised about the extent to which the interests of the tourism and leisure industy dominate the planning process. For example, a proposed traffic management scheme in Borrowdale in the Lake District, designed to reduce the environmental impact of traffic congestion, foundered on the oposition of local traders who feared a loss of business. It has been suggested that community involvement should be the very foundation of sustainable development (see Murphy 1983, 1985 and 1988 and Haywood 1988). Procedures have been proposed for a community based planning procedure (Godfrey 1990), but due to the difficulty in obtaining representative views and involvement it is unlikely that such an approach would be workable for anything but small scale, localised schemes, such as Country Village Weekend Breaks. Nevertheless, the partnership approach signifies a positive planning and management process, taking into account broader environmental and social issues, that goes some way to achieving sustainable development objectives.

UPLAND MANAGEMENT SCHEMES
One of the first attempts to resolve the conflict between recreation, conservation and other land use and to take a more positive approach to countryside management was established in the late 1960s. Experimental schemes, known as the Upland Management Experiments, were set up in the Lake District and Snowdonia National Parks in 1969 (Countryside Commission 1976 and 1979a). Their primary purpose was to resolve the conflicts between the needs of visitors and upland farmers, in particular addressing localised problems of trespass, vandalism, litter and damage to footpaths and walls.

Each experiment centred on the appointment of a project officer who had sufficient funding and autonomy to assist farmers in small scale conservation work, such as repairing gates, stiles and dry stone walls. The success of the experiments, however, depended on the ability of the project officers to establish effective working relationships with all the parties involved in particular conflicts. Thus, the officer would identify a potential area of conflict, bring together the relevant parties, such as landowners, farmers, local authorities and national park authorities, and implement practical solutions. Positive results were achieved, both in conservation work and in improved understanding and relationships between farmers and visitors, but the success was largely attributable to the local, small scale nature of the experiments and the ability of the officers to take immediate, autonomous action on the ground. Nevertheless, the Countryside Commission used the basic principles of the experiments to implement similar countryside management schemes on a larger scale. Project officers, for example, were appointed in 1972 to resolve the serious conflicts between farmers and recreationists in the Bollin Valley near Manchester.

Larger scale countryside management schemes were found to be less immediately successful owing to the length of time it took the project officers to familiarise themselves with an area and to develop effective relationships with landowners and local authorities. Therefore, later schemes were based on area management plans adopted by local authorities.

AREA MANAGEMENT IN THE COUNTRYSIDE
There are relatively few area management schemes in the UK. Those that do exist have been developed close to urban areas to protect threatened landscapes, to regenerate derelict industrial land and to provide new recreational opportunities. They also vary widely in their administrative structure. Some schemes are an association between constituent local authorities working to an agreed plan whereas, uniquely, the Lee Valley Regional Park is managed by an authority which was created by the Lee Valley Regional Park Act 1966.

One example of an area management scheme is the Blackwater Valley Project which is designed to promote conservation and recreation in the

Blackwater River Valley. The area covered by the project lies on the borders of Hampshire, Surrey and Berkshire, is about 14 miles (22 km) long and includes semi-urban and degraded landscapes and unspoilt countryside. The valley was traditionally agricultural but urban development and sand and gravel extraction have changed its character. An estimated 200,000 people live within 1.5 miles (2.5 km) of the river in a number of towns and villages in or near the project area.

The County Councils of Hampshire, Surrey and Berkshire first produced a joint report in 1971 which looked at the likely development of the gravel pits and possible uses, including recreation, once gravel extraction was complete. It was not until 1979, however, that the three County Councils combined with seven district councils and the Countryside Commission to establish the Blackwater Valley Project. Between 1979 and 1986 over 250 acres (101 hectares) were restored, 8 miles (13 km) of riverside path constructed and over 20,000 trees planted. A number of recreational programmes were organised and the valley has increasingly come into recreational use. A survey in 1986 found that recreation had, in fact, become the major land use in the valley, in particular around the worked-out gravel pits which had been restored as lakes. Furthermore, although much development had taken place in the surrounding areas, there had been little development in the valley itself. The future development of the valley as a resource for recreation, building on the Project's initial success, was outlined in the 1987 Blackwater Valley Recreation Strategy. This highlighted the need to develop the image and identity of the valley as an attractive recreational area for local residents and to realise the full potential of the area.

A similar approach, but on a larger scale, was adopted for the development of the Colne Valley Park west of London. In the late 1960s the then Greater London Council and other district authorities set out policies for developing the recreational potential of the area, although the prime purpose was the conservation of the remaining undeveloped rural areas within the park. From 1978 the Countryside Commission has funded a Colne Valley Countryside Management Project to encourage landscape and access improvements. In contrast, the Lee Valley Regional

251

Park, which stretches for 23 miles (37 km) along the River Lee from Ware in Hertfordsire to Limehouse in East London, is controlled by the statutory Lee Valley Regional Park Authority. The main purpose of the Authority is to develop the park as a place for leisure, recreation and sport, and to undertake conservation work including the provision of nature reserves. To this end the Authority is empowered to acquire land and by 1986 over thirty per cent of the park area was under its control. It has been successful in developing a range of leisure facilities, including sports centres, horse-riding facilities and leisure centres, but it has been criticised for its autonomy and lack of an overall landscape strategy (for a full assessment of the Lee Valley Regional Park, see Harrison 1991).

THE NEW NATIONAL FOREST AND COMMUNITY FORESTS
In 1987 the Countryside Commission published a policy document, *Forestry in the Countryside* , calling for a review of existing forestry policy and proposing a new approach to forestry in England. The Commission's proposals were based on the notion that forestry should be multi-purpose. In other words, trees should be planted not only for timber production but also to serve a variety of other purposes, including recreation provision, nature and wildlife conservation, landscape reclamation and enhancement, and alternative agricultural use. The Commission also proposed two major new forestry initiatives; the establishment of a new National Forest in the Midlands and the creation of Community Forests in the countryside bordering a number of major urban centres. The forests were to be similar to the New Forest in Hampshire, that is, a combination of woods, open land, farms, villages and commercial developments rather than simply an area of dense woodland.

There was an enthusiastic response from both national and local government and, following applications from a large number of local authorities, by early 1991 the location of the new National Forest between Leicester, Nottingham and Derby and 12 regional Community Forests had been announced (see Fig.8.3.).

i   The New National Forest
The location of the new National Forest, which includes the sites of the

252

two historic forests of Needwood and Charnwood, has been chosen *because of the widespread and lasting environmental improvement that can be achieved there* (Countryside Commission 1990b). Covering an area of some 200 square miles (502 square km), the dominant land use is agriculture although a significant proportion of the landscape suffers from industrial dereliction. The reclamation of this derelict land will be a primary aim of new woodland planting but the longer term aim of the project is to plant trees in about one third of the total land area of the forest, compared to the current six per cent of the area which is wooded. The objective is to establish seventy per cent of this within the first ten years. It has been estimated that creating the forest will cost an average of £2 million to £3 million over the 30 year development period, with funding coming from a variety of public and private sector and voluntary sources. Farmers and landowners will be given incentives to plant and manage trees and it is expected that a variety of organisations will contribute to the planting and management programme.

The major purposes of the new National Forest are landscape and wildlife conservation, land reclamation, job creation and the provision of a valuable leisure resource in a part of the country that is relatively lacking in countryside recreation opportunities. In 1994 it was announced that a new independent body will be formed to oversee the creation of the forest, beginning its operations in 1995. It will not have any powers; the development of the forest will be dependent on the voluntary co-operation of farmers and landowners, many of whom might perceive tree planting as reducing the flexibility of land use and the capital value of the land. On the other hand, the Ramblers Association see the purpose of the forest as primarily a resource for recreation. Trails, bridleways and cycle routes will form a strategic network of access routes through the forest, linking more major recreational facilities which may be developed on old mineral workings and other derelict land (Countryside Commission 1994b). A variety of quiet, passive activities and more active sports will be catered for and thus, despite widespread public and government support for the project, it is likely to give rise to conflicts similar to those experienced in the wider countryside.

FIGURE 8.3. THE NEW NATIONAL FOREST AND THE TWELVE COMMUNITY FORESTS IN ENGLAND

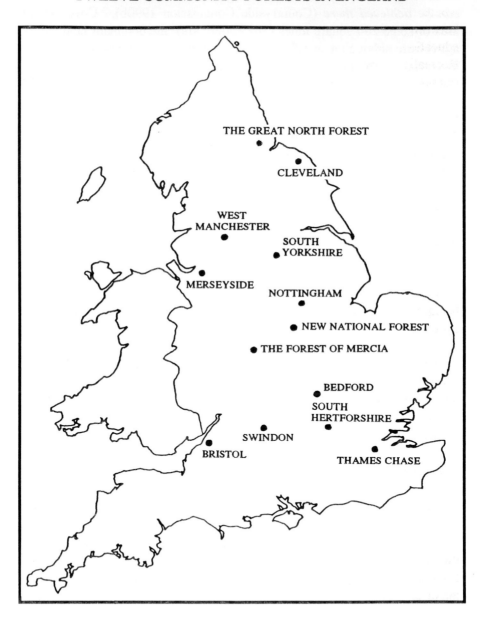

THE GREAT NORTH FOREST

CLEVELAND

WEST MANCHESTER

SOUTH YORKSHIRE

MERSEYSIDE

NOTTINGHAM

NEW NATIONAL FOREST

THE FOREST OF MERCIA

BEDFORD

SOUTH HERTFORSHIRE

SWINDON

BRISTOL

THAMES CHASE

ii Community Forests

The 12 Community Forests are all to be developed on the edges of cities where there is potential for landscape reclamation. Covering areas of between 40 and 80 square miles, they will create a wooded landscape for education, nature conservation, housing, industry and timber production. Recreation provision is also a major objective, with each forest affording opportunities for a variety of informal and organised leisure activities. As with the National Forest, farmers and landowners are expected to make a significant contribution to the creation of the forests by planting trees on marginal or derelict land. However, the main aim of the Community Forest programme is, as the name suggests, to involve local communities. Thus, local schools, amenity societies, churches and voluntary groups and also local businesses will be encouraged to participate in the planning and creation of the forests. Financial support will be provided by the Countryside and Forestry Commissions and by local authorities, although the main burden will fall upon local, as opposed to national, government.

One such forest is the Marston Vale Community Forest in central Bedfordshire. Covering an area of some 61 squre miles (16,000m hectares), the proposed forest will cover a variety of landscapes including up to 4900 acres (2000 hectares) of derelict and damaged land, much of which was used for the extraction of clay for brickmaking. The objectives of the Marston Vale project are to develop and attractive area of woods, lakes and open farmland, to reclaim and conserve the derelict and damaged lands in the 'Brickfield' area and on the Bedford urban fringe, to create a variety of recreational opportunities for local people, and to substantially improve the image of Bedfordshire to potential investors.

The creation of the National and Community Forests are a manifestation of the Countryside Commission's longer term objective of working towards a thriving, multi-purpose, accessible and environmentally healthy countryside (Countryside Comission 1989d). Undoubtedly the primary aims of the forests are conservation and landscape improvement yet, over the 25 to 30 year period during which the forests will develop, they will become an increasingly important new resource for recreation close to major centres of population.

COUNTRYSIDE STEWARDSHIP

Following the publication of its White Paper on the Environment, *This Common Inheritance: Britain's Environmental Strategy* (HMSO 1990), the government invited the Countryside Commission to develop a new strategy for the conservation, re-creation and management of certain areas of the countryside. For this purpose, £13 million was made available to the Commission over a period of three years. As a result, the Commission, in collaboration with English Nature and English Heritage, announced the Countryside Stewardship Scheme in 1991.

In essence the scheme, based on a system of incentive payments and agreements, is designed to combine the interests of conservation and recreation with practical land management and farming. It has four main purposes (Countryside Commission 1991).

(a) **Landscape** To restore characteristic qualities and features to intensively farmed landscape.

(b) **Wildlife** To restore, protect and improve important wildlife habitats.

(c) **History** To protect and maintain important historical and archaeological sites in the countryside.

(d) **Access** To create opportunities for visitors to enjoy the countryside on existing rights of way, through the sensitive provision of new access, and by helping to manage land under visitor pressure.

The scheme is voluntary and open to all farmers, landowners, voluntary organisations and local authorities who are willing to enter into a ten year agreement with the Countryside Commission. Priority is given to those proposals which offer the greatest potential for environmental improvement and public benefit. Indeed, public access and enjoyment is of fundamental importance to the scheme.

Five categories of landscape have been initially targeted to pilot the Countryside Stewardship Scheme, namely chalk and limestone grassland, lowland heath, waterside landscapes, coastal areas and uplands. In each case, incentive payments are available to undertake one or more courses of action. For the uplands, for example, the scheme offers incentive payments for:

(a) the management and restoration of upland meadows, pastures and areas of rough grazing,

(b) the regeneration of heather and other moorland vegetation on enclosed and agriculturally improved land, and

(c) improved access where land is under visitor pressure or where new permissive routes would be beneficial.

Incentive payments for conservation, restoration and allowing access and capital payments for particular work, from waymarking a path to tree and shrub planting, are set out in a schedule and are paid each year in arrears. To receive payments the landowner must fulfil all the conditions in the agreement. Thus, with regard to access, the landowner must allow free access to all the designated land and signpost and waymark routes where appropriate. The land may be closed for up to ten days each year, except on public holidays, and the Countryside Commission may publicise the availability of access to the land.

Since it was established, the Countryside Stewardship Scheme has attracted widespread interest and participation. It has been extended beyond its original three years and is now supported directly by the Ministry of Agriculture, Fisheries and Food. It is a good example of how countryside conservation and recreation can be mutually beneficial to both visitors and landowners with the resource being sustained and enhanced for the enjoyment of future generations. It is not self-sustaining, however; its future success is dependent on the continuing financial support from the government.

RECREATION ON THE URBAN/RURAL FRINGE

As is discussed in Chapter Three, surveys have shown that the majority of visits to the countryside are made by a relatively small proportion of the population. The demand for countryside recreation is largely determined by occupation, income, car ownership and housing location and, as a result, it may be concluded that countryside recreation is a middle class activity. On the other hand, it has also been found that there is little distinction, in terms of occupation and social class, between those who actually participate in recreational activities in the countryside. By inference, therefore, it may be argued that there is a significant proportion of the population, in particular inner city residents on lower incomes who are dependent on public transport, who would visit the countryside if they were able to do so.

Since the 1970s the Countryside Commission has been paying greater attention to improving not only access within the countryside but also the accessibility of the countryside. Indeed, the Commission re-affirmed its commitment to improving the accessibility of the countryside in its 1991 consultation paper, *Visitors to the Countryside*, in which it highlighted the need for better information provision and for fostering greater understanding and confidence amongst infrequent countryside visitors. At a practical level, however, much attention has been focussed on developing recreational opportunities in the urban/rural fringe. In other words, the policy has been to bring the countryside closer to towns and cities to satisfy the perceived supressed and latent demand amongst urban dwellers.

The value of urban fringes, in particular green belts, as a resource for recreation has been recognised for many years. The original purpose of the creation of green belts was to limit the expansion of major urban centres but many are now popular leisure destinations. Derelict industrial areas on the edge of towns and cities are also increasingly becoming the subject of countryside management schemes. The Countryside Commission supports a number of local countryside projects, all of which are involved in both conservation and recreation provision on the urban fringe. On a larger scale, the proposed creation of Community Forests (see above) is evidence of the emphasis being placed on conservation and recreation provision close to major centres of population.

A complete appraisal of the development of urban fringes is beyond the scope of this chapter (see, for example, Elson 1986). Nevertheless, it is important to consider the degree to which the promotion of countryside recreation in the rural fringe actually increases participation amongst disadvantaged or infrequent visitor groups. The provision of facilities or new recreational opportunities on the edge of towns and cities should, logically, appeal to those people who are unable to visit the wider countryside, in particular those who do not have use of a car. Studies have shown, however, that the use of the countryside on the urban fringe is generally local. That is, relatively few inner city residents travel to the urban/rural fringe for recreational purposes. Barnet in Hertfordshire, for example, was the site of a major countryside management experiment in the mid -1970s and yet a later survey found that most visitors came from the immediate vicinity and over fifty per cent of those had walked. Very few visitors came from inner London and only five per cent had travelled by public transport.

A further insight into the value of promoting countryside recreation amongst particular groups was provided by the Operation Gateway experiment in Nottingham in 1983. The purpose of this was encourage low income, non-car owning residents to visit the countryside. With the support of the Countryside Commission, an officer was appointed to set up an information centre, to arrange events for groups as requested, to arrange subsidised transport and to organise host rangers to meet groups at selected sites. Although some success was achieved, the scheme indicated that greater participation in countryside recreation is not necessarily dependent on simply the provision and promotion of facilities and opportunities. In other words, many people prefer to participate in other forms of leisure activity and that, for a variety of reasons, recreation in the countryside does not satisfy their needs. By implication, therefore, the emphasis placed on the promotion of countryside recreation in the urban/rural fringe to satisfy perceived latent or supressed demand may need to be re-assessed in the overall planning and management of tourism and leisure in the countryside (see Countryside Commission 1987e).

TRANSPORT IN THE COUNTRYSIDE

Tourism is synonymous with transport and, in the context of recreation in the countryside, the dominant mode of transport is the motor car. About eighty per cent of all visits to the countryside are made by car and in some areas, such as the Peak District National Park, the proportion of visitors arriving by car is as high as ninety per cent (PPJPB 1989). Nor is the car simply a means of travelling *to* the countryside; touring is one of the most popular recreational activities in the countryside and, for many visitors, the car is an essential element of their enjoyment. It is not surprising, therefore, that road traffic on non-urban roads increased by one third between 1987 and 1994 (Cross 1995).

The car is also the greatest potential threat to the sustainable planning and management of recreation in the countryside and, therefore, effective transport policies are seen as an essential ingredient of sustainable rural tourism development (Countryside Commission 1995c). The car is a major source of pollution, congestion and physical damage and, if current forecasts of car ownership are proved to be correct, the regular traffic jams that now plague towns and cities may soon become commonplace in the countryside. For example, it has been predicted that, in terms of vehicle miles, traffic is likely to increase by between 83 per cent and 142 per cent by 2025; given that 57 per cent of all motorised traffic is on rural roads and and mororways (although only eleven per cent of the population lives outside urban areas), it has been suggested that rural traffic in particular may grow by between 127 per cent and 267 per cent (Countryside Commission 1992c and 1992d). In recent years some popular areas of the countryside, such as the Lake District, have already come close to being gridlocked at peak periods in the summer. Furthermore, widespread car ownership has been instrumental in the reduction in the level of public transport services, severely restricting the mobility of both rural and urban residents who do not own, or do not wish to use, a car.

It is not only the sheer volume of cars that is a threat to the rural environment. As long ago as 1945, when car ownership was enjoyed by only a small minority of the population, John Dower voiced his concern about the potentially destructive effects of expanding and improving the road network to accommodate more vehicles.

That great damage, direct and indirect, to landscape beauty, to farming, to the peace and quiet of the country and to its enjoyment by visitors and residents, must follow - and has followed - from wholesale widenings, straightenings and flattenings, and from the encouragement they give to ever-heavier and ever-faster traffic, is plain enough from examples in many parts of the country.

(Dower 1945)

Yet, despite recommendations from successive national park review committees (Sandford 1974 and Edwards 1991) that the preservation of the rural environment should take precedence over road building and improvement, the government has, until recently, continued to pursue an extensive road building programme both in the national parks and in the wider countryside. The 1989 White Paper *Roads to Prosperity,* for example, announced a ten year, £20 billion road building scheme, justifying the investment on the perceived environmental benefit of transferring traffic from towns and villages onto bypasses through the countryside. In October 1994, however, the Royal Commission on Environmental Pollution published its long awaited report in which it was suggested that building more roads is not the solution; transport needs to be managed by encouraging the use of public transport and other, greener forms of transport, such as cycling. It confirmed the widely held view that road building does not simply accommodate, but also creates traffic (the M25, for example, created forty per cent more traffic within five years) and the report also challenged the traditional arguments concerning the benefits of a car-dominated society. Recent reductions in public expenditure have signalled a reduction in new road developments and the £42.5 grant from the Millenium Commission to the development of the National Cycle Network in 1995 (Sustrans 1995) indicates support for alternative forms of transport, but it remains to be seen to what extent the Government is adopting a *transport*, as opposed to a *roads*, policy (Cross 1995).

Effective transport policies are, therefore, of central importance to the sustainable planning and management of countryside recreation but, for the organisations responsible for balancing recreation provision with conservation, transport is probably the most difficult issue to resolve. In the more popular areas of the countryside the presence of large numbers of cars is contrary to the notion of quiet enjoyment and the conservation and enhancement of the natural scenery. Yet any policy designed to reduce the volume of traffic, and hence visitors, in the countryside is likely to be seen as a threat to the livelihood of rural tourism and leisure businesses, although many car-borne day visitors contribute relatively little to the local economy. The problem is particularly acute in the national parks. The national park authorities have no power to restrict traffic or parking and, in response to the overwhelming use of the car, most amenities and facilities are, in fact, designed for the motorist. Visitor centres, for example, are often only accessible by car and many publicised walks are circular routes which start and finish at a car park.

There are a number of potential solutions to the problem of road congestion in the countryside. Before considering these, it is useful to outline the direct and indirect impacts of the motor car on the rural environment.

i The Impact of the Motor Car
The most commonly quoted environmental impact of cars is pollution. It has been found that, of the gases that contribute to the greenhouse effect and/or acid rain, vehicle emissions account for 16 per cent of the total UK production of carbon dioxide, 45 per cent of nitrogen oxides, 28 per cent of hydrocarbons, and 85 per cent of carbon monoxide (Transport 2000, 1989). The level of emissions is greater when traffic is slow moving or static and such pollution is known to have destroyed thousands of acres of woodland in Scandinavia and Germany. The effects are also cumulative, countering the arguments that traffic is only a seasonal or peak period problem in the countryside.

Illegal roadside parking when car parks are full causes extensive damage to verges. Despite large car parks in the tiny village of Malham in the

Yorkshire Dales, for example, it is not unusual to see a line of cars parked on the grass verges for up to a quarter of a mile along the country lanes. Long queues of slow moving or stationary vehicles visually intrude on the scenic quality of the countryside whilst excessive noise levels can also disturb the peace of the rural environment. Traffic congestion can disrupt the lives of local communities; many villages suffer from intolerable levels of traffic, causing noise and inconvenience and, in some cases, endangering local residents.

The by-products of motorised transport impact on the rural environment. Car parks, lay-bys, traffic signs, facilities, such as roadside restaurants and garages, and new roads are all intrusive, man-made creations designed to serve the needs of a car dependent society. They can also have indirect impacts. Car parks, for example, tend to concentrate visitors at particular sites, thereby causing excessive erosion on nearby footpaths.

In a more general sense, the motor car is the least sustainable mode of transport in terms of its impact on the enviroment and society. For the individual traveller it is one of the cheapest forms of motorised transport and is becoming increasingly so. Yet the costs to society in terms of energy use, pollution, land use, health care and, of course, road building are virtually incalulable. It has been traditionally argued that society benefits as only about forty per cent of the income from road tax (about £16 billion each year) is put back in to road building, maintenance and policing, but it has been estimated that the costs of congestion, pollution and traffic accidents cost the country in excess of £24 billion a year (Pearce 1993). It has also been estimated that the taxation on car use (eg duty on petrol and road tax) would have to be increased by a factor of five for these costs to be met (Whitelegg 1992).

Despite these acknowledged and well publicised disbenefits of the widespread use of the motor car it remains the most popular and flexible means of transport. Moreover, it is likely to remain so while the government continues to pursue the policy of building more roads to accommodate greater levels of traffic. It is generally accepted that providing more roads on the grounds of economic efficiency simply increases the level of car usage; more roads means more cars, more pollution and more damage to the environment, and it may not be long before the joke about motorways being no more than linear car parks becomes an everyday reality.

ii Solutions to the Traffic Problem
Much attention has been recently focused on the problem of traffic congestion in towns and cities. Proposed solutions have ranged from the implementation of park-and-ride schemes, already successful in Oxford and York, to the introduction of road tolls. The problem is perceived to be less severe in the countryside but, nevertheless, it is equally vital that a solution is found. There are four possible courses of action.

(a) To allow congestion to act as its own deterrent.
The simplest course of action may be to do nothing and allow the countryside to become so busy that people no longer wish to visit it. However, although some potential visitors may decide not to visit the countryside at popular times of the year, such as summer bank holiday weekends, sitting in traffic jams seems to have become an accepted aspect of leisure travel. Furthermore, throughout much of the year the countryside is relatively uncongested with traffic and, therefore, a more positive approach is required to address the longer term negative impacts.

(b) To improve the road network and car park provision.
The straightening and widening of roads, the building of bypasses, and the provision of more car parks in rural destinations improves accessibility to and within the countryside. These have a physical impact on the countryside, however, diminishing the character of an area and encouraging yet more visitors to travel by car. Since the 1970s it has been accepted, particularly in the national parks, that appropriate transport management schemes should be established to suit the level of traffic to the existing road network rather than adapting roads to handle greater volumes of traffic.

(c) To restrict or regulate car access.
The restriction or regulation of traffic is commonplace in many towns and

cities. One way systems, barriers to entry and restricted parking are all measures to improve the flow of traffic through urban centres and to restrict access through residential areas. Park-and-ride systems have been successful in limiting the amount of traffic in a number of towns and it is likely that experimental schemes, such as road tolls, will be implemented in the near future. One of the first traffic regulation schemes in the countryside was the Goyt Valley Traffic Experiment in the Peak District in 1972 (PPJPB 1972). At peak periods the road through the valley was closed and visitors were required to park their cars and continue their journey on a free mini-bus service. More recently there have been road closures in the Derwent Valley in the Peak District with visitors being encouraged to explore the region on bicycles. These schemes, however, have only a local and temporary beneficial impact and do not provide a real solution, or alternative, to the use of the car in the countryside.

(d) To promote and develop effective public transport services.
Throughout the first half of the twentieth century most people travelled to the countryside by train or bus but the rapid increase in car ownership from 1950 onwards steadily reduced the number of passengers on public transport. The 1963 Beeching Report led to the closure of over one third of the existing rural railways and stations and road building programmes overtook the investment in public transport systems. By the 1970s the high cost of imported oil, increasing road congestion and a greater awareness of the needs of non-car owners renewed official interest in public transport (DART 1976). However, the deregulation, or privatisation, of bus companies following the Transport Act 1985 did not favour rural areas where competition for routes was not viable. Many routes were closed on economic grounds, fares increased and passenger number fell by up to 25 per cent (Speakman 1995), resulting in yet greater dependence on the car for both visitors and rural communities.

An integrated and efficient public transport system is seen by many as the only realistic solution to the problem of transport to and in the countryside (see, for example, Speakman 1989). The next section considers the advantages and problems associated with the development of recreational public transport.

265

iii Public Transport in the Countryside
(a) Advantages
Public transport to the countryside brings both social and environmental benefits. Although, on average, about 66 per cent of the population own, or have use of, a car, it is by no means an even spread. In 1987, for example, the proportion of people living in households without a car was as low as 20 to 25 per cent in certain prosperous urban or and rural areas. In Manchester, however, the figure was 47 per cent. Also, the concept of *car in household* can be misleading; teenage children or the elderly, for example, may not have the ability or opportunity to drive a car (Countryside Commission 1987). Thus, the provision of an integrated public transport network would improve the accessibility of the countryside to a significant proportion of the population.

Environmentally, public transport is much less harmful. A large coach, for example, can carry the equivalent number of passengers as perhaps 30 cars yet uses much less road space. Nor do buses have to be parked in a car park or on the roadside all day. The damaging effects of the motor car are further reduced if rail transport and local, sustainable forms of transport, such as cycling, are linked into the overall network. Public transport can also improve the enjoyment of a visit to the countryside. The opportunity to enjoy the scenery without the responsibility of driving or parking can be an attraction in itself whilst public transport also enables visitors to explore the wider countryside rather than being tied to circular walks based on a car park. Yet, despite these advantages, there are a number of problems associated with the development of public transport.

(b) The Viability of Public Transport.
Economic Viability A major hurdle to be overcome is the economic viability of public transport. Following deregulation, bus companies have to be profitable and, therefore, there is little financial incentive to provide a service in areas where there is limited local demand and only irregular, sesasonal demand from visitors. In rural Wales, for example, deregulation of the buses led to redundancies, lower wages, and a choice of different coloured buses, but no increase in the level of service (Moyes 1988). The Kentmere Valley, a popular walking destination in the Lake District, has

no bus service as the route is considered to be uneconomic (Bingham 1990). The national park authority has, therefore, proposed the building of a car park to accommodate car-borne visitors.

Even the popular Hadrian's Wall bus service is unprofitable. Launched in 1974 by the Northumberland National Park and linking with regular rail services, it enables visitors to walk along the wall and to catch a bus back to their cars. During its six week annual operating period, the service covers between 50 and 60 per cent of its operating costs with the shortfall covered by the park authority and the Countryside Commission (Countryside Commission 1987). Thus, a substantial degree of financial support is required for any rural public transport service to be viable, support that is unlikely to be forthcoming under the present national transport policy.

Integration In order for public transport to provide an efficient alternative mode of transport, in particular matching the flexibility of the car, the system must be regular, economical and, above all, integrated. That is, different services must be co-ordinated so that the visitor is able to travel to his or her destination without undue delays when changing buses or changing from a train to a bus. Deregulation, however. has led to bus companies becoming subject to Competition Law. As a result, the degree of co-operation necessary between separate bus companies for the provision of integrated regional, or even national, sevices might be deemed unfair competition and has, therefore, suffered. Likewise, publicity for bus services has diminished since deregulation. A fully integrated, national public transport service is also dependent on co-operation between different modes of transport. Visitors may wish, for example, to travel to a region by train and then on to their destination by bus. Although inter-modal services, such as the Wayfarer Project, have been created regionally, it is unlikely that national integration could be achieved.

Public Attitudes Since the 1950s, British society has become increasingly car dependent. Even the shortest journeys are now made by car and, for example, the development of vast, out-of-town hypermarkets and leisure centres has further increased the perceived dependence on the car. No other form of transport can match its flexibility, privacy and comfort and it has become, in effect, *a detachable extension to the home* (Bannister 1988). If the expense and inconvenience of the existing public transport system is taken into account it is, perhaps, not surprising that eighty per cent of countryside visitors travel by car.

The question that must be addressed is, would the provision of an efficient, cheap, regular and reliable public transport service to the countryside induce sufficient numbers of visitors to leave their car at home? Recent surveys have indicated that, on the one hand, many motorists would prefer to use public transport, on the other hand, it has also been found that the majority of motorists would still drive their own cars even if significant improvements were made to public transport services. Therefore, even though there is more widespread acceptance of the environmental benefits of public transport, few people are prepared to leave their car at home. In other words, an improved public transport service is unlikely to attract a significant number of new customers unless measures, such as large increases in road tax or restrictions on access, are also introduced.

iv   Public Transport in Action
Despite the inherent problems in developing and promoting a rural public transport system and the government's commitment to road building and improvement programmes, a number of public transport schemes have been established in the countryside. For example, the Snowdon Sherpa, which operates in the Snowdonia National Park in the summer months, is a network of three services with day and family rover tickets providing an economical means of travelling to and around the park. The Sherwood Forester, run by Nottinghamshire County Council, links Nottingham with five country parks. In 1985 it carried over 60,000 passengers, forty per cent of whom came from car owning households. On the other hand, in 1990 a new Sunday afternoon bus service between Ambleside and Coniston in the Lake District was, ironically, abandoned because traffic congestion made it impossible to run a regular, efficient service. Many other counties have established seasonal or weekend services but the Wayfarer Project, initiated by the Countryside Commission in 1981, has

been the most comprehensive attempt yet to promote recreational public transport (Countryside Commission 1985).

The Project was a three year transport experiment involving buses, trains and canals throughout Greater Manchester and West Yorkshire. It was designed to encourage people to visit countryside attractions and destinations, including the Peak District and Yorkshire Dales National Parks, using existing public transport services. The scheme was sponsored jointly by Tatton Park in Cheshire, the National Museum of Film, Photography and Television in Bradford and the relevant county councils. The ability to offer through tickets and daily and weekly passes was also considered essential to the success of the project. However, the most significant feature of the Wayfarer Project and, indeed, of other successful public transport schemes, was a strong marketing campaign. In other words, *any recreational transport scheme is only as good as its marketing* (Countryside Commission 1985).

Most public transport schemes are also heavily subsidised, seasonal and localised. Therefore, given the perceived dependence on the motor car, it is likely that a widespread shift to the development and use of recreational public transport in the countryside will be dependent on a combination of measures, including higher taxes on motoring, restrictions on car access, greater investment and co-ordination in public transport, a radical alteration in national transport policies, and, of course, a change in the attitudes of the motorist. In some areas, a proactive approach is being taken to solve some of these problems; the Lake District Traffic Management Initiative, for example, is an integrated project based upon the development of a roads hierarchy, linking public transport to countryside access needs, and effective marketing. However, unless all these issues are overcome, the use of the car in the countryside will remain the greatest obstacle to sustainable planning and management.

SUMMARY
The planning and management of recreation in the countryside has, in the past, usually been in response to increasing demands and pressures. In recent years, however, recreation has impinged on many other aspects of

countryside planning, necessitating a more positive, proactive approach. The first attempt to resolve potential conflicts between visitors and oher countryside users were local countryside management schemes, such as the Upland Management Experiments. The success of these led to similar schemes being established inother areas, including the urban/rural fringe.

Because of the need to maintain a balance between the needs of visitors, local communities, and the conservation of the environment as the basic resource that attracts and supports tourism and leisure, a sustainable approach to planning and management has now been adopted. That is, recreation is planned so that the benefits to visitors and local people are optimised whilst he impacts on the environment are minimised. At the same time, it has been recognised that tourism and leisure can play a positive role in the conservation of the countryside. Some smaller scale projects, such as Country Village Weekend Breaks, embrace the principles of sustainable development and a number of other schemes, including the partnership approach, community forests, area management and countryside stewardship, attempt to integrate the provision of recreation with conservation and the needs of local people.

Nevertheless, questions need to be raised about the viability of sustainable planning and management. The tourism and leisure industry comprises thousands of small, private businesses, many of which may be influenced more by short-term financial considerations rather than longer-term environmental planning. The success of sustainable development is also dependent on the full co-operation and involvement of local communities. This might be difficult, if not impossible, to achieve except in the most smallest of schemes. Perhaps most importantly, sustainable tourism and leisure in the countryside is dependent on sustainable transport policies which, in short, require an alternative to the private motor car. Thus, although there is widespread support for the adoption of sustainable planning and management principles, putting them into practice may be more difficult.

Case Study: The Settle-Carlisle Railway

On April 11th 1989 it was announced that, after a six year battle, the 72 mile (116 km) railway line between Settle in North Yorkshire and Carlisle in Cumbria (Figure 8.4.) would not be closed. The announcement was a victory for the Settle-Carlisle Joint Action Committee which had campaigned vigorously against British Rail's proposal to close the line but, more importantly, it demonstrated that the social benefits of retaining a public transport service through a remote rural area can outweigh the financial arguments for closure.

Built between 1869 and 1876, the Settle to Carlisle railway is a monument to Victorian civil engineering.   Along its route it passes through 14 tunnels, crosses 21 bridges, including the famous Ribblehead Viaduct, and at Dent it is proclaimed to be the highest railway in England. The line is not, however, simply an attraction; it is a lifeline for the people who live in the isolated upland Yorkshire and Cumbrian villages. Reduced bus services and poor roads mean that, for many people, the train is the only way of reaching schools, shops or hospitals. During the winter months, when the roads are often impassable, the rail link is even more important.

Despite the dependence of local communities, on the railway the level of service, in terms of both the number of trains and the number of stations, was gradually reduced during the 1960s and 1970s. As a result the route suffered a serious fall in income and in 1983 British Rail announced its intention to close the line. The decision was taken on financial grounds because, by 1982, the line was losing an estimated £1 million annually. Many of its large, stone-built viaducts were also in need of urgent repair, in particular the Ribblehead Viaduct which, at over 1310 feet (400 meters) long, 110 feet (30 meters) high and with 24 arches, is the centrepiece of the line. British Rail claimed that to repair this one structure would cost up to £6 million, although this later proved to be a gross over-estimate. By 1989 the cost had come down to £1.5 million.

The closure announcement was immediately opposed by both local and national groups. Not only were the financial figures disputed, but to counter British Rail's argument that most passengers on the Settle-Carlisle route would simply transfer to other lines it was also found that up to eighty per cent of passengers would not travel on another rail route. In other words, they travelled on the Settle-Carlisle train because they liked the journey.

The closure proposal was subject to public hearings which were conducted by the Transport Users' Consultative Committees (TUCCs) for north-east and north-west England in 1986. A total of 22,000 objections were received and the hearings lasted twenty days. Most of the evidence was concerned with the problems that closure would cause to local communities but it was also pointed out that the town of Settle is highly dependent on the income from tourists. A survey in 1985 had found that 36 per cent of visitors would not have gone to Settle had there been no rail service. Therefore, the impending closure of the line presented a serious threat to the local economy.

The TUCCs concluded that, on the basis of the hardship that would be caused to local communities, the line should not be closed. The route was also becoming much more popular; between 1983 and 1989 passenger journeys rose from 90,000 to about 500,000 annually, and revenue for 1988-89 was £1.4 million. Some 27 months after the hearings the government announced that permission to close the line was to be refused. The decision was based on social and economic considerations, improved numbers of passengers, the reduced cost of repairing the Ribblehead Viaduct and the willingness of local authorities and other organisations to support the line.

Much of the increasing success of the Settle-Carlisle line is attributable to the level of publicity its impending closure caused and, at the same time, a strong marketing campaign. The route is now a major tourist attraction in its own right as well as being an environmentally friendly means of transporting large numbers of visitors through some of Englands finest upland country. Since 1992, the line has been run by the Settle and Carlisle Railway Development Company, a limited company with a Board of Directors made up of representatives from the Cumbria Tourist Board, the Rural Development Commission, the English Tourist Board, Regional Railways and other public and private sector organisations. Its mission is to safeguard the future of the railway whilst seeking out opportunities to promote development and bring economic and social benefits to the region. Rail privatisation represents a further threat to the long term future of the line, but there is no doubt that the Settle-Carlisle route fulfils a vital social role for the local communities, that the level of service has improved since the early 1980s, that the success of line is proof that the demand for rail travel exists and, finally, that a well-marketed, quality public transport service is still viable.

FIGURE 8.4. THE SETTLE-CARLISLE RAILWAY

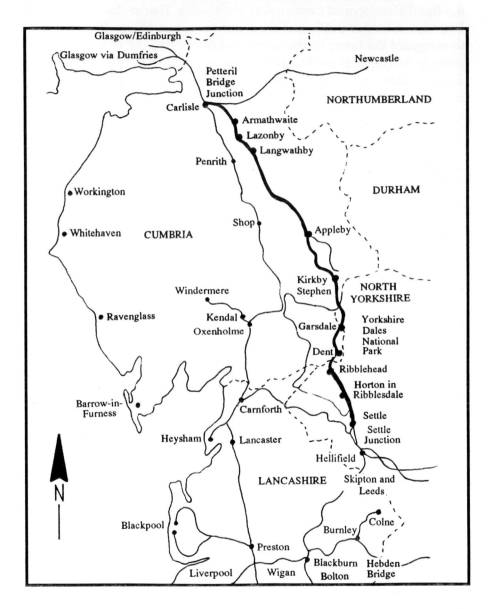

Chapter Nine

Visitor Management in the Countryside

INTRODUCTION

The idea that some degree of control or influence should be imposed on visitors in the countryside is an anathema to many people. The supporters of the freedom to roam campaigns would, in particular, find the notion of visitor management a direct contradiction to the ethos of countryside recreation. Indeed, *regulations are the antithesis of recreation, which connotes the spirit of freedom and spontaneity in the voluntary pursuit of pleasurable and rewarding experience in a preferred setting* (Jim 1989).

Nevertheless, such is the level and diversity of demand for tourism and leisure in the countryside that some form of visitor management is a vital ingredient of sustainable planning and management. In other words, the policies and plans of the organisations concerned with the promotion and provision of countryside recreation are just one side of the sustainable development coin. Countryside recreation is about people visiting the countryside and it is equally important that their activities and behaviour are also appropriate and sustainable.

Visitor management is necessary for a number of reasons. All visitors, knowingly or unknowingly, have an impact on the rural environment and in the more popular areas, in particular the national parks, the quality and attractiveness of the countryside is in danger of becoming seriously degraded. Thus, steps must be taken to minimise any further damage to the physical fabric of the countryside. (See Sidaway 1988 for an examination of the conflicts between recreation and nature conservation). Some areas are also more robust and better able to withstand visitor pressures than others and it is, therefore, essential that both the level and type of activity are appropriate to the capacity (see Chapter Two) and the character of the destination area. On the other hand, in comparison to the honeypot destinations, some parts of the countryside are relatively under-utilised for recreation and visitor management can play a role in the redistribution of recreational use. The activities of some visitors may also lessen the enjoyment or experience of other visitors and so it is necessary to ensure that the recreational use of the countryside is managed so that the benefits to all visitors are optimised.

In short, both the planning and development of the countryside and its recreational use require careful and effective management to ensure that the quality and character of the resource are maintained for the enjoyment and well-being of future generations of visitors and rural communities. This final chapter explores the concept of visitor management in the countryside and considers the ways in which it can contribute to the sustainable development of tourism and leisure. In conclusion, the controversial notion that the recreational use of the countryside incurs costs which should be borne by visitors is also discussed.

PRINCIPLES OF VISITOR MANAGEMENT
Visitor management encompasses a range of measures that may be introduced to directly or indirectly influence the activities and behaviour of visitors in the countryside. In other words, it is concerned with exerting varying degrees of control over where people go in the countryside and what they do when they get there.

Countryside recreation, however, is generally synonymous with unplanned, informal activities and, for many people, the attraction of the countryside as a recreational destination is the contrast it offers to the order and constraints of everyday urban life. Thus, although the overall aims of visitor management are to minimise the negative impacts of recreation on the environment and to enhance the enjoyment and experience of visitors, it must be implemented in a manner which maintains the sense of freedom, choice and spontaneity that is the basis of countryside recreation. That is, whilst visitor management is a necessary aspect of the management of tourism and leisure, it should take into account the needs and motivations of visitors, it should be as unobtrusive as possible, and it should not reduce the attraction of the countryside to potential visitors.

Depending on the level of use and the character of an area this might not always be possible but, in general, there are three categories, or levels, of visitor management (Jim 1989). At its least regulatory level, visitor management may simply be a means of influencing visitor behaviour through, for example, publicity campaigns or the provision of information services. The impacts of the popularity or over-use of some areas, on the other hand, may be reduced by redistributing use. That is, the purpose of visitor management may be to encourage people to visit other, less popular destinations. In the extreme, visitor management may take form of controls and measures designed to limit or ration use by, for example, restricting access. The following sections consider each of these methods in turn, giving examples of how they may be put into practice.

i Influencing Visitor Behaviour
In many cases the harmful impacts of tourism and leisure in the countryside result from the inappropriate behaviour or activities of individual visitors rather than the overall number or volume of visitors at any one site. The problems of litter and pollution, for example, would be minimised if all visitors put their rubbish into litter bins or took it home with them. People listening to loud transistor radios can spoil the peaceful enjoyment of the countryside for large numbers of visitors and some activities, such as certain motorised sports, can both impact on the environment and conflict with other activities. A common example of the latter is the conflict between water sports enthusiasts, such as jet skiers, and people participating in quieter activities, such as fishing or sailing.

Whilst some impacts and conflicts arise from selfish or thoughtless behaviour, most visitors may simply be unaware of the potentially harmful environmental effects of their recreational activities in the countryside. Wandering off designated footpaths, leaving gates open allowing animals to stray or lighting camp fires can all have serious impacts on the environment and give rise to conflicts between visitors and landowners or farmers yet, more often than not, such behaviour is a result of ignorance rather than malicious intent. Thus, influencing visitor behaviour is concerned with both improving visitors' attitudes towards the recreational use of the countryside and the enjoyment of other visitors, and increasing people's awareness of conservation issues and the need to respect, and contribute to, the rural environment.

These objectives may be achieved in a number of ways.

(a) Codes of Conduct

One of the earliest attempts to influence the behaviour of visitors in the countryside was the introduction of the Country Code in 1953 (see Figure 9.1.).

FIGURE 9.1. THE COUNTRY CODE

Enjoy the countryside and respect its life and work
Guard against all risk of fire
Fasten all gates
Keep your dogs under close control
Keep to public paths across farmland
Use gates and stiles to cross fences, hedges and walls
Leave livestock, crops and machinery alone
Take your litter home
Help to keep all water clean
Protect wildlife, plants and trees
Take special care on country roads
Make no unnecessary noise

Many people are aware of the Country Code and research has shown that up to 75 per cent of visitors in the countryside can recall at least one of its points. It is, however, very general in its approach, it concentrates mainly on visitor behaviour on agricultural land and it does little to raise visitors' awareness of the broader issues related to the sustainable use of the countryside as a resource for recreation. The Countryside Commission has, therefore, propose a new code for the "green" countryside visitor (see Figure 9.2.).

FIGURE 9.2. GUIDE FOR THE GREEN TOURIST

Consider the effect of your visit wherever you travel - at home, abroad and especially in the world's most beautiful places

Take time to learn in advance about the place you are going to visit

Wherever possible, stay in small-scale, locally owned accommodation

Show friendship, respect local custom and lifestyles, support skills, services and produce

Whenever possible, travel by your own muscle power - on foot or cycle - or use public transport

Spend sufficient time in an area to get to know and understand it

Support the conservation of natural beauty throughout the world

Source: Countryside Commission 1991a

The purpose of the "green" code of conduct is to encourage visitors to act responsibly in the countryside at the same time as supporting the conservation of the rural resource and contributing to the economic and social well-being of rural communities. In other words, it is a set of guidelines for the sustainable use of the countryside.

In line with the growing awareness of the need to minimise the impacts of recreational activities on the countryside and to reduce conflicts with other users, codes of conduct have been introduced for specific activities and sports. The National Caving Association, for example, has published a conservation code which lists ways in which cavers should behave to ensure that caves and cave wildlife are maintained and protected from damage or destruction. Many other countryside activities, including climbing and mountain biking, are also subject to codes of conduct. Similarly, sustainable tourism development projects have highlighted the need to encourage visitors to be environmentally responsible. For example, the Dartmoor Area Tourism Initiative Project published the *Green Visitor Guide* and the Norfolk Coast Project placed emphasis on drawing up and publicising codes of practice in holiday guides and other publicity material. Unfortunately, however, the major drawback of all such codes as a visitor management tool is, of course, that they are not legally binding and, furthermore, their effectiveness is difficult to monitor. That is, codes of conduct are, essentially, a set of guidelines for responsible or appropriate behaviour. The degree to which they are adhered to is totally dependent on the willingness of individual visitors to adapt their behaviour and their ability to accept their responsibility to the environment.

(b) Marketing and Information
Marketing and information provision are two important means of changing or influencing the behaviour of visitors to the countryside. The difference between the two is not always distinct; the provision of information is often an element of the broader marketing process but, generally, marketing can have an influence on who visits the countryside and where they go whereas information provision is designed to influence the behaviour of visitors once they have arrived in the countryside. Together they play an important role in vistor management, minimising the negative impacts of tourism and leisure whilst encouraging the sustainable use of the countryside for recreation.

The marketing of tourism and leisure is a broad subject beyond the scope of this chapter (see, for example, Middleton 1988 or Holloway and Plant 1992). Within the context of visitor management, however, it can have an important influence on visitor behaviour. Alternative under-utilised or more robust areas of the countryside can be heavily promoted to encourage visitors away from the more traditional, popular destinations, thereby reducing the impacts of visitor pressure. The Cumbria Tourist Board, for example, is committed to promoting tourism and leisure in areas outside the Lake District National Park, such as the Eden Valley and the Cumbrian coast, in order to alleviate the problems of excessive numbers of visitors within the park. This strategy is combined with the policy of promoting the Lake District as a destination for longer staying, higher spending visitors to optimise the economic benefits of tourism (CTB 1990). Similarly, since the late 1980s, South Somerset District Council has been promoting the district for tourism in an attempt, although primarily for economic reasons, to gain a bigger share of the county's tourism, most of which was going to Exmoor or the coast. On the other hand, the marketing of alternative destinations in an attempt to relieve visitor pressure in popular areas is considered by some to be an undesirable course of action. It is seen as a way of spreading, rather than containing, the impacts of tourism and leisure and so, for example, the Friends of the Lake District, the major conservation organisation in the region, is firmly opposed to the Cumbria Tourist Board's strategy.

Effective marketing can also influence the type, or mix, of visitors in the countryside. Depending on its characteristics, a particular area or attraction can be marketed to specific target groups. Thus, staying visitors as opposed to day visitors, special interest groups as opposed to general recreationists, or public transport users as opposed to car drivers may be encouraged to visit a destination in order to ensure its sustainable recreational use. At the same time, seasonal variations in demand, and the resulting economic uncertainty, may be reduced through the marketing and promotion of low season breaks.

Marketing as a visitor management tool is not always a positive activity. That is, popular or over-visited sites or areas can be de-marketed to reduce demand. For example, some popular National Trust properties, such as Sissinghurst Gardens in Kent, are no longer actively promoted by the Trust and the famous Lyke Wake Walk in North Yorkshire is now omitted from Ordnance Survey maps owing to the serious erosion problems caused by thousands of walkers. The plethora of guide books now available, other information sources and the reputation of particular sites, however, renders de-marketing a less effective means of influencing visitor behaviour. Furthermore, marketing as a means of influencing visitor behaviour is only likely to be effective when it is directed towards new or infrequent countryside visitors. That is, regular visitors who are familiar with a site or area are unlikely to be influenced by marketing or information campaigns.

Once visitors have arrived in the countryside the provision of information can modify or change their behaviour at the same time as enhancing their enjoyment or experience. At the simplest level, information points, display boards, maps and signs direct visitors along certain routes and to particular sites whilst other areas are protected. In most cases, visitors are unaware that their freedom of choice has been restricted. The use of signs, for example, was an important element in the successful Tarn Hows management scheme which was designed to conserve and protect one of the Lake District's most popular beauty spots (Countryside Commission 1977). In recent years, however, information provision has evolved into the process of interpretation.

Whilst it is difficult to accurately define interpretation as a visitor management tool it is, nevertheless, becoming an increasingly popular means of both informing and educating visitors and influencing their opinions and attitudes. In essence, interpretation is an extension of the provision of information. However, rather than simply conveying facts by traditional methods it seeks to explain and generate an understanding of the countryside, presenting a complete picture through a variety of media. In particular, it is designed to be a two-way process which involves the visitor and elicits a response. In other words, interpretation is a vistor experience which describes the countryside and the relationship between its historical, geographical, geological, wildlife and human characteristics. By involving the visitor in the interpretation process it seeks to develop an appreciation of the countryside which, in turn, leads to more appropriate and considerate behaviour in the countryside.

Interpretation can be presented in a number of ways. It can involve visitor participation, such as guided nature walks or self-directed walks using maps, printed information or listening posts, or it can take the form of lectures or slide shows. Static displays, such as photographs, models and life-size reconstructions, are common interpretative techniques whilst various forms of audio visual presentations are widely used. At certain sites, such as at Fountains Abbey in North Yorkshire, purpose built visitor centres house interpretative displays. Technology has provided new interpretative techniques; sounds and smells are recreated to increase realism whilst at the Jorvik Centre in York visitors are transported back through time to the Viking era in specially designed 'time capsules'. Live performances, such as mock battles by the Sealed Knot or working museums with staff in period costume, also form part of the interpretative process.

Little information is available as to how far interpretation influences or modifies visitor behaviour and there are two inherent problems in using interpretation as a visitor management tool. Firstly, its popularity might lead to some locations or sites being unnecessarily interpreted and, secondly, as interpretation techniques become more sophisticated there is a danger that the display itself becomes the visitor attraction rather than the site that it is designed to interpret.

(c) Countryside Rangers

Countryside rangers are an important link in the visitor management process. Their original function, as defined in the National Parks and Access to the Countryside Act 1949, was to enforce bye-laws and to assist the public where necessary. Since then their role has developed and much of their work is now concerned with practical, on the ground activities such as essential conservation and repair work, footpath maintenance and waymarking, and general site management. Within their position as the link between visitors and farmers, landowners and local communities, however, personal, rather than practical, skills are becoming an increasingly important requirement and one of their prime tasks, as defined by the Countryside Commission, is to enhance visitors' enjoyment through interpretation and information provision (Countryside Commission 1979b). They are also expected to protect visitors from known hazards and to ensure that vistors behave in a manner that is appropriate to the characteristics of the site and other people's enjoyment of it.

Thus, countryside rangers are able to influence visitor behaviour through interpretative activities, such as leading guided walks, giving lectures and talks to vaious groups, and involving local groups and communities in countryside management schemes. They are also able to take immediate, on-site action to ensure that visitors behave in a responsible manner. In most cases, inappropriate behaviour, such as straying onto private land, can be rectified by giving advice although certain bye-laws which, for example, forbid fishing ot the use of motorised transport, may need to be enforced. In the extreme, stronger action and he involvement of the police may be necessary to prevent illegal activities, such as poaching.

Given the drawbacks of codes of conduct and marketing and information as visitor management tools, the most effective and immediate way of influencing visitor behaviour is, therefore, through the work of countryside rangers. Although information or education programmes are necessary to ensure widespread appreciation of the need for sustainable recreational activities in the countryside, they may take a long time to bear fruit. Rangers, on the other hand, are able to take immediate action to rectify inappropriate activities but, inevitably, their effectiveness is constrained by the number of rangers it is possible to employ and the need to minimise the apparent policing of the countryside.

ii Redistributing Visitor Demand

Influencing visitor behaviour is, perhaps, the most desirable form of visitor management as it limits the extent to which the enjoyment and recreational use of the countryside is perceived to be regulated or controlled. In the more popular areas of the countryside or at popular attractions and destinations, however, where the impacts of tourism and leisure are greatest, informal visitor management is often insufficient to ensure the sustainable use of the resource. That is, where excessive numbers of visitors are degrading both the physical and social environment and the enjoyment of visitors it may be necessary to redistribute use to other areas or destinations. Furthermore, some areas are less or better able to sustain different types of activity or levels of use than others, whilst conflict can also arise between different recreational activities. The purpose of the redistribution of visitor demand is, therefore, to match recreational demand with the carrying capacity of a destination or attraction at the same time as ensuring that the type of activity undertaken is appropriate to both the setting and the enjoyment of other visitors.

Visitor redistribution can be applied at a regional level or on a local, site basis. However, it is important to consider the total recreational use of the countryside when managing the distribution or spread of demand. In some cases, for example, redistributing use may simply spread the impacts of tourism and leisure to other, previously unaffected, areas. Thus, visitor redistribution can involve both the dispertion of visitors away from fragile areas and concentration of demand at more robust sites. The policy of the Lake District National Park Authority, for example, is to concentrate and contain higher levels of recreational use in the popular honeypot areas, such as Windermere and Ambleside, whilst discouraging the spread of visitors into identified quieter areas (LDNPP 1986).

One of the earliest attempts to redistribute visitor demand in the wider countryside was the creation of country parks. The original objective of country parks was bring the countryside closer to major urban centres, thereby reducing the level of demand for recreation in the more traditional and fragile areas of the countryside, in particular the national parks. As is discussed in Chapter Six, country parks, generally, failed to achieve this objective although they have been successful in absorbing and concentrating demand at purpose designed and managed sites. More recently, marketing and other forms of information provision, as described in the previous section, have been used to influence the distributon of visitors in the countryside. Car tourists, for example, are frequently directed along selected scenic routes in order to both enhance visitor enjoyment and to relieve congestion on major routes whilst the inceasingly common white-on-brown tourist signs play a role in diverting visitors to a variety of attractions and destinations in the countryside. The marketing activities of tourism development partnerships (see Chapter Eight) also contribute to visitor redistribution. The purpose of the North Pennines Tourism Partnership, for example, is to tap some of the high level of demand for recreation in the surrounding national parks.

285

At a local or site level there is a variety of ways in which visitor redistribution can be achieved. Differential pricing schemes at historic properties, for example, with reduced prices in the off season or higher prices at peak periods, are an effective means of spreading demand throughout the year, thereby limiting the detrimental effects of excessive demand. The use of directional signs at a countryside site channels visitors away from damaged or ecologically sensitive areas and a reduction or increase in the range of facilities and amenities provided is a powerful visitor management tool. At Warwick Castle, for example, the provision of new attractions in the grounds has spread demand away from the central site and at Woburn Abbey in Bedfordshire there is a variety of visitor attractions, including a pottery wokshop, an antiques centre and the safari park, in addition to the main house. The provision of facilities is a popular visitor management technique. Car parks, toilets, visitor centres, picnic sites and tea rooms are a natural draw to visitors whilst, conversely, limiting the range of facilities tends to reduce the level of visitor demand. However, one of the most important methods of redistibuting demand to ensure the sustainable use of the countryside is zoning.

(a) Zoning

Zoning is the method by which different areas of a countryside destination are classified according to their physical and ecological characteristics and their ability to sustain different levels and types of recreational use. It has two main purposes. Firstly, it is designed to ensure the appropriate and sustainable use of different areas of the countryside and, secondly, it is a means of minimising the potential conflicts between different types of activity. In other words, zoning designates particular areas of the countryside for specific uses, redistributing and managing demand by separating recreational activities according to the capacity and character of the landscape and the need for conservation. Thus, for example, different areas of a lake may be designated for nature conservation, quieter activities, such as fishing, or for motorised water sports.

The Canadian national parks authority, Parks Canada, has devised a five-class zoning system that gives priority to various land uses in different areas of a park (Murphy 1985). It ranges from special preservation areas, where the primary purpose is conservation with limited public access, through wilderness areas (used for hiking and primitive camping), the natural environment zone, where a balance is sought between conservation and more general recreational use, to recreation and park services areas where tourism and leisure are the dominant functions.

Similar schemes have also been implemented in some of the UK national parks. The National Park Plan for the Peak District, for example, identifies five zones where the appropriate level and type of recreational use are defined according to the character of the landscape and the needs of local communities and industries (PDNPP 1988).

Zone 1. Wild Areas
These areas show relatively little evidence of human influence. Access is only allowed on foot along public rights of way.

Zone 2. Remoter Areas of Farmland and Woodland
Activities such as walking, riding, cycling are permitted and camping and farmhouse accommodation may be provided.

Zone 3. The Majority of the Park
Limited recreational facilities, such as caravan sites and small car parks, are permitted to support appropriate, quiet activities.

Zone 4. Specific Locations
These are suitable for a reasonable level of recreational use. Car parks and picnic sites are provided.

Zone 5. Areas of Highest Intensity Recreational Use
These are the most robust areas of the park containing major facilities such as visitor centres, large car parks and refreshment facilities.

The Park Plan also includes a presumption against certain intensive activities and major sporting events which are considered to be inappropriate to the character of the park.

A similar system has been adopted in the Snowdonia National Park where four different zones have been identified. Zone A includes the most popular peaks of Snowdon and Cadair Idris where, although there is a pressing need for conservation, there is little chance of reducing visitor demand. The policy is, therefore, to concentrate demand in Zone A to protect other, less popular areas. Zones B and C are areas with intermediate visitor pressure where conservation and repair work is undertaken and Zone D contains those remote areas which are of prime conservation interest and support a low level of recreational use. Zone D is not, therefore, publicised by the park authorities.

Zoning, then, is normally based on the characteristics of an area and is, therefore, spatially defined. An alternative system of zoning to reduce conflicts between different recreational activities and between recreation and conservation is temporal, or time, zoning. That is, different activities may be permitted at different times of the day, week or year or there may be a restriction on all recreational activities at certain periods in the interests of conservation or the protection of wildlife.

iii Rationing Visitor Demand

In extreme cases, where the capacity of a site has been exceeded and where the redistribution of demand or other, less regulatory forms of visitor management are insufficient to ensure the sustainable use of attractions or destinations in the countryside, it may be necessary to regulate, or impose a limit on, the number of visitors at any one time. Such an approach is, of course, the least desirable as it contradicts the ethos of countryside recreation but, on the other hand, it is only applicable to managed or enclosed sites. That is, with a few exceptions, it is virtually impossible to regulate the number of people visiting the wider countryside whereas it is possible to limit the number of visitors to, for example, a country park or an historic site.

A prerequisite of any method of rationing use is that it should be, as far as possible, non-discriminatory. In other words, all visitors should be given an equal chance of gaining access. Ideally, the reason for limiting use should also be communicated to avoid resentment on the part of visitors.

A number of direct and indirect methods can be used to ration the demand at countryside recreation sites.

(a) Limiting Car Parking

Any reduction in the number of car parking spaces will, consequently, reduce the number of visitors able to visit a site. Dovedale, for example, is one of the most popular destinations in the Peak District. It used to attract up to one million visitors annually, the great majority of whom travelled to the valley by car and used a car park which had a capacity for 900 vehicles. The excessive level of use meant that the footpaths in the area were becoming seriously eroded and it was decided, therefore, that visitor numbers should be restricted by reducing the capacity of the car park to 500 cars. The owner of the car park was compensated for the loss of revenue and a significant sum of money was invested in repairing and strengthening the paths. As a result, the sustainable use of Dovedale has been limited to an estimated half a million visitors a year.

(b) Time-Tickets

At some sites, the number of visitors is regulated by tickets which permit entry at specified times only. Such a system ensures that the capacity of the site is not exceeded, thereby limiting the damaging impacts of large numbers of visitors, and maintains a regular and even flow of people at the site. Chartwell, in Kent, is a National Trust property which attracts about 180,000 visitors each year. Owing to severe problems of overcrowding and long queues at peak periods time-ticketing was introduced in 1968. Visitors purchase tickets which permit entry at a specified time at 15 minute intervals. Up to sixty tickets are sold for each 15 minute period and the system has successfully reduced waiting times, improved visitors' enjoyment of the visit and limited damage to the house itself.

(c) Advance Booking/Permits

The notion of pre-booking or obtaining permits for certain recreational activities in the countryside is a common means of rationing use. Fishing and hunting generally require a permit or licence, as does the use of most inland waterways. Visits to nature reserves and other protected areas are often subject to obtaining permission and many historical attractions require advance booking for groups to plan for, and minimise the impacts of, large parties of visitors.

(d) Guided Tours

The requirement that visitors should be escorted around a site or attraction by an official guide provides the twin benefits of limiting the number of visitors at any one time and ensuring that their behaviour is appropriate. At Dove Cottage in the Lake District, for example, all visitors are shown around in small groups.

(e) Denying Access

In exceptional circumstances it may be necessary to deny access to a site or location to prevent further congestion or damage. At the simplest level, entrances to sites can closed if there are too many visitors and in 1989 the police found it necessary to 'close' the Lake District to further vehicular access owing to cars queueing on the M6 motorway. At Stonehenge, visitors are no longer allowed access within the stone circle to prevent further damage to the ancient stones. Such measures, however, are taken in the last resort and tend to be a solution to a temporary problem of excessive visitor demand.

(f) Pricing

At some sites and attractions, introducing or increasing entry charges is often considered as a means of rationing demand. The simple economic theory is that if prices are raised then demand will fall. The issue is, however, both complex and emotive. For example, if an entry fee constitutes a relatively small proportion of the overall costs of a trip then it is unlikely to act as a deterrent. Costs are also one of a number of factors that influence demand for countryside recreation. Accessibility, trends in leisure and tourism, the weather, and the personal characteristics of individual visitors (see Chapter Three) all have a bearing on the level of demand and it is, therefore, uncertain to what degree pricing is an effective visitor management tool. The experience of British museums gives credence to the notion that charging entry fees reduces demand; both the Natural History Museum and the Science Museum in London suffered an immediate forty per cent drop in attendances following the introduction of charges (Yale 1990), yet limited research in the UK has shown that, in the longer term, the introduction or raising of entry charges will have little significant effect on visitor levels at countryside attractions (see Bovaird *et al* 1984).

There is also a more general debate about whether the sustainable use of the wider countryside, as opposed to visits to specific sites, should be paid for. The underlying economic theory is that the countryside, like any other scarce resource, is not a free good and that its use should be paid for by the consumer (i.e. the visitor). It may be argued that the recreational use of the countryside can only be truly sustainable if the cost of maintaining and conserving the resource is paid for by those who benefit from it. Therefore the concluding section of this book considers the issue of pricing as a future management tool for tourism and leisure in the countryside (See also Sharpley 1993).

SHOULD THE COUNTRYSIDE BE PRICED?

Virtually every type of tourism and leisure activity requires some degree of payment by the visitor or recreationist. Whether a game of golf, a visit to a sports centre, a meal at a restaurant, or an annual holiday, the privilege of enjoying such activities must be paid for. On the other hand the countryside, as a resource for recreation, has long been regarded as a free good. However, in the face of increasing impacts on the environment, and the consequent costs of repair and maintenance, the question that must be addressed is, should visitors to the countryside be required to contribute towards the costs that their activities incur?

i Pricing and Sustainable Countryside Recreation

Throughout this book it has been emphasised that the level and range of recreational activities in the countryside should be such that the harmful impacts on the character and quality are minimised, whilst the potential benefits to the rural environment and local communities are optimised. That is, a harmonious relationship should exist between the needs of visitors, the tourism and leisure industries, rural communities, and the countryside itself to ensure that the resource is maintained and protected for the benefit of future generations. In short, tourism and leisure in the countryside must be sustainable.

Central to the concept of sustainable use and development is the notion that all natural resources, including the countryside, are scarce and finite and that the use of any one resource should not deplete its overall stock. As a simple example, sustainable forestry means that, for every tree that is cut down for timber or the manufacture of paper, a new tree should be planted, financed by the profits of the forestry industry. Thus, in the longer term, the overall supply of trees is maintained and, ideally, increased. At the same time, environmental economics proposes that the price of any good or service should include not only the direct costs of production, such as materials and labour, but also the indirect costs of the production process on the environment, such as water or air pollution.

The same principles may be applied to the recreational use of the countryside. That is, areas of the countryside that are damaged or used up by tourism and leisure should be repaired or replenished. As is discussed in Chapter Five, much of the work undertaken by countryside organisations is concerned with land conservation, reclamation and repair, ensuring that the overall amount of countryside available for recreation is maintained. The major issue is, however, who should bear the costs of this work? Many countryside facilities, such as car parks, restaurants or camp sites, are paid for by visitors yet, at present, the cost of repairing environmental damage in the wider countryside, such as footpath erosion, is borne not by the visitor but by public sector or voluntary organisations. Furthermore, the capacity of many popular countryside areas and destinations has been exceeded, resulting in unsustainable levels of recreational use and serious damage to the physical fabric of the countryside.

It has been suggested, therefore, that a price should be put on the recreational use of the countryside or, in other words, people should pay to visit the countryside. This, it is argued, would serve two purposes. Firstly, it would act as a visitor management tool, rationing demand by price, and, secondly, it would be a significant source of revenue against which the costs of conserving and maintaining the countryside may be offset.

ii Pricing for Visitor Management

The concept of charging people to visit the countryside is not new. In the United States, for example, entry fees were first collected at Mount Rainer National Park in 1908 (Harris and Driver 1987). By 1916, the fee at Mount Rainer was $6 per vehicle whilst Yosemite and Yellowstone National Parks charged $8 and $10 respectively (Walsh 1986). Entrance fees are now collected at about twenty per cent of the 330 American national parks.

Whilst the original purpose of entry fees to national parks in the United States was to contribute towards their running costs, attention has increasingly been focused on their role in visitor management. As the demand for countryside recreation, both nationally and internationally, has increased, support for the use of pricing as a means of limiting demand, hence reducing environmental impacts, has become more widespread (see, for example, Cullen 1985, Fractor 1982, and Rosenthal et al 1984).

The use of pricing to ration demand is based on the premise that recreation in the countryside is an economic activity and that people, therefore, place a value on visiting the countryside. Thus, if a visit to the countryside is free then, in economics theory, the benefits to the consumer are maximised and everyone who wishes to visit the countryside will do so. On the other hand, different people place different values on visiting the countryside, both as a distinct activity and also in relation to other forms of recreation. If the costs of countryside recreation begin to outweigh the perceived benefits, then those people who place a relatively low value on a visit to the countryside are more likely to participate in other activities. Conversely, those who place a high value on countryside recreation, to whom the perceived benefits remain greater than the costs of a visit, will continue to visit the countryside. In short, *rationing by price guarantees that those who most avidly desire wilderness access, as measured by willingness to pay, will obtain it* (Fractor 1982).

Pricing may also be used as a visitor management tool within the countryside. If charges are introduced at certain popular or over-used areas, people with a low preference for a particular site or destination will, in theory, go elsewhere in the countryside where there are no charges. However, for those *individuals who feel that a site is unique and that there are very few good substitute sites, a price change will have little effect on the use of that site* (Rosenthal *et al* 1984). Research into trends in international tourism tends to support this theory. The demand for traditional short-haul, sun-sea-sand package holidays has been found to be susceptible to changes in price, particularly where substitute destinations exist (Gerakis 1965 and Edwards 1987), whereas the demand for long-haul, individual holidays is less affected by price.

In practice, however, the effect of charging for countryside recreation does not conform to economic theory. Studies in the United States have shown that substantial increases in camping fees in national parks have had little effect on levels of demand. Furthermore, if entry fees are introduced, *once visitors become accustomed to paying a reasonable entry fee, recreation use is expected to increase above pre-entrance fee levels* (Walsh 1986). Indeed, it has been found that the introduction of pricing is strongly supported if it is seen by visitors to be a means of preventing further deterioration in the quality of the countryside (Leuschner *et al* 1987).

Countryside recreation in the UK is not, of course, free. Even with informal activities in the wider countryside, as opposed visits to managed sites with entry fees, there are the associated costs of transport, refreshments, equipment, such as clothing, and time. Thus, any visitor fee or charge, unless it is significantly high, will represent a relatively small proportion of the total cost of a visit to the countryside. Furthermore, the demand for countryside recreation is determined by a variety of factors in addition to the cost of a visit and, therefore, the introduction of pricing is unlikely to reduce the level or spread of tourism and leisure in the countryside.

iii Pricing for Countryside Conservation
The countryside is a fragile, scarce resource. If the level of recreational

use was such that little damage was caused and that little of the countryside was required for the provision of recreation then, in theory,, there would be no need for sustainable planning and management. In many areas, however, in particular the national parks and the more popular Areas of Outstanding Natural Beauty, the demand for recreation has exceeded the capacity for sustainable use. As a result, there are serious problems of footpath erosion, pollution, litter and damage to flora and fauna.

In short, countryside recreation incurs a huge cost on the environment. It has been estimated, for example, that repairing the damage to the Pennine Way alone will cost about £5 million. If this is translated into repairing and maintaining all the footpaths and other rights of way in the countryside, then the cost will be many times greater. To this must be also added the costs of litter collection, nature conservation, countryside rangers, national park authorities, highway authorities and a variety of other services, as well as the longer term environmental costs of, for example, the effects of car exhaust pollution. Together, the costs of providing for sustainable countryside recreation are virtually incalculable.

It is necessary, therefore, to look at the complete picture in assessing the costs and benefits of tourism and leisure in the countryside. Visitors benefit from a healthy and attractrive environment. The tourism and leisure industries benefit from an estimated £500 million to £800 million of visitor spending in the countryside. Yet neither visitors, nor the businesses they support, contribute directly towards the costs of conserving and maintaining the resource on which they depend. The burden falls, instead, upon farmers, landowners, voluntary organisations, such as the National Trust, and the public sector.

Sustainable development policies are, increasingly, adopting the *polluter pays* principle. That is, the costs of production of any good or service should include environmental costs, the total cost being reflected, inevitably, in the price to the consumer. If the same principle is applied to the countryside, it may be argued that both visitors and the businesses that benefit from tourism and leisure should be required to pay for the damage caused by recreational activities. In other words, those who benefit, directly or indirectly, from countryside recreation should contribute towards the conservation of the resource. It would not be unjustifiable, for example, to charge people to walk on the Pennine Way, contributing to both the costs of repairing the path and the enjoyment of future generations of walkers.

iv Pricing: Issues and Problems

There would, inevitably, be much opposition to any attempt to impose charges for countryside recreation. Many people, for example, consider free access to the countryside to be a moral right; charging would be seen as an infringement or restriction on personal freedom. Thus, a wide variety of organisations, from the Ramblers Association to motoring and camping clubs, would be firmly opposed to any restriction on access. The opportunity to participate in countryside recreation has also been traditionally regarded as being good for both the individual and for society as a whole or, in other words, a merit good. Just as free education and a health service, two commonly quoted examples of merit goods, contibute to a healthier and better educated society, so too is a rested, re-created worker assumed to be more productive and, therefore, a benefit to society.

If countryside recreation is, indeed, a merit good then, by implication, the responsibility for its funding lies with central government. However, whilst the merit good argument can be applied to the state owned, wilderness areas of the United States, it is of less relevance in the context of countryside recreation in the UK. Most of the countryside is privately owned, inhabited, and used for a variety of purposes, and many rural communities depend on tourism and leisure as a source of employment and income. It would, therefore, be illogical to extend the involvement of the public sector beyond its present statutory responsibilities.

A further argument against the imposition of a pricing system is that it would be elitist. That is, it would discriminate against those people less able to pay for the privilege of enjoying the countryside. As is discussed in Chapter Three, however, the demand for recreation is determined by a variety of factors, including occupation, income, car ownership, and social class, implying that those who would be most affected, or discriminated against, by charging for countryside recreation tend not to visit the countryside anyway. Interestingly, research into countryside recreation the United States has demonstrated a similar visitor profile as in the UK and that, as a consequence, *the imposition of...user-fees would not tend to discriminate against the poor* (Vaux 1975).

At a practical level, the major hurdle inherent in introducing a pricing system in the wider countryside would be the legal implications. The public have a legal right of free access along all public rights of way and charging for access or use on heavily used roads or footpaths by, for example, the introduction of tolls, would require significant and far reaching changes to the law. Even if it was legally possible, collecting an entry fee would be an enormous and expensive task. Except in the case of enclosed sites it would be impossible to restrict access and so to charge for the use of popular trails or footpaths, such as the Pennine Way, would necessitate a large number of rangers to ensure widespread compliance. On the other hand, it is frequently argued that car-borne visitors have the greatest impact on the countryside but, certainly in the case of day visitors, contribute least to the local economy. It has, therefore, been proposed that charges should be levied on cars arriving in, or passing through, popular countryside destinations. Again, however, the expense and difficulty in collecting fees would outweigh any benefits. It has been estimated, for example, that barriers would have to be erected on over 120 roads leading into the Lake District (Toothill 1991), to say nothing of the difficulty in making a distinction between local car owners, their friends and relatives, and genuine countryside recreationists.

Perhaps the most practical way of charging for countryside recreation would be to levy a conservation tax on tourism and leisure businesses, expanding on the concept of the bed-tax that operates in many European countries. The cost would, inevitably, be passed onto the consumer in higher prices for meals, overnight stays, guide books and outdoor leisure equipment, significant sums could be generated to contribute towards countryside conservation, and it would, relatively, be the simplest method of developing a system of pricing countryside recreation. Indeed, a number of small businesses already operate a voluntary conservation charge on goods and services, raising funds for local conservation projects.

Despite the growing recognition that visitors should, in some way or another, make a contribution towards the conservation and upkeep of the countryside which they enjoy, the practical difficulties and the undoubted opposition from visitors, pressure groups and the tourism and leisure industries mean that it is unlikely that any form of charging will be implemented in the foreseeable future. Nevertheless, various organisations are increasingly questioning whether visitors to the countryside should be required to pay towards the maintenance of the countryside (see Beard 1995). Generally, the present legal and administrative structure is, in itself, not sufficient to guarantee the management and development of sustainable countryside recreation. Organisations, such as the Countryside Commission and local authorities, are increasingly looking to the general public to support their countryside management work and it is, arguably, in the hands of the visiting public that the future of the countryside lies. In other words, sustainable tourism and leisure in the countryside is dependent on the co-operation and support of those who visit and enjoy the countryside and, in particular, the acceptance of their responsibility for its protection and future survival.

SUMMARY

Although any form of visitor management contradicts the meaning and spirit of countryside recreation, such is the level and diversity of demand that it has become increasingly necessary to exert some degree of control over the behaviour and activities of visitors in the countryside. The purpose of visitor management is to minimise the negative impacts of recreation on the environment and to enhance the recreational experience by attempting to match the level and type of use to the capacity and characteristics of a site or destination.

In order to maintain the sense of freedom and spontaneity inherent in countryside recreation, any form of visitor management should be as unobtrusive as possible, taking into account the motivation and enjoyment of visitors. At the same time, it should be sufficient to ensure the appropriate and sustainable use of the countryside. There are, in effect, three levels, or degrees, of control that may be exercised.

i Influencing Visitor Behaviour At the simplest level, appropriate visitor behaviour may be achieved through the provision of information, effective marketing, the development of codes of conduct, and the work of countryside rangers.

ii Redistributing Use The recreational use of the countryside may be made more sustainable by redistributing the demand for recreation either spatially or temporally. An increasingly popular method of redistribution is through zoning areas of the countryside according to its capacity and physical characteristics.

iii Rationing Use In some popular areas and destinations it has become necessary to ration the demand for recreation to reduce the harmful impacts on the environment. Methods of rationing include limiting car parking, issuing time-tickets, differential pricing, guided tours and advance booking.

The management, planning and development of sustainable tourism and leisure in the countryside is dependent on effective policies and management schemes and the co-operation and support of visitors. It has become increasingly recognised, therefore, that the responsibility for the sustainable recreational use of the countryside lies with countryside organisations, landowners, rural communities, and visitors themselves. In particular, there is growing support for the notion that both visitors and the tourism and leisure industries should contribute financially to the conservation and upkeep of the resource on which they depend.

Case Study: Cannock Chase Country Park

During the early 1980s, Cannock Chase Country Park, situated in the larger Cannock Chase Area of Outstanding Natural Beauty, was the site of an experimental management plan based largely on the redistribution of visitor demand. The aim of the plan was to provide for recreation in the relatively under-used areas of the park, to minimise conflicts between different user groups, to maintain the existing level of demand and to achieve certain conservation objectives.

The park was divided into three areas, or zones, each with a separate management policy. The first area was the most popular for recreation whereas the second was the most important in terms of conservation. The third area, on the other hand, was of limited conservation value yet relatively under-utilised by visitors. The plan proposed that the recreational purpose of the first area should be maintained and visitor enjoyment enhanced by the provision of extra facilities, such as more toilets and refreshment facilities, and by improving waymarking, but that the level of demand in both the first and the second areas should be redistributed to the third area. This was to be achieved by providing extra parking, waymarked trails, picnic areas, and toilet and refreshment facilities in the third, under-utilised area at the same time as limiting access to the second area.

Over a five year period the aim of the plan was largely achieved. There was a significant increase in the recreational use of the third area whilst the first and second areas experienced a decline in use. Furthermore, the needs of different user groups, such as people who sought more solitary activities and those who preferred a more crowded environment, were also catered for. Thus, a variety of visitor management techniques were used to achieve the desired level of redistribution of demand.

References and Further Reading

Titles marked with an asterisk (*) are references in the text. Other titles are suggested further reading.

*Albright, H. and Cahn, R., *The Birth of the National Park Service*, Howe Brothers, Utah, 1985

*Ashcroft, P., Love Affair with the Countryside, *Countryside*, No.77, Countryside Commission, January/February 1996

*Bannister, D., Congestion and Gridlock in Britain, *Built Environment*, Vol 15, No. 3, 1988

*Baty, B. and Richards, S., Results from the Leisure Day Visits Survey 1988-89, *Employment Gazette*, pp257-268, May 1991

*Beard, C., Countryside Access - A Commodity to Sell?, *Countryside Recreation Network News*, Vol 3, No.2, pp20-23, 1995

*Berry, G. and Beard, G., *The Lake District - A Century of Conservation*, Bartholomew, 1980

*Bingham, H., *A Fragile Environment?*, GCSE Resource Guide 2, Lake District National Park, 1988

Biss, A., Perspectives on Leisure, *Countryside Campaigner*, CPRE, Summer 1994

Blunden, J. and Curry, N., *The Changing Countryside*, Open University, 1985

Blunden, J. and Curry, N., *A People's Charter?*, Countryside Commission, HMSO, 1990
Borrett, N., (Editor), *Leisure Services UK*, Macmillan, 1991

*Bovaird, A., Tricker, M. and Stoakes, R., *Recreation Management and Pricing*, Gower Publishing, 1984

British Moutaineering Council, *Tread Lightly: Conserving Britain's Mountains and Crags*, BMC, 1988

*British Tourist Authority, *Tourism Intelligence Quarterly*, BTA, August 1992

*Bromley, P., *Countryside Management*, E. & F.N. Spon, 1990

*Brundtland, G., (Chair), *Our Common Future-World Commission on the Environment*, OUP, 1987

*Clark, G., Darrall, J., Grove-White, R., Macnaughten, P. and Urry, J., *Leisure Landscapes. Leisure, Culture and the English Countryside: Challenges and Conflicts*, CPRE, 1994

Cope, J., *Eden Tourism*, ETB Insights, C1-5, 1991

Corke, J., *Tourism Law*, 2nd Edition, Elm Publications, 1993

*Country Landowners Association, *Recreation and Access in the Countryside: A Better Way Forward*, CLA, 1991

Countryside Commission, *The Coastal Heritage*, HMSO, 1970

Countryside Commission, *The Upland Management Experiment*, CCP 82, Countryside Commission, 1974

*Countryside Commission, *The Lake District Upland Management Experiment*, CCP 93, Countryside Commission, 1976

*Countryside Commission, *Tarn Hows: An Approach to the Management of a Popular Beauty Spot*, CCP 106, Countryside Commission, 1977

*Countryside Commission, *The Snowdonia Upland Management Experiment*, CCP122, Countryside Commission, 1979a

*Countryside Commission, *Countryside Rangers and Related Staff*, Advisory Series No.7, Countryside Commission, 1979b

*Countryside Commission, *Country Park Visitor Surveys*, CCP 180, Countryside Commission, 1984

*Countryside Commission, *National Countryside Recreation Survey 1984*, CCP 201, Countryside Commission, 1985

*Countryside Commission, *Access Study Summary Report*, CCP 216, Countryside Commission, 1986a

*Countryside Commission, *Access to the Countryside for Recreation and Sport*, CCP217, Countryside Commission, 1986b

*Countryside Commission, *Policies for Enjoying the Countryside*, CCP 234, Countryside Commission, 1987a

*Countryside Commission, *Public Transport to the Countryside*, CCP 227, Countryside Commission, 1987b

Countryside Commission, *A Compendium of Recreation Statistics 1984-1986*, CCD 16, Countryside Commission, 1987c

*Countryside Commission, *Forestry in the Countryside*, CCP245, Countryside Commission, 1987d

*Countryside Commission, *Planning for Countryside in Metropolitan Areas*, CCP 244, Countryside Commission, 1987e

Countryside Commission, *Heritage Coasts in England and Wales*, CCP252, Countryside Commission,1988

*Countryside Commission, *Welcoming Visitors to Country Parks*, CCD 40, Countryside Commission, 1989a

*Countryside Commission, *Managing Rights of Way: An Agenda for Action*, CCP 273, Countryside Commission, 1989b

*Countryside Commission, *Common Knowledge?*, CCP 281, Countryside Commission, 1989c

*Countryside Commission, *Planning for a Greener Countryside*, CCP 264, Countryside Commission, 1989d

Countryside Commission, *Areas of Outstanding Natural Beauty* , CCP 276, Countryside Commission, 1989

*Countryside Commission, *Paths, Routes and Trails: Policies and Priorities*, CCP 266, Countryside Commission 1990a

Countryside Commission, *Out in the Country*, CCP 186, Countryside Commission, 1990

Countryside Commission, *The Rights of Way Act 1990*, CCP 301, Countryside Commission, 1990

*Countryside Commission, *The New National Forest*, CCP 328, Countryside Commission, 1990b

Countryside Commission, *Forests for the Community*, CCP 340, Countryside Commission, 1991

*Countryside Commission, *Visitors to the Countryside*, CCP 341, Countryside Commission, 1991a

*Countryside Commission, *Heritage Coasts: Policies and Priorities*, CCP 305, Countryside Commission, 1991b

Countryside Commission, *Countryside Stewardship: an Outline*, CCP346, Countryside Commission, 1991c

Countryside Commission, *Caring for the Countryside*, CCP 351, Countryside Commission, 1991d

Countryside Commission, *Your Countryside, Our Concern*, CCP338, Countryside Commission, 1991

*Countryside Commission, *Enjoying the Countryside: Policies for People*, CCP 371, Countryside Commission, 1992a

*Countryside Commission, *Pennine Way Survey: 1990 Use and Economic Impact*, CCP 361, Countryside Commission, 1992b

*Countryside Commission, *Trends in Transport in the Countryside*, CCP 382, Countryside Commission, 1992c

*Countryside Commission, *Road Traffic and the Countryside*, CCP387, Countryside Commission, 1992d

Countryside Commission, *Parish Paths Partnership: An Outline*, CCP 380, Countryside Commission, 1992

*Countryside Commission, *Managing Public Access: a guide for farmers and landowners*, CCP 450, Countryside Commission, 1994a

*Countryside Commission, *The National Forest: The Strategy*, Countryside Commission, 1994b

*Countryside Commission, *National Survey of Countryside Recreation 1990: Summary of Results*, Countryside Commission, 1995a

*Countryside Commission, *Quality of Countryside: Quality of Life*, CCP 470, Countryside Commission, 1995b

*Countryside Commission, *Sustainable Rural Tourism: Opportunities for local action*, CCP 483, Countryside Commission, 1995c

*Countryside Commission, *Public Attitudes to the Countryside*, CCP 481, Countryside Commission, 1996

*Countryside Commission/ETB, *Principles for Tourism in National Parks*, Countryside Commission, 1989

*Countryside Commission/ETB, *Principles for Tourism in the Countryside*, Countryside Commission, 1989

Countryside Commission/Tourist Boards, *Tourism in the National Parks: A Guide to Good Practice*, Countryside Commission, 1991

Countryside Recreation Research Advisory Group, *Our Priceless Countryside: Should it be Priced?*, 1991 Countryside Recreation Conference Papers, CRRAG, 1992

*CPRE, *Green Belts: Response to the Draft Revised PPG2*, Council for the Protection of Rural England, May 1994

*CRN, *UK Day Visits Survey 1993*, Countryside Recreation Network, 1995

*Cross, T., Trends, Problems and Approaches to Policy, *A Drive in the Country: Examining the problems of recreational travel and working towards solutions*, CRN workshop proceedings, Countryside Recreation Network, 1995

*Cullen, R., Rationing Recreation Use of Public Land, *Journal of Environmental Management*, Vol 21, pp213-224, 1985

*Cumbria Tourist Board, *Regional Tourism Srategy for Cumbria*, CTB, 1990

*Curry, N., *Countryside Recreation, Access and Land Use Planning*, E & FN Spon, 1984

*Dartington Amenity Research Trust, *Public Transport for Countryside Recreation*, DART, 1976

*Davidson, R., *Tourism in Europe*, Pitman, 1992

*Defoe, D., *A Tour through the whole island of Great Britain*, J.M. Dent, 1974

Denman, R., *Tourism in the National Parks: A Guide to Good Practice*,The Tourism Company, 1991

Denman, R., *The Farm Tourism Market: A Market Study of Fram Tourism in England*, The Tourism Company, 1993

Denman, R., *The Farm Tourism Market*, ETB Insights, B49-64, 1994

Department of the Environment, *The New Forest: The Government's Proposals*, DOE, 1992

*Department of National Heritage, *Tourism: Competing with the Best*, DNH, 1995

*Dower, J., *National Parks in England and Wales*, Cmnd. 6378, HMSO, 1945

Dower, M., *The Challenge of Leisure: The Fourth Wave*, Architectural Press, 1965

*Eade, F., Land in Many Hands, *National Parks Today*, Winter 1987

Eden TAP, *Eden Tourism Action Programme*, Eden TAP, 1991

*Edwards, A., *Choosing Holiday Destinations*, Special Report No. 1109, Economic Intelligence Unit, 1987

*Edwards, R., (Chair), *Fit for the Future: Report of the National Parks Review Panel*, CCP 334, Countryside Commission, 1991

Elson, M., *Green Belts: Conflict Mediation in the Urban Fringe*, Heinemann, 1986

*English Tourist Board, *Tourism and the Environment: Maintaining the Balance*, ETB, 1991a

English Tourist Board, *Visitors in the Countryside: A Development Strategy*, ETB, 1991b

English Tourist Board/Countryside Commission/Rural Development Commission, *The Green Light: A Guide to Sustainable Tourism*

*Fairbrother, N., *New Lives, New landscapes*, Penguin, 1972

*Fitton, M., Countryside Recreation: The Problems of Opportunity, *Local Government Studies*, Vol 5, pp57-90, 1979

*Forestry Commission, *Great Britain, Great Forest*, Forestry Commission, 1989

*Forestry Commission,*The Forestry Commission of Great Britain*, Forestry Commission, 1993

*Fractor, D., Evaluating Alternative Methods for Rationing Wilderness Use, *Journal of Leisure Research*, Vol 14, No.4, pp341-349, 1982

*Garner, J. and Jones, B., *Countryside Law*, 2nd Edition, Shaw & Sons, 1993

*Gerakis, A., The Effects of Exchange Rate Devaluation and Revaluation on Receipts from Tourism, *IMF Papers*, Vol 12, No.1, 1965

Gilmour, W., The Making of the Rother Valley Country Park, *Journal of the Institute of Leisure Amenity Management* Vol 1, No.10, pp14-18, 1983

*Glyptis, S., *Countryside Recreation*, Longman/ILAM, 1991

*Godfrey, K., *The Tourism Planning Charette, A Strategy Model for Community Based Tourism Planning and Management*,Tourism Research into the 1990s Conference, Durham University, December 1990

*Gray, T., *Journal in the Lakes*, Macmillan, 1884

Green, B., *Countryside Conservation*, Allen and Unwin, 1981

*Grolleau, H., *Rural Tourism in the 12 Member States of the European Economic Community*, EEC, 1987

Gunn, C., *Tourism Planning*, Taylor and Francis, 1988

*Harris, C. and Driver, B., Recreation User Fees Pros and Cons, *Journal of Forestry*, Vol 85, No.5, pp25-29, 1987

*Harrison, C., *Countryside Recreation in a Changing Society*, TMS Partnership, 1991

*Harrison, C., Limb, M. and Burgess, J., *Popular Values for the Countryside*, UCL London, 1986

*Haywood, M., Responsible and Responsive Tourism Planning in the Community, *Tourism Management*, pp105-118, June 1988

*Hewison, R., *The Heritage Industry*, Methuen, 1987

Hill, H., *Freedom to Roam*, Moorland Publishing, 1980

*HMSO, *Forestry Act*, HMSO, 1942

*HMSO, *The Scott Report (Report of the Committee on Land Utilisation in Rural Areas)*, HMSO, 1942

*HMSO, *Town and Country Planning Act*, HMSO, 1947

*HMSO, *National P*HMSOarks and Access to the Countryside Act*, HMSO, 1949

*HMSO, *Countryside (Scotland) Act*, HMSO, 1967

*HMSO, *Forestry Act*, HMSO, 1967

*HMSO, *Countryside Act*, HMSO, 1968

*HMSO, *Development of Tourism Act*, HMSO, 1969

*HMSO, *Town and Country Planning (Scotland) Act*, HMSO, 1978

*HMSO, *Highways Act*, HMSO, 1980

*HMSO, *Wildlife and Countryside Act*, HMSO, 1981

*HMSO, *Agriculture Act*, HMSO, 1986

*HMSO, *Roads to Prosperity*, HMSO, 1989

*HMSO, *Environmental Protection Act*, HMSO, 1990

*HMSO, *This Common Inheritance: Britain's Environmental Strategy*, HMSO 1990

*HMSO, *General Household Survey 1986*, HMSO, 1989

*HMSO, *Social Trends 21*, HMSO, 1991

*HMSO, *The Effectiveness of Green Belts*, HMSO, 1993

*Hobhouse, Sir A., (Chair), *Report on the National Park Committee*, Cmnd. 6628, HMSO, 1947

*Hoggart, K., Buller, H. and Black, R., *Rural Europe: Identity and Change*, Arnold, 1995

Holloway, J.C., *The Business of Tourism*, 4th Edition, Pitman,1994

Holloway, J.C. and Plant, R., *Marketing for Tourism*, 2nd Edition, Pitman, 1992

Hoskins, W., *The Making of the English Landscape*, Hodder and Stoughton, 1955

*Huxley, Sir J., Chair, *Report of the Committee on the Conservation of Nature in England and Wales*, Cmnd. 7122, HMSO, 1947

Inder, A., *Blackwater Valley Recreation Strategy*, Hampshire County Recreation Department, 1987

*IUCN, *World Directory of National Parks and Other Protected Areas*, IUCN, 1975

*IUCN, *Protected Landscapes: The United Kingdom Experience*, IUCN, 1987

*Jim, C., Visitor Management in Recreation Areas, *Environmental Conservation*, Vol 16, No.1, pp19-34, 1989

KCC, *Public Rights of Way Strategy 1992*, Kent County Council, 1992

KCC, *Kent for Walking: Guided Walks in Kent*, Kent County Council, 1992

*Krippendorf, J., *The Holiday Makers*, Heinemann, 1984

Lane, B., *The Future for Rural Tourism*, ETB Insights, ETB, 1989

*Lane, B., What is Rural Tourism?, *Journal of Sustainable Tourism*, Vol 2, Nos. 1 & 2, pp7-21, 1994

*Lake District Special Planning Board, *Lake District National Park Plan*, LDSPB, 1986

*Lavery, P., *Travel and Tourism*, ELM Publications, 1990

*Leuschner, W., Cook, D., Roggenbuck, J. and Oderwald, R. A., Comparative Analysis for Wilderness User Fee Policy, *Journal, of Leisure Research*, Vol 19, No.2, pp105-115, 1987

*Lowenthall, D. and Prince, H., English Landscape Tastes, *Geographical Review*, Vol 55, pp186-222, 1965

MacEwan, A. and MacEwan, M., *National Parks: Conservation or Cosmetics?*, Allen and Unwin, 1982

MacEwan, A. and MacEwan, M., *Greenprints for the Countryside*, Allen and Unwin, 1987

Mather, A., *Land Use*, Longman, 1986

*Mathieson, A. and Wall, G., *Tourism: Economic, Physical and Social Impacts*, Longman, 1982

McCallum, J. and Adams, J., Charging for Countryside Recreation: A Review with Implications for Scotland, *Transactions of the Institute of British Geographers*, Vol 5, pp350-368, 1980

*McCormack, F., *Water Based Recreation: Managing Water Resources for Recreation*, ELM Publications, 1994

Mercer, D. and Puttman, D., *Rural England: Our Countryside at the Crossroads*, CPRE/ Queen Anne Press, 1988

*Middleton, V., *Marketing in Travel and Tourism*, Heinemann, 1988

*Ministry of Defence, *Walks on Ministry of Defence Lands*, MOD, 1992

*Moyes, A., Travellers Tales in Rural Wales, *The Geographical Magazine*, June 1988

*Murphy, P., Tourism as a Community Industry, *Tourism Management*, pp180-193, September 1983

*Murphy, P., *Tourism: A Community Approach*, Routledge, 1985

*Murphy, P., Community Driven Tourism Planning, *Tourism Management*, pp96-104, June 1988

*National Tourist Boards, *The Countryside Directory*, Sphere, 1991

National Trust, *The National Trust - an Introduction*, The National Trust, 1980

National Trust, *North-West Regional Review*, The National Trust, 1989

National Trust, *Footpath Repair and Erosion Control in Mountain Situations*, The National Trust, 1990

*Newby, H., *Green and Pleasant Land? Social Change in Rural England*, Wildwood House Ltd, 1985

*NPTP, *North Pennines Tourism Partnership Constitution*, North Pennines Tourism Partnership, 1991

OECD, *What Future for Our Countryside? A Rural Development Policy*, Organisation for Economic Co-operation and Development, 1993

OECD, *Tourism Policy and International Tourism in OECD Countries 1991-1992*, Organisation for Economic Co-operation and Development, 1994

Patmore, J., *Recreation and Resources*, Blackwell, 1983

*Peak Park Joint Planning Board, *The Goyt Valley Traffic Experiment*, A Report to the Countryside Commission, PPJPB, 1972

*Peak Park Joint Planning Board, *Peak District National Park Plan*, PPJPB, 1989

*Pearce, D., *Blueprint 3*, Earthscan Publications, 1993

*Pearce, D., Markandya, A. and Barbier, E., *Blueprint for a Green Economy*, Earthscan Publications, 1989

Pimlott, J., *The Englishman's Holiday*, Faber and Faber, 1947

*Porritt, J., Conference Address, *Managing Tourism: Education and Regulation for Sustainability*, London, 1995

*Ramblers Association, Loss of Access to our Forest Lands, *Rambling Today*, p5, Autumn 1992

*Ramsay, Sir J., (Chair), *National Parks and the Conservation of Nature in Scotland*, Cmnd. 7235, HMSO, 1947

*Riddall, J. and Trevelyan, J., *Rights of Way: A Guide to Law and Practice*, Open Spaces Society/Ramblers Association, 1992

*Rollinson, W., *A History of Man in the Lake District*, J.M. Dent, 1967

Rosenthal, D. Loomis, J. and Petersen, C., Pricing for Efficiency and Revenue in Public Recreation Areas, *Journal of Leisure Research*, Vol 16, No.3. pp195-209, 1984

Rural Development Commission, *Tourism in the Countryside - A Policy Document*, RDC, 1992

Rural Development Commission, *Promoting Jobs and Communities in Rural England*, RDC

*Sandford, Lord., (Chair), *Report of the National Park Policy Review Committee*, HMSO, 1974

*Scottish Rights of Way Society, *Rights of Way: A Guide to Law in Scotland*, SRWS, 1986

*Sharpley, R., Sustainable Tourism in the English Countryside - Should the User Pay?, *Sustainable Development*, Vol 1, No.3, pp49-63, 1993

*Sharpley, R., *Tourism, Tourists and Society*, ELM Publications, 1994

*Shoard, M., *The Theft of the Countryside*, Temple Smith,1980

Shoard, M., *This Land is our Land*, Paladin, 1987

*Short, J., *Imagined Country: society, culture and environment*, Routledge, 1991

*Sidaway, R., *Sport, Recreation and Nature Conservation*, Sports Council, 1988

*Speakman, C., *Public Transport in National Parks*, Transport for Leisure, 1989

*Speakman, C., Integrating Transport Policies in the Countryside, *A Drive in the Country: Examining the problems of recreational travel and working towards solutions*, CRN workshop proceedings, Countryside Recreation Network, 1995

*Sports Council, *A Countryside for Sport: Towards a Policy for Sport and Recreation in the Countryside*, Sports Council, 1991

*Sports Council, *Annual Report 1990-1991*, Sports Council, 1992

*Sports Council, *A Countryside for Sport: A Policy for Sport and Recreation*, Sports Council, 1992

Stokes, R., National Parks - Who Pays?, *Environmental Education and Information*, Vol 8, No.4, pp225-235, 1988

*Sustrans, *The National Cycle Network*, Sustrans, 1995

Town and Country Planning Association, *The Future Planning of the Countryside*, TCPA, 1989

*Toothill, J., *Charge or Tax? - The Practicalities*, CCRAG 1991 Conference Paper, 1992

*Torkildsen, G., *Leisure and Recreation Management* , E & F.N. Spon, 1992

Transport 2000, *No Through Road*, Transport 2000, 1989

*Vaux, H., The Distribution of Income among Wilderness Users, *Journal of Leisure Research*, Vol 7, No.1, pp29-37, 1975

*Walsh, R., *Recreation Economic Decisions*, Venture Publishing, State College, Pennsylvania, 1986

Ward, C. and Hardy, D., *Goodnight Campers!*, Mansell Publishing, 1986

*Weideger, P., *Gilding the Acorn: behind the facade of the National Trust*, Simon & Schuster, 1994

*Wheeller, B. *Is Responsible Tourism Appropriate?*, Tourism Research into the 1990s Conference Paper, Durham University, December 1990

*Wheeller, B., Tourism's Troubled Times, *Tourism Management*, Vol 12, No. 3, pp91-96, 1991

*Wheeller, B., Alternative Tourism: A Deceptive Ploy, in *Progress in Tourism, Recreation and Hopitality Management Vol IV*, Cooper, C. (ed), Bellhaven Press, 1992

*Whitelegg, J., Jammed in a Cul-dc-Sac, *Times Higher Education Supplement*, April 24th, 1992

Whitelegg, J., *Transport for a Sustainable Future: The Case for Europe*, Bellhaven Press, 1993

*Wordsworth, W., *Guide to the Lakes*, (Ed, De Selincourt), OUP, 1977

*World Tourism Organisation, *Manila Declaration on World Tourism*, WTO, 1980

*Yale, P., *From Tourist Attractions to Heritage Tourism*, ELM Publications, 1990

*Yale, P., *Tourism in the UK*, ELM Publications, 1992

*Yearley, S., *The Green Case: A Sociology of Environmental Issues, Arguments and Politics*, Routledge, 1991

*Young, K., Rural Prospects, *British Social Attitudes: the 5th Report*, Ch.9, Jowell, R., Witherspoon, S. and Brook, L., (Editors), Gower, 1989

*Young, Lord., *Pleasure, Leisure - and Jobs: The Business of Tourism*, HMSO, 1985

Index

317